CU00705255

Robert Mitchum
on the Screen

Also by ALVIN H. MARILL:

Samuel Goldwyn Presents
The Films of Sidney Poitier
The Films of Anthony Quinn
Katharine Hepburn: A Pictorial Study
The Cinema of Edward G. Robinson

Robert Mitchum on the Screen

ALVIN H. MARILL

South Brunswick and New York:
A. S. Barnes and Company
London: Thomas Yoseloff Ltd.

© 1978 by Alvin H. Marill

A. S. Barnes and Co., Inc.
Cranbury, New Jersey 08512

Thomas Yoseloff Ltd
Magdalen House
136–148 Tooley Street
London SE12TT, England

Library of Congress Cataloging in Publication Data

Marill, Alvin H
  Robert Mitchum on the screen.

  1. Mitchum, Robert. I. Title.
PN2287.M648M36   791.43′028′0924   76-50203
ISBN 0-498-01847-4

PRINTED IN THE UNITED STATES OF AMERICA

Contents

	Foreword	9
	Acknowledgments	13
Part I	**The Robert Mitchum Story**	19
Part II	**The Robert Mitchum Movies**	45
	1 *Border Patrol*	47
	2 *Hoppy Serves a Writ*	49
	3 *The Leather Burners*	50
	4 *The Human Comedy*	51
	5 *Aerial Gunner*	53
	6 *Follow the Band*	54
	7 *Colt Comrades*	55
	8 *Bar 20*	57
	9 *We've Never Been Licked*	59
	10 *Corvette K-225*	60
	11 *The Lone Star Trail*	62
	12 *Cry Havoc*	63
	13 *False Colors*	64
	14 *Minesweeper*	65
	15 *Beyond the Last Frontier*	66
	16 *The Dancing Masters*	68
	17 *Doughboys in Ireland*	70
	18 *Riders of the Deadline*	71
	19 *Gung Ho!*	72
	20 *Mr. Winkle Goes To War*	74
	21 *Girl Rush*	75
	22 *Johnny Doesn't Live Here Anymore*	77
	23 *Nevada*	79
	24 *When Strangers Marry*	80
	25 *Thirty Seconds Over Tokyo*	82
	26 *West of the Pecos*	84
	27 *The Story of G.I. Joe*	86
	28 *Till the End of Time*	88
	29 *Undercurrent*	90

30 *The Locket*   91
31 *Crossfire*   93
32 *Pursued*   95
33 *Desire Me*   97
34 *Out of the Past*   100
35 *Rachel and the Stranger*   102
36 *Blood on the Moon*   104
37 *The Red Pony*   106
38 *The Big Steal*   108
39 *Holiday Affair*   110
40 *Where Danger Lives*   112
41 *My Forbidden Past*   114
42 *His Kind of Woman*   116
43 *The Racket*   118
44 *Macao*   120
45 *One Minute to Zero*   122
46 *The Lusty Men*   124
47 *Angel Face*   126
48 *White Witch Doctor*   128
49 *Second Chance*   129
50 *She Couldn't Say No*   132
51 *River of No Return*   134
52 *Track of the Cat*   136
53 *Not As a Stranger*   138
54 *The Night of the Hunter*   140
55 *Man with the Gun*   142
56 *Foreign Intrigue*   145
57 *Bandido!*   147
58 *Heaven Knows, Mr. Allison*   149
59 *Fire Down Below*   151
60 *The Enemy Below*   154
61 *Thunder Road*   155
62 *The Hunters*   158
63 *The Angry Hills*   160
64 *The Wonderful Country*   162
65 *Home from the Hill*   164
66 *The Sundowners*   166
67 *The Night Fighters*   169
68 *The Grass Is Greener*   171
69 *The Last Time I Saw Archie*   173
70 *Cape Fear*   175
71 *The Longest Day*   177
72 *Two for the Seesaw*   180
73 *The List of Adrian Messenger*   182
74 *Rampage*   185
75 *Man in the Middle*   187
76 *What a Way To Go!*   189
77 *Mister Moses*   191
78 *The Way West*   193
79 *El Dorado*   195
80 *Anzio*   198
81 *Five Card Stud*   200
82 *Villa Rides!*   202
83 *Secret Ceremony*   205
84 *Young Billy Young*   207
85 *The Good Guys and the Bad Guys*   209
86 *Ryan's Daughter*   212
87 *Going Home*   214
88 *The Wrath of God*   217
89 *The Friends of Eddie Coyle*   220

90 *The Yakuza*   222
91 *Farewell, My Lovely*   225
92 *Midway*   228
93 *The Last Tycoon*   230
94 *The Amsterdam Kill*   233
95 *The Big Sleep*   234

A Mitchum Portrait Gallery   236

Appendix   242

Index   244

Foreword

I was tremendously pleased to have been asked to write a foreword to this book on Robert Mitchum, and I accepted readily and happily. Now, with my typewriter staring aggressively at me, I only hope that I can do him justice! Because Bob is not easy to write about. He is a far more complex person than his lazy, relaxed manner would have you believe, and so much of his colorful way of expressing himself is totally unrepeatable. But that is a great part of his own personal charm. He can use language and expressions that, coming from anyone else, would shake even a Marine. He has a knack of replying to some rather trite question from a journalist with a series of ingeniously couched expletives that completely enchant the questioner until he looks at his notes and realizes that what Bob has said is unprintable.

But I should not dwell on this aspect of Bob's personality, since it might give the reader a totally false picture of him. I mention it only to illustrate that it is extremely difficult to recount anecdotes or quote him accurately. What I can write about is his work. I have had the good fortune to work with him three times—in *Heaven Knows, Mr. Allison, The Sundowners,* and *The Grass Is Greener.* The first of these was shot entirely on location on the tiny, beautiful island of Tobago, off the coast of Trinidad. I remember well the slight trepidation that I felt at the prospect of working with him . . . his reputation as a bit of a bad boy was naturally well known, but I had always admired his work and felt he was a highly underrated actor. I need not have worried. Within hours, we were sitting on the soft, pink sand and I was listening to an extremely sensitive, poetic, extraordinarily interesting man. Not just a vain

Deborah Kerr with Robert Mitchum in *The Sundowners.*

9

actor concerned only with his role and his looks, but a perceptive, amusing person with a great gift for telling a story, and possessed of a completely unexpected, vast fund of knowledge. Throughout the shooting of the movie, which was a particularly rugged one, Bob was at all times patient, concerned, and completely professional, always in a good humor, and always ready to make a joke when things became trying, as they so often can on location. Here on this remote island in the Caribbean, I came to know and admire his facile acting. We discovered we could work together like a good doubles pair at tennis. His timing is always perfect and he makes the very difficult task of "acting" seem as easy as falling off a log. But that has always been the trademark of a good performer.

Heaven Knows, Mr. Allison was a charming, touching, unusual story that could have verged on the tasteless in less sensitive hands, since it told of a nun and a Marine cast away on a Pacific Island during the war. But Bob's wonderfully innocent bewilderment at his own predicament made the relationship between the two human beings a most moving and gently humorous happening. Something of the same quality also enriched my favorite movie with Bob, *The Sundowners*. We were once more on a very rugged location—in Australia—where the heat has to be experienced to be believed. In this movie, Bob and I had more dramatic scope, and we had some beautiful scenes to play . . . some funny, some angry, and of course, the unforgettable scene where Paddy (Bob) comes home late and drunk and has to confess to Ida, his wife, that he has lost all her savings at "Two-up," an Australian gambling game relying on the toss of a coin. Here again, we worked together with ease and awareness, that exciting giving-and-taking that is a delight to be able to execute, and that one finds so rarely . . . so many actors—and actresses—being concerned only with themselves.

Good performances, especially in films, are interrelated. They depend a great deal on the director, of course, but much more, I feel, on the "playing together" of the actors. I was nominated for an Academy Award for this movie, but Bob should have been as well. It was a joint and shared effort, each performance complementing the other. Bob puts up a very effective smokescreen of casual, don't-give-a-damn-if-I'm-an-actor-or-not attitude, but at heart he *does* care. He can be colored by other's attitudes, and if *they* don't care then neither will he. He is always at heart a professional, though. Consequently, he always emerges well.

Perhaps I should elaborate on what I believe to be the meaning of the word *professional*. To me, it means that no matter how rough the situation, how hung-over you are, how many problems you may be grappling with at home or within yourself, you are on time at work, you have learned your words and given thought to them, and you are patient with your fellow workers. Such a "pro" is Bob. True, he can have downed half a bottle of Scotch the night before, or even that morning! But in no way does it influence his work. I can quite honestly say that in the three movies we worked on together, I only remember *one* occasion when Bob did not turn up on time in the morning. It was during the shooting of *The Sundowners*, and since the setup was a particularly complicated one involving, sheep, horses, and dogs, our director, Fred Zinnemann—also a very stern "pro"—was beginning to get quietly angered. He came to me and said, "Deborah, you've worked with Bob before. Now is this going to go on happening? I'm afraid I am very, very angry." I told him, "Please, Fred, just ignore it if you can. Just go on as if nothing had happened . . . he'll turn up." And he did. Not a word was exchanged as to why or what. And it never happened again. Nor did I ask what had happened.

Other people on other movies may have had different experiences. I am aware of that. Bob is deeply conditioned by how much or how little he respects the actors and directors he is working with. If that quality is lacking, then he will reply in kind. He does not tolerate fools either gladly or politely. He is amazingly tolerant of the fawning adulation of hysterical women, and is invariably picked on by men who are jealous of his success. He is very slow to move to retaliate, though. In Tobago, I remember, an American destroyer appeared out of the blue and anchored in the harbor. Naturally the small seaport town of Scarborough was inundated with sailors on leave, and a few found their way to the bar at the hotel where Bob was staying. Bob was peacefully and quietly propped against the bar, where we were all having a drink after the day's work. One of the four sailors who came in looked pugnaciously at him and made some disparaging remarks about Bob's much-publicized toughness. Bob lazily proferred his chin and said, "Okay, go on, hit." The hugh hulking sailor took him at his word and landed one on Bob's jaw. The blow made not the slightest impression. Warming to the enjoyment of hitting a movie star, the poor, guileless creature said, "Yah! I'm gonna hit you again." Bob silently and politely offered the other cheek.

Another vast swing came to the jaw, making the same impression as the one before it. Enraged, the sailor started to haul off once more, and Bob said, "Whoa, there, friend. This time, do you mind if I defend myself?" Speechless, the sailor took a third swing, and quickly found himself flying across the floor, through the veranda door, down a flight of steps, and into the garden. Bob quietly dusted off his hands, turned to the astounded barman, and ordered drinks all around—"particularly to the gentleman who seems to have fallen down the steps." I think the story is appropriate because it illustrates well the kind of man Bob is.

Stories about Bob Mitchum are legion, but deep down, he is a gentle, obliquely witty man, possessed of many, many more talents than the acting by which he is known. Enormous musical knowledge and a sense of rhythm—he had mastered all of the local West Indian songs with their complicated rhythms before a week was out in Tobago—a poet who won't show his poetry, a writer who won't show his writings, a man who hides many lights under many bushels, a human being of whose longtime friendship I am very proud. One of my fondest hopes is that we can work together again.

DEBORAH KERR
Marbella, Malaga, Spain

Acknowledgments

John Quincy Adams
Lewis Archibald
Alan G. Barbour
Dennis Belafonte
John Cocchi
Guy Giampapa
Maralee Hastings
Stephen Klain
Leonard Maltin
Doug McClelland
David McGillivray
Leo Pachter
James Robert Parish
Charles Reilly
Bob Smith
Lou Valentino
and
Deborah Kerr and Robert Mitchum
and to the staff of
the Theatre Collection of the Lincoln Center
Library for the Performing Arts in New York and
to Airlie Productions, Bruco Enterprises, and
Film Favorites
　　—for their assistance, my deep appreciation

Robert Mitchum on the Screen

"Other actors act. Mitchum is. He has true delicacy and expressiveness but his forte is his indelible identity. Mitchum can, simply by being there, make almost any other actor look like a hole in the screen."　　　　　　—David Lean

"All the tough talk is a blind. He is a literate, gracious, kind man with wonderful manners and he speaks beautifully—when he wants to. He would make the best Macbeth of any actor living."　　　　　　—Charles Laughton

"I don't know why Bob puts on his act. Few actors I've worked with bring so much of themselves to a picture, and none do it with such total lack of affectation as Mitchum does."　　　　　　—Vincente Minnelli

"There are only a few stars left who I'd go out to see in a picture but I never fail to see Mitchum. There's something about him that just thrills me to death. I think he's one of the finest, most solid and real actors we have in the world."　　　　　　—William Wellman

"He is a rarity among actors, hard-working, noncomplaining, amazingly perceptive, one of the most shockingly underrated stars in the business."　　　　　　—John Huston

"He is one of the finest instinctive actors in the business, almost in the same class as Spencer Tracy."　　　　　　—Fred Zinnemann

PART I

The Robert Mitchum Story

"I've still got the same attitude I had when I started. I haven't changed anything but my underwear."

—Robert Mitchum

"I decided to play dead," Robert Mitchum as Philip Marlowe confesses at one point when being menaced by a couple of goons in *Farewell, My Lovely*. "I didn't have to be a hell of an actor."

Slowly over the latter part of his thirty-odd-year film career have critics—many reluctantly—come around to discovering that Robert Mitchum was, and is, a hell of an actor. They'd been judging him simply as a popular movie star—a villain in "B" westerns originally, then a soft-spoken menace with sex appeal, a heart-throb to groupies in bobby-sox, the male Jane Russell (his own term), leading man, and finally charismatic superstar with the instinct to survive. Along the way, a couple of varying terms in the slammer and an intriguing touch of scandal that made good newspaper copy. Since all this fit his screen image, though, no big deal.

And Mitchum himself always has been the last to admit his talent. "I don't even like acting," he confides to one interviewer, "I just do it for the money." Another time his tactic is, "I have two acting styles—with and without a horse." A third: "I do a picture just because I have to get out of the house. When I choose a script, I just look to see if I have to run up any stairs and how many days I get off."

"To Mitchum, acting is strictly journeyman stuff," *Time Magazine* wrote. " 'I just fall in and fall out,' he claims, and even though he maintains he so often plays the same role, described as being beaten to death by gorillas—'when I get a script, the first thing I do is thumb through it and find the gorilla'—not everyone is conned by his non-chalant, sleepy-eyed putdowns of his abilities not only as an actor but, in recent years, as a larger-than-life screen presence."

He is, in the words of *Rolling Stone*, "the last celluloid desperado."

Robert Charles Mitchum was born in Bridgeport, Connecticut, on August 6, 1917. His father, James, was a railroad switchman; his mother, Anne (Gundarson), the daughter of a Norwegian merchant seaman. He was two when word came to his mother and his older sister, Julie, then living in Charleston, South Carolina, that James Mitchum had met with a fatal accident at work in one of the marshaling yards. Anne at the time was seven months pregnant with the couple's third child—to be named John (a heavyweight boxer during World War II and later a character actor in films).

The family went through the accident compensation money fairly quickly, and then Anne went to work as a typesetter and parttime reporter for the *Post-Telegram* back in Bridgeport. In 1927, she remarried. Her new husband was the paper's feature editor, Hugh Cunningham-Morris, an Englishman with a colorful war background, who came to be known among the Mitchums as the Major. "A totally fearless, indomitable man with a tremendous personality and not a nerve in his entire body," was John Mitchum's admiring description of his stepfather. The year after her second marriage, Anne moved the children to her parents' farm in Delaware after Robert had become increasingly difficult to handle, made a great deal of mischief, and finally was expelled from school. In Delaware, Robert's half-sister, Carol, was born, and his stepfather, staying at his newspaper desk in Bridgeport, sent his family whatever money he could spare.

Years later, Mitchum spoke of the Major: "He took on quite a task marrying a woman with three

Mitchum's first publicity photo (circa 1943).

children, but you know how it is with stepparents. I'm afraid we kids didn't give him much of a break for a long time. He had a box filled with medals from World War I, photos of himself on camels in Egypt, climbing out of old bi-planes in France, saluting the quarter deck on windjammers in Australia. When we were very small, we couldn't understand that he was full of shrapnel and couldn't work hard enough to keep us all together as a family unit. Of course, he was a very interesting man, but I couldn't see it at first."

Julie Mitchum was the first in the family to display any show business talent at fourteen, she was a fully accomplished young entertainer. She obtained a work permit, left high school, and got herself a club job in New York. To be with her, her mother and brothers moved to Manhattan in 1930, and Robert was enrolled in Haaren High School, a vocational school in New York's tough "Hell's Kitchen" area. To survive, Robert quickly became one of the boys—as belligerent and aggressive as any around him, and when his natural leadership qualities began to emerge, he was in trouble again.

In desperation after Robert again was expelled, Anne took him, John, and Carol to Felton, Delaware, to live with her mother, but neither she nor Robert's grandmother was able to cope with the rebellious teenager who refused to attend school.

Robert then ran away to Fall River, Massachusetts. He was fourteen, and by lying about his age, obtained work as a deckhand. Hoping a job might mature him and offer some stability, his parents reluctantly agreed to falsify his application so that he could get seaman's papers. He worked one trip on a salvage vessel but was fired when his true age was discovered. The keel-hauled teenager decided not to return to his family and, instead, rode freight trains and his thumb to Los Angeles, washing dishes, hauling slop, and rolling drunks along the way.

After the first few months on the West Coast, though, Mitchum became homesick and headed back East. In a railroad yard in Savannah, he was caught hopping a boxcar and arrested for vagrancy. For a week, he did hard labor, shackled at the ankles, in the Chatham County Camp chain gang, before his parents could get him released as a minor.

"In those days," Mitchum recalled, "if you made a run for it, they wouldn't spend fifty cents to catch you if they missed you with a rifle. They just went out and rounded up someone else to take your place on the chain gang. Probably by

telling the same sort of lie they used to get me."

Mitchum hitchhiked his way up to Delaware, suffering from ankle bruises and sores from the chains.

The physical hardships Mitchum had faced shocked his family when he finally turned up. "His left leg had swelled up huge," John remembered, "as big around as a tree stump, where the shackle marks had let in dirt and poisoned it." Robert nearly lost the leg, but his mother refused to let the doctors amputate.

At the time, John was attending Caesar Rodney High School near Camden and was right guard on the football team. He invited his adventurous older brother to visit his school and meet some of his friends, and Robert, still on crutches, was introduced to a tall, fourteen-year-old girl from Camden, Dorothy Spence. Within a few weeks, young Robert and Dorothy found themselves in love.

For a few restless months before hitting the road again, Mitchum toiled on a soil reclamation project, digging ditches and planting trees for the Civilian Conservation Corps, but finally grew tired of the regimented work schedule. He promised Dorothy he'd return and then headed West once more, taking John with him this time. The brothers decided to visit sister Julie in Long Beach who was now living there with her sailor husband. Robert became a longshoreman, but after about a year of living in a cramped, two-room bungalow (the rest of his family had come West in September, 1934, and all had crowded into Julie's place), he felt he could relieve the situation by working elsewhere and contributing to family expenses.

Back on the bum, Mitchum took a job in the Toledo auto factory run by the father of an old pal from Long Beach, Fred Fast. He was put on a power punch press, but soon found himself at odds with his conservative boss and was fired. It was in Toledo that Mitchum first smoked marijuana. A dozen years later he wrote in a probation report: "My first use of marijuana was an isolated instance in 1936 while I worked in Toledo." Losing his factory job, he continued East to visit his grandmother and resume courting Dorothy Spence, then working as a stenographer for an insurance company. He reassured Dorothy he still loved her and would be back for her when he had some more money behind him.

Bumming his way cross-country once more, he landed in Sparks, Nevada, where he drifted into another short-lived profession as a heavyweight boxer with really only one punch—a hard, looping right. The Mitchum face still bears the scars from his twenty-seven-fight career. By the time he returned to Long Beach, his sister Julie had become involved in the local Civic Theater group and, knowing of her brother's stifled creative talents, encouraged him to audition for the company. He was accepted and worked first as a stagehand and then in small acting roles, and finally writing children's plays and directing. Mitchum's earliest roles were in plays such as *The Petrified Forest, Remember the Day,* and *Rebound.*

For the first time, apparently, Mitchum discovered something he really enjoyed. "I'd never had so much fun before," he said. "I got sort of hooked on it right there and then. Well, there were a lot of amusing people backstage. It was real fun, and I figured that one of the biggest movie stars at the time was Rin Tin Tin, a mother dog. I reckoned if he could hack it maybe even a turtle could make out."

He also began devising comedy material and song lyrics for his sister's club act that were so good other entertainers began buying his ideas. Some of his risqué songs became part of the repertoires of Nan Blackstone, Peggy Fears, and Ray Bourbon, a noted female impersonator. Mitchum also wrote and composed an oratorio about European Jewish refugees that was produced by Orson Welles in a 1939 fund-raising benefit at the Hollywood Bowl. And then he was hired to ghostwrite the forecast columns of astrologer Carroll Richter and organize his tours.

During late 1939 and early 1940, Mitchum worked the Florida resort circuit with Richter. Then, after saving up $2300, he took a leave of absence and headed North to ask Dorothy Spence to be his wife. After examining Mitchum's charts, though, Richter warned him that their horoscopes were completely incompatible and that there would be great conflict in their marriage. Dorothy's family, it is said, shared Richter's opinion. Mitchum went to Delaware anyway, and on March 16, 1940, he and Dorothy were married. Theirs remains among the longer unions in Hollywood, another anomaly in the image Mitchum has developed during his lengthy screen career.

The couple headed West by Greyhound after the wedding and arrived at Julie's bungalow broke and exhausted. Shortly after returning to California, Mitchum dissolved his agreement with Richter, and, for a year, went back to turning out songs and special materials for Sunset Strip nightclub acts as well as doing some acting in small theatrical productions. Then he lived off

Dorothy and Robert Mitchum in 1946.

unemployment checks until landing a job as a sheet-metal worker at Lockheed in Burbank. He worked next to a shaper, James Doherty, who then was married to a girl named Norma Jean Baker. Later she would become Marilyn Monroe, opposite whom big movie star Robert Mitchum would act a decade hence.

Mitchum counteracted the tedium of the day shift at Lockheed by doing some theater work at night, acting in plays such as Gorky's *The Lower Depths.* "I spoke with a thick Russian accent, like Gregory Ratoff, and while we were on stage odd things would happen, like the lights would suddenly all go out. It would be somebody plugging in a hot plate to warm up some blintzes! We'd hear director Mike Stanislavsky arguing backstage, 'To hell with the blintzes!' and then he'd stick his head out through the curtain and ask the audience to bear with him."

A month after his job at Lockheed had begun, Mitchum's first son, Josh (later James) was born—on May 8, 1941. The year at Lockheed, however, is one Mitchum recalls as one of his most joyless. "It was like something out of Edgar Allen Poe's *The Fall of the House of Usher,*" he said, recalling his rapidly developing hatred of the metal-shaping machine he was on. "I was running this horrible monster of an infernal machine and I was afraid of it. I couldn't eat or sleep and I was finally living on No-Doz and chewing tobacco with hot sauce sprinkled on it to keep me awake." He was working the graveyard shift—midnight to morning—and with a baby in the house, he was unable to get much sleep during the day. He developed chronic insomnia and, when his eyesight began to fail, the company doctor told him his physical deterioration was the result of mental stress, caused by working at a job he hated. Torn between the work he dreaded and the responsibility of providing for his family, Mitchum was in a quandary. His mother suggested that he try the movies.

"I had no burning ambitions to be an actor," Mitchum had said, "and I wasn't much good at reading lines, but I was big and looked like I could handle myself in a brawl. I thought maybe I'd be good enough in professional movies to pick up some work as an extra." His acting in his little theater group had brought him to the attention of Paul Wilkins, an agent, who encouraged Mitchum to merchandise his talents and began taking him around on interviews. Mitchum lied to Wilkins that he could ride a horse, and he was sent to see Harry "Pop" Sherman, who then was turning out Hopalong Cassidy westerns at Paramount.

Mitchum ran down his credits for Sherman—deckhand, dishwasher, rodriding hobo, ditchdigger, longshoreman, pro boxer, sheet-metal worker—and a cowpuncher in Laredo. Sherman observed that Mitchum had no great ambitions to

be a star but looked tough and would probably be happy as an extra. He told Mitchum: "Okay, don't shave or cut your hair until you hear from us." Mitchum raced home, told Dorothy the news, borrowed against his grandmother's coffin fund to pay his way into the union, and waited for the call.

Wilkins sent Mitchum to Bakersfield by Greyhound and by local bus to Kernville, in the desert, where a Hopalong Cassidy movie was being made. "I didn't know whether I was supposed to bring my own makeup or horse or what." He was put on a horse by an old wrangler, who immediately spotted Mitchum as a greenhorn. The animal bucked and threw Mitchum to the ground. Gamely, the would-be actor climbed back into the saddle again and again before realizing he had been given a trick horse. Mitchum finally stayed aboard and made his less-than-auspicious screen debut as a minor villain in *Border Patrol*. Then he appeared in *Hoppy Serves A Writ* and *Colt Comrades*, all made in late 1942, and even managed to get a nice bit in MGM's *The Human Comedy* as a lonely soldier on leave. "I was working in movies and getting a hundred bucks a week plus all the horse manure I could take home," he explained characteristically. In the first eighteen months of his film career, he appeared in twenty-three movies!

There were seven Hopalong Cassidy movies with Mitchum usually a bearded bad guy. Once, however, he was cast as the (more-or-less) romantic lead—a law-abiding rancher in *Bar 20*. He also played in a couple of minor musicals, *Follow the Band* and *Doughboys in Ireland*; enacted an outlaw who turns honest in *Beyond the Last Frontier*; and had feature roles in flagwavers such as *We've Never Been Licked, Gung Ho!*, and *Corvette K-225*. And he was a crewman aboard the *Ruptured Duck*, the B-25 that bombed Japan in *Thirty Seconds Over Tokyo*.

Mitchum's first important role was in *When Strangers Marry*, a trim little thriller that William Castle turned out for Monogram Pictures on Hollywood's Poverty Row. His part: the second lead—a salesman who helps a former girlfriend trace her husband, a suspect in a brutal killing. "I never went after a movie job," he remembered. "They just seemed to come after me, the bread kept getting better, and it sure as hell beat punching a time clock." If his roles were getting bigger, so, too, was his family: his second son, Christopher, was born on October 16, 1943.

Mitchum's work in *Thirty Seconds Over Tokyo* impressed producer Sid Rogell, who liked the

With sons Jim and Chris (1946).

Spinning yarns for fellow RKO players Jim Warren, John Laurenz, Nan Leslie, Bob Clarke, Barbara Hale, Bill Williams, Steve Brodie, Jane Greer, and Anne Jeffreys.

young actor's rugged, offbeat style and, in June 1944, signed him to a long-term contract at RKO. The deal would last for ten years and keep Mitchum in bondage for the first and last time. By now, though, Mitchum had received his draft notice, but a regulation exempting fathers indefinitely postponed his induction, and the RKO contract he had signed assured his family of an income when he was called up.

Of his RKO days, Mitchum had these words: "They were looking for a journeyman actor and like everyone else had a lot of attractive people on their books. But these actors didn't have, I suppose, enough versatility. They felt I could do a number of things, so by hiring me they'd be getting a lot for the same money. I was a sort of utility man there for ten years." He continued: "I kept telling them I couldn't ride a horse or anything, but they went through all the old Hopalong Cassidy movies, then dressed everyone

else up very badly and marched me out before the cameras in a tailor-made outfit. After that I was sort of on the hook. RKO opened the door for me, and I became their workhorse."

Mitchum's first for RKO was *The Girl Rush*, a B musical set in the Old West. The studio's house comics, Wally Brown and Alan Carney, were the stars, and Mitchum was the romantic lead opposite singer Frances Langford. Studio head Sid Rogell then arranged for Mitchum to meet Frank Ross, then an RKO producer, who was preparing to bring Lloyd C. Douglas's *The Robe* to the screen. Rogell thought that Mitchum might be right for the role of Demetrius the Gladiator. When *The Robe* had to be shelved because of the war, RKO instead put Mitchum into a couple of Zane Grey yarns, *Nevada* and *West of the Pecos*, and discovered that their new talent had what it takes to be a two-fisted, if somewhat offbeat and sleepy-eyed, western hero. In both, he played the tough, lackadaisical cowpoke that, in several variations, would establish his screen personality for years to come.

Then William A. Wellman convinced independent producer Lester Cowan to borrow Mitchum from RKO to play the battle-hardened commander of Infantry Company C in *The Story of G.I. Joe*. Wellman's confidence in the actor paid off in an outstanding performance as the officer who united and inspired his men before being killed in the Battle of Cassino. The portrayal won Mitchum an Academy Award nomination as Best Supporting Actor.

While filming *G.I. Joe*, Mitchum was called to active duty by the draft board, but received a deferment until the movie was completed. Then, after eight months as an Army private, first at Fort MacArthur and then at Camp Roberts in California, he was given (in October 1945) a hardship discharge because of his six dependents. If his own war service was uneventful, his stepfather's certainly was not. Hugh Cunningham-Morris volunteered, was turned down, but lied about his age by knocking off a good ten years. He became a deckhand on a freighter, later received a captain's commission, and took part in the Philippines and Okinawa invasions.

Mitchum, meanwhile, returned to civilian life and found himself being hailed as Hollywood's newest male star. "After the war, suddenly there was this thing for ugly heroes, so I started going around in profile." Characteristically, he didn't bother showing up for the Oscar ceremonies in the spring of 1946. Of his work in *G.I. Joe*, Mitchum says with a shrug: "I was lucky. No one

Rehearsing with Guy Madison for the "Lux Radio Theater" adaptation of *Till the End of Time* (1947).

could have missed in such a role. Coming down off a mountain strapped to a mule and having the camera panned right onto my kisser—I was bound to click. But that doesn't mean I did any acting."

The postwar Mitchum got himself a new agent, Phil Berg, who negotiated a new contract shared equally by RKO and David O. Selznick. His first part under this agreement was as an ex-rodeo rider whose war injuries stop him from returning to his old life. The film, Dore Schary's *Till the End of Time* (the title taken from Perry Como's hit record of the day), reintroduced Mitchum as the screen's new heartthrob but was merely a slick, synthetic account of three war veterans readjusting to civilian life—sort of a traveling company of *The Best Years of Our Lives*. "I was now a leading man, a cause for apprehension and embarrassment, and it was much too late to start pursuing any particular design or direction. I knew I'd be a leading man until the string ran out."*

Next, RKO loaned him to MGM to co-star with

*Mitchum re-created his role of Bill Tabeshaw in the "Lux Radio Theater" adaptation of *Till the End of Time* (1/6/47) opposite Laraine Day, Guy Madison, and Bill Williams. It was his only appearance on the fondly remembered radio series.

Katharine Hepburn and returning veteran Robert Taylor in Vincente Minnelli's *Undercurrent*. Mitchum recalls that his off-camera pranks and bawdy jokes were met with scorn from the film's leading lady, who cut him down with the comment: "You know you can't act, and if you hadn't been good looking, you never would have gotten the picture. I'm tired of playing with people who have nothing to offer."

Katharine Hepburn notwithstanding, *Motion Picture Herald* named him one of the "Stars of Tomorrow" in its national poll in 1946. Simultaneously with the filming of *Undercurrent*, Mitchum co-starred with Greer Garson and, first Robert Montgomery, then his replacement, Richard Hart, in MGM's *Desire Me*. The film, plagued by script rewrites and constant reshooting of scenes, went on for so long and was such a mess that directors George Cukor and Mervyn LeRoy each disowned it. When it finally was released after a lengthy repose in MGM's vaults, Mitchum told the press irreverently: "It was so bad when they first ran it that after the first reel people walked out. So I put my collar up, sneaked out, and pretended I was never there. But I'm surprised with what Mervyn LeRoy has been able to do with it. You'd never know it was the same picture. In the original, we were made to act like Shakespearean actors. Now there's some comedy in it." Unintentional, of course.

RKO then cast Mitchum as a suicidal Greenwich Village artist hopelessly in love with thieving psycho Laraine Day in *The Locket*. This was followed by Edward Dmytryk's gritty *Crossfire*. The Mitchum name rapidly was beginning to mean something on the marquee, and the fact did

Relaxing with Robert Taylor and director Vincente Minnelli between scenes of *Undercurrent* (1946).

With director George Cukor and Greer Garson during the filming of *Desire Me*.

portrayed the strong, silent, quick-on-the-trigger cowboy type.

RKO then loaned him (for the last time) to producer/director Lewis Milestone for the film version of John Steinbeck's *The Red Pony*. In his first Technicolor movie, Mitchum played affable ranchhand Billy Buck. By 1948, the actor was earning nearly $250,000 a year, and his life-style, if not really normal by Hollywood standards, was still unconventional. When he discovered that his business representative had misued most of his money, Mitchum refused to prosecute. Instead he took Dorothy and their sons to Delaware in the spring of 1948 for a long vacation. "Following a quarrel concerning the continuation of my career," Mitchum recalled, "I left to return to Los Angeles, expecting to begin work in a film on the fifteenth of June." After weeks of tests and fittings, though, the picture was cancelled, and, hoping for a reconciliation with Dorothy, Mitchum started looking for a new house with more rooms. "I was somewhat depressed over the lack of communication with my wife, who was adamant in her refusal to melt, and I began drinking a great deal more than was good for me."

Shortly after midnight, in the early hours of

not escape the RKO front-office boys. "People started talking about Mitchum-type roles," Mitchum said, "but I still don't know what they mean. They'd paint the eyes on my eyelids, man, and I'd walk through the part. The least work for the most reward."

Mitchum quickly became RKO's top attraction. His lazy eyes and laconic acting style, together with his naturally powerful torso, exposed frequently in "beefcake" shots became his trademarks, and the studio turned him into the prototype of the screen hero. One woman fan told a reporter: "Mitchum has the most immoral face I've ever seen." The publicity people, naturally, were delighted, except, of course, when he became impatient with interviewers' questions and began making irreverent statements about his—and the studio's—work.

Jacques Tourneur's grim melodrama *Out of the Past* was the film that confirmed RKO's confidence that Mitchum could carry a film. He now was box office. It was his first private-eye-in-the-trenchcoat role, the type constantly and erroneously identified with him. In his next, *Rachel and the Stranger*, he co-starred with Loretta Young and William Holden, playing a handsome vagabond, strumming a guitar and singing several "frontier" ballads, and in Robert Wise's *Blood on the Moon* (Wise's first "A" movie), he again

A free moment on the set of *Out of the Past* (1947).

The Mitchums in 1948.

September 1, 1948, Mitchum was arrested in the Laurel Canyon cottage of actress Lila Leeds and charged with possession of marijuana cigarettes. Also taken into custody with them were Vicki Evans, a dancer, and Robin Ford, a real estate buddy from Mitchum's army days. Mitchum, then making $3,700 a week, told the press: "Well, this is the bitter end of everything—my career, my home, my marriage."

After his arraignment, he was freed on bail and reunited with Dorothy. Howard Hughes, who recently had taken charge at RKO, dragged out the script of a gangster film that had been gathering dust, hired Don Siegel to "save" Mitchum, and rushed the actor into the production as soon as he hit the street after bail was posted. The movie, *The Big Steal*, was a robbery caper tale with so many auto chases it often is referred to as a live-action *Roadrunner* cartoon, making little or no sense. It was shot around Mitchum when he was unavailable, and his scenes

At his well-publicized marijuana trial in 1948 with lawyer Jerry Geisler.

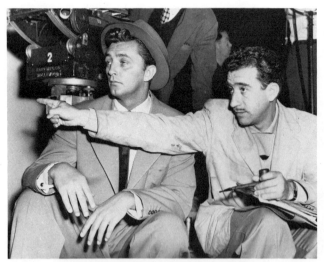

On the set of *The Big Steal* (1948) with director Don Siegel.

At his sentencing in February, 1949, with actress Lila Leeds, her attorney, Grant D. Cooper, and his counsel, Jerry Geisler.

Bidding the press goodbye before being locked up.

were later patched in, according to director Siegel.

Meanwhile, Mitchum had become a serious problem for the industry, particularly since RKO had two Mitchum films on the shelf, and Republic had lots invested in the unreleased *The Red Pony.* "Clearly a serious industrial crisis was in the making," *Time Magazine* wrote. "The problem was much bigger than salvaging a valuable property named Mitchum—a star of the first magnitude and an idol of organized bobby-soxers who call themselves Bob Mitchum's Droolettes—who'd been unused to stardom. It was even bigger than protecting some $5-million riding on three unreleased Mitchum films." Mitchum's ex-boss, Dore Schary, now with MGM, spoke for the industry and pleaded with the public not to "indict the entire working personnel of 32,000 well-disciplined and clean-living American citizens."

Howard Hughes advanced Mitchum $50,000 (at six percent interest, to be deducted from his future pay) for defense counsel, and the actor hired two noted attorneys, Jerry Geisler and Norman Tyre. In his memoirs, Giesler reminded Mitchum's critics that his client had waved a jury trial and was convicted only of conspiracy to possess marijuana. "Perhaps it has been forgotten," Geisler wrote, "that Mitchum never did plead guilty. . . . He served his time without complaining. By taking his medicine like a man, he gained rather than lost public sympathy. Instead of boycotting his films afterward, people flocked to see him in greater numbers than before." Geisler also alluded to a possible frame-up in the case. Mitchum was sentenced to sixty days in the Los Angeles county jail, plus a one-year suspended sentence and two years probation.

RKO gambled on Mitchum's star status and rushed *Rachel and the Stranger* into release. Kate Cameron, in the New York *Daily News*, wrote: "You'll forget while watching Robert Mitchum in the role of Jim Fairways that his is anything but the man he appears on the screen."

Howard Hughes could have dropped Mitchum under the morals clause, but he realized what he had in his contract player and shrewdly bought out David O. Selznick's share. (Mitchum later commented: "Selznick was always loaning me out. Maybe he thought I wasn't good enough to be in his own pictures! Sometimes I was loaned for roles I didn't want to do, but I was too new in this business to be temperamental, so I did what I was told.") Under Hughes, Robert Mitchum emerged as RKO's top star.

Immediately on his release—with ten days off for good behavior—from the honor farm in Castaic, California ("It's just like Palm Springs," the actor explained, "without the riff-raff"), Mitchum was rushed to Mexico to complete *The Big Steal*, which then was hurried into July release and was a box-office smash. Talking to the press shortly after its premiere, Mitchum grouched: "I didn't like *The Big Steal*, but it's making a barrel of money so I'll be doing *The Big Steal* from now on. When a studio comes up with a musty old script that brings in the shekels, the actor hasn't got much of an argument. So I don't bother the studio and it doesn't bother me. Somebody hands me a script, I look at it and ask, 'When do I start?' If there *is* a good story on the lot, you've got to smuggle it out to read it. And I do mean smuggle."

Mitchum's acting career was not impaired by his brush with the law, which seemed in keeping with the rugged individualism of his screen image. The Mitchum case remained in the papers, via two sequels. In September 1949, Los Angeles District Attorney William E. Simpson had his office launch an investigation into persistent rumors that the actor had been framed and that organized crime, various blackmailers, and assorted extortionists had been involved, or that the Los Angeles police department had been looking for headlines to obscure inaction against narcotics rackets. And why had the newspapers been tipped off to an impending raid on Lila Leeds's home long before Mitchum had arrived? The results of the investigation were never publicly announced, but, on January 31, 1951, the court quietly reviewed Mitchum's case, and

his conviction was expunged from the records.

"It took me from 1948 to 1951 before I was on my feet financially again," Mitchum recalled. During this time, he was the bankable commodity on which RKO sold a wide range of films; *Holiday Affair*, an offbeat (for Mitchum) romantic comedy; *Where Danger Lives*, a suspense drama that Howard Hughes assembled as a vehicle to promote (unsuccessfully) his newest leading lady, Faith Domergue; *My Forbidden Past*, a dreary nineteenth-century costume melodrama that teamed Mitchum with Ava Gardner; and *His Kind of Woman* and *Macao*, sexy adventure films in which he and Jane Russell became a team. By this time, Mitchum had paid off his financial debt to Hughes—with interest—but he still had several years to go on his contract, so his parade of films continued—although he occasionally was spelled by fellow beefcake star, Victor Mature, the studio's backup for Mitchum.

Mitchum starred as an incorruptible police captain in the crime drama, *The Racket*, which Hughes had filmed once before (in 1928); a stalwart infantry colonel in *One Minute to Zero*, one of the few big studio films about the Korean War; a washed-up bronco buster in *The Lusty Men*, Nicholas Ray's underrated rodeo movie; an ambulance driver-cum-chauffeur for mentally deranged heiress, Jean Simmons, in *Angel Face*, for Otto Preminger; a country doctor in Hughes's attempt to bring back screwball comedy, *She Couldn't Say No*, again playing opposite Jean Simmons (whose talents, like Mitchum's had been grossly misused by Howard Hughes at RKO); a great white hunter in *White Witch Doctor*, again with Susan Hayward—on loan-out to 20th Century-Fox; and finally an ex-boxer trying to lose himself somewhere in the Andes in a 3-D thriller, *Second Chance*. Then he balked when Hughes asked him to do *The French Line* with Jane Russell, and sat out his contract on suspension for next refusing to co-star with Barbara Stanwyck in *Cattle Queen of Montana* (Ronald Reagan finally did the part).

When Hedda Hopper asked Mitchum whether he'd be re-signing with RKO, he complained that he was sick of doing the same picture over and over again. "I wear the same suit, speak the same lines, throw the same punches. All they do is change the girl. I'd like to do some wonderfully important parts, difficult parts that require three-days' work with a ten-week guarantee," he told her sarcastically. "I'd go in, do my bit, pack up my makeup, and go back to the farm. I'd be brilliant in a three-day part. When I'm interested,

Discussing a scene from *The Racket* (1951) with director
John Cromwell and Joyce MacKenzie.

I know my lines and everybody else's. When I'm
not, I go on the set and announce, 'Tell me what
to say.' No fret, no strain, no pain. If you want my
interest, interest me. If you just want my presence, pay me."

During his RKO days under the Hughes
regime, he had a private detective assigned to him
to keep him out of trouble. "The shamus" (as
Mitchum has referred to his shadow) failed to
prevent the surfacing of the image of Mitchum as
a rough-and-tumble bucko whose tendancies to
tangle with cops and other two-fisted types dogged
the actor through the 1950s. In November 1951,
while filming in Colorado Springs, Mitchum
decked a soldier named Bernard B. Reynolds,
a professional boxer, in the bar of a local hotel.
According to the military police, Mitchum kicked
the soldier in the head—an allegation the actor
denied, claiming they both fell to the floor during
the scuffle. "If I hadn't decked him, he might
have decked me—might have been real painful,"
Mitchum said. In 1953, he outraced a Los Angeles motorcycle cop in his sports car and was
charged with "evading arrest" and "resisting and
obstructing an officer." The following year, he
was hauled into court for ramming into the rear
of another car at an intersection, and was sued
for $50,000. The case was settled out of court for

With son Jim and costar Arthur Kennedy on the set of
The Lusty Men (1952).

The Mitchum family in mid-1952: Chris, Dorothy, Petrina, Robert, and Jim.

an undisclosed amount. And in 1956, he flattened a couple of American sailors in a barroom brawl on the island of Tobago in the Caribbean and became involved with the Navy Shore Patrol.

Mitchum's home life during this period ranged from welcoming a new arrival, daughter Petrine, born March 3, 1952, to, because of his continued carousing, a brief separation from his wife, Dorothy, a year later.

Mitchum worked once again with Otto Preminger, appearing opposite Marilyn Monroe in the rugged outdoor drama, *River of No Return*, his first film as a free agent. Playing a laconic backwoodsman with a young son, fighting dangerous rapids, Indian attacks, and Ms. Monroe, Mitchum starred in his first CinemaScope movie, and commented: "This new medium is going to turn a lot of actors gray overnight. The new lens brings you so close to the audience it's impossible to use doubles or stuntmen. I've done

things in this picture which would give stuntmen the shivers." He later recalled: "That was some movie. Otto tried to alter Marilyn's carriage, the way she walked. He would mince about showing her the way he wanted it. He only stopped when she turned her ankle over and twisted it." And there was this classic Mitchum comment about a love scene with Monroe: He grasped the lush body; her moist lips parted in anticipation; and Mitchum asked irritably, "How can I take aim when she's undulating that way?"

In April 1954, Mitchum again became front-page news. He and Dorothy were attending the Cannes Film Festival, and, on the beach, he found himself next to a shapely French starlet, Simone Silva. Without warning, she yielded to a sudden urge and dropped the top of her two-piece bathing suit—in the presence of about fifty photographers. Several fell into the sea in the ensuing scramble, one fractured his ankle, and another broke an elbow. Dozens of shots were taken, though, and the recorded scene—with

33

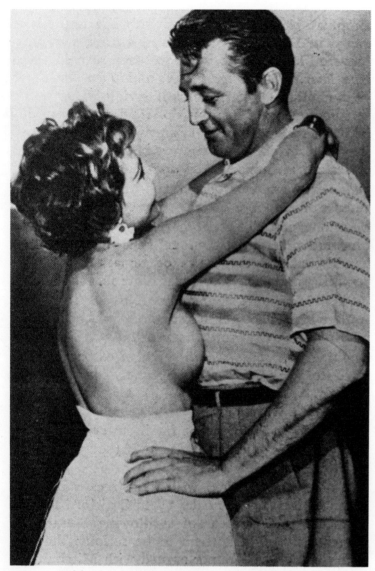

With Simone Silva at the Cannes Film Festival "incident" in 1954.

willed, evil son of a mountain family. Britain's *Monthly Film Bulletin* categorized the film as "CinemaScope's first real weirdie." Then, Mitchum was prepared to costar with Lauren Bacall in *Blood Alley* but, on January 12, 1955, he was back on page one when, after a week's worth of shooting on the film, he was fired for reportedly shoving a studio functionary into San Francisco Bay. "It was just a bit of horseplay," Mitchum claimed.

Between *Track of the Cat* and *Blood Alley*, Mitchum had gone to Mexico to scout locations for a movie he had planned to get his own newly founded film company, DRM Productions, off the ground. Then he returned to play the idealistic Dr. Lucas Marsh in *Not As a Stranger*, which marked producer Stanley Kramer's directorial debut. Most reviewers felt Mitchum was completely miscast although he himself described his performance as "all right," and commented that with a top-heavy lineup of actors with whom he worked: Sinatra, Lee Marvin, and Broderick Crawford, "it wasn't a cast so much as a brewery." Director Stanley Kramer later remembered the film as "ten weeks of hell." Following the incident at *Blood Alley*, Mitchum was hired by stage producer Paul Gregory for his maiden film, *The*

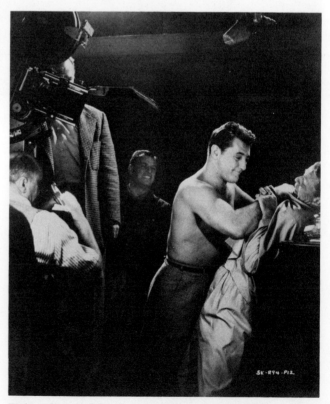

Being directed by Stanley Kramer (center) in a scene with Frank Sinatra for *Not As a Stranger* (1955).

Mitchum's arms around the seminude actress—made front page news around the world. "Simone must have been lowered by helicopter because I never saw her coming," Mitchum said. "I had my back to the sea and I could either stay put or leap into the ocean to get out of her way." Later he shrugged, "If a girl wants to have her picture taken like that, it's none of my affair."

Back in the United States, Mitchum signed to do two pictures for Batjac Productions, John Wayne's company. Both were to be directed by William A. Wellman, who had worked with Mitchum on *The Story of G.I. Joe*. First: *Track of the Cat*, an intriguing allegorical thriller with arty touches—the color photography was primarily black and white—and Mitchum as the strong-

With Charles Laughton on the set of *The Night of the Hunter* (1955).

mitted: "Most stars prefer to ignore the whole thing rather than get tangled up in a dirty court fight. Personally I don't feel that way about it. I think it's a case of fighting for your good name. You know, there is tremendous power in the written word, and people are inclined to believe what they read. They say, 'If it's printed, it must be true. And if it's not true, how come they are able to get away with it?' And that's the whole point. They should not be allowed to get away with it . . . to get rich by printing lies and smut." The whole *Confidential* affair riled Mitchum and his wife more than any of the other printed off-screen Mitchum peccadillos.

His film career, after *The Night of the Hunter*, settled into a string of routine programmers. In *Man with the Gun*, Samuel Goldwyn Jr.'s maiden production, he starred as a hired gun and self-proclaimed town-tamer in the Old West; in *Foreign Intrigue*, Sheldon Reynolds's full-length expansion of his successful television series, Mitchum donned a trenchcoat and became involved in espionage in Europe's back alleys; in *Bandido*, for his own company, DRM Productions, he portrayed—with tongue firmly in cheek—a renegade gun-runner supplying arms to both sides in the Mexican Rebellion of 1916.

Night of the Hunter, which would also mark Charles Laughton's first and only film as a director. Mitchum's performance as a psychopathic circuit-riding preacher in the Depression south certainly was his most original portrayal and one of his most memorable. He received the best notices he had gotten since *The Story of G.I. Joe*.

Not long after completing *The Night of the Hunter*, Mitchum again found himself in the headlines—this time on the cover of *Confidential*, the infamous magazine of the 1950s that specialized in lurid exposes of noted personalities. In May 1955 Mitchum surprised Hollywood by a million-dollar damage suit against the publication, denying the story it had printed that he had been invited to a post-production masquerade party co-hosted by Charles Laughton and Paul Gregory and had shown up completely nude, covered merely by a layer of ketchup and pretending to be a hamburger. The lengthy litigation, one of the last cases handled by lawyer Jerry Giesler before he died, dragged on for some time and cost the magazine as well as Mitchum a small fortune, but it encouraged other stars to press similar charges against *Confidential* and help put it out of business. Mitchum ad-

With producer Samuel Goldwyn, Jr., on Goldwyn's first movie, *Man with the Gun* (1955).

While in New York for the premiere of *Man with the Gun* in October 1955, Mitchum made his television debut—singing! He guest-starred on CBS' *Stage Show*, hosted by Tommy and Jimmy Dorsey (it was the same show on which Elvis Presley made *his* nationwide television debut three months later). Mitchum's vocal efforts were received with enough initial enthusiasm to convince him to continue a spasmotic secondary career as a singer. He had sung in films previously—three songs in *Rachel and the Stranger* and "harmonizing" with Lillian Gish in *The Night of the Hunter* and with Ann Blyth in *One Minute to Zero*—but he now was urged to try his hand (voice?) at recording an album. In March of 1957, Mitchum surprised the music industry (and probably himself as well) by coming up with a hit record, a calypso number called "Mama Look A Boo-Boo." and beating Harry Belafonte, who also had recorded it, at his own game. And the following year, Mitchum's recording of "The Ballad of Thunder Road," which he had written for his lively "moonshiner" picture, became an unexpected hit and remained, surprisingly, in *Cash Box* magazine's Top 100 records for several years thereafter.

On the screen, Mitchum was seen in *Fire Down Below*, as a small-time smuggler in the West Indies, competing with his partner, Jack Lemmon, for the affections of shady-lady Rita Hayworth (in her first film in several years). Then he did three in a row for 20th Century-Fox: John Huston's *Heaven Knows, Mr. Allison*, for which he got his best notices in some time, and co-starring with Deborah Kerr—who subsequently became one of the business' foremost Mitchum boosters, and two war movies for actor-turned producer/director, Dick Powell, *The Enemy Below* and *The Hunters*. For DRM Productions, he made the memorably off-beat *Thunder Road*, an engaging little action film about a free-thinking Tennessee moonshiner. Mitchum wrote the original story, the title song, and a tune called "Whippoorwill," sung in the film by Keely Smith—who also played his girl at one end of his run. Mitchum's son, Jim, made his debut in this movie, playing his younger brother.*

In 1957, amid all of the screen activity laced with occasional, vaguely newsworthy off-camera

*James Mitchum, a dead-ringer for his father, went on to appear in a number of forgettable youth-oriented films, such as *The Beat Generation, Young Guns of Texas*, and *Ride the Wild Surf*. He also had roles in *The Last Time I Saw Archie* (with his father), Carl Foreman's *The Victors*, Otto Preminger's *In Harm's Way*, Jean Negulesco's *The Invincible Six*, and in 1975 starred in *Moonrunners*—as a whisky-runner, a la *Thunder Road*.

With son Jim and Sandra Knight during the filming of *Thunder Road* (1958).

contretemps, he was vetoed by Korean War fighter pilot/clergyman Col. Dean Hess when Universal proposed signing Mitchum to star in *Battle Hymn*, the film story of Hess's life (Rock Hudson got the role). And in 1959, he found himself in litigation once more when agent Paul Wilkins, who had put Mitchum into films in 1942, filed suit in Superior Court seeking to collect five percent of the actor's earnings dating back a dozen years. The matter was settled amicably between Wilkins and Mitchum's new agents, the William Morris Agency, which had taken the actor on as a client after he had become an international star.

And international was the correct word for Mitchum. In the summer of 1958, he flew to Athens to star in Robert Aldrich's *The Angry Hills*, a rather routine drama of wartime intrigue. (Originally Alan Ladd was to have played the role of the war correspondent before being replaced by Mitchum. A couple of years earlier, Mitchum had been scheduled to star in *Boy on a Dolphin*, but Alan Ladd ultimately got that part.) Next, Mitchum went to Mexico for *The Wonderful Country*, an exciting, magnificently photographed western made for his DRM Productions.

Two great Mitchum performances followed, and for them he was named Best Actor of 1960 by the National Board of Review of Motion Pictures. In Vincente Minnelli's *Home from the Hill*, he played Captain Wade Hunnicutt, the wealthy, womanizing Texas landowner. It was a role reportedly written for Clark Gable, but Mitchum made it his own with a sensitive, moving performance that reflected a growing maturity in his acting. Equally as exciting was his acting in Fred Zinnemann's *The Sundowners* as Paddy Carmody, the Australian sheepdrover who loves his freedom, his wife (Deborah Kerr), and his teenaged son (Michael Anderson, Jr.).

Mitchum also played an Irish rebel in *The Night Fighters* (called *A Terrible Beauty* in Great Britain) and a wealthy American sightseer in *The Grass Is Greener*, both of which were filmed before *The Sundowners*. All opened in New York within a nine-day period during the 1960 Christmas season. Deborah Kerr and he acted together in *The Grass Is Greener* and *The Sundowners*, and a few years earlier in *Heaven Knows, Mr. Allison*. "I adore her," Mitchum has said. "We have such a rapport professionally we could phone it in. We can anticipate that much."

In the early sixties, Mitchum renamed his DRM movie outfit Talbot Productions after his new country home at Belmont Farm in Talbot County, Maryland—a haven of privacy for Dorothy and a place away from Hollywood between films for him. Talbot Productions put Mitchum on a strict budget. Previously he had been commanding more than $400,000 per film, plus a hefty percentage of the gross. "Talbot cut me down to $100,000 and they take the rest," he said. "Now I have my own production company so I at least own what's left of my soul. I work all the time because I've got a wife and three kids to support and obligations to meet and taxes to pay. But I'm not much of an actor. I'm in demand because I don't waste the producers' money. I'm too middle class for that. I've got all the middle class virtues. That's why I laugh when people call me a rebel. I'm no rebel. So I once went to jail on a marijuana rap. Ever since I've been so damn middle class it hurts. Also lucky. Just look at my record. Look at the racing form and study my past performances, and you've got to come to the conclusion that I'm the luckiest sonofabitch ever born."

In 1961, he turned down John Huston who wanted him to star opposite Marilyn Monroe in *The Misfits*. "I was sure the script I read wouldn't play and I was right, and I was afraid Huston

With wife, Dorothy, during the filming of *The Wonderful Country* (1959).

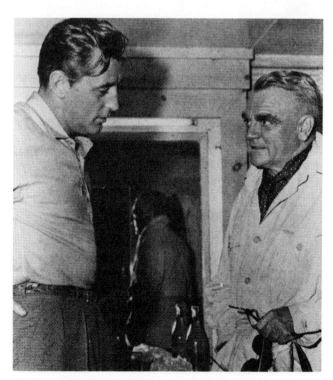

Visiting with James Cagney on the set of *Home from the Hill*. Cagney, then starring as Admiral Halsey in *The Gallant Hours*, might have been offering tips to Mitchum who would portray Halsey in *Midway* sixteen years later.

Between scenes of *The Grass Is Greener* (1960) with Deborah Kerr and director Stanley Donen.

would kill me! That guy demands more of his actors than any other director I ever worked with." Instead he teamed with Jack Webb (an unlikely combination) for a broad service comedy called *The Last Time I Saw Archie*, playing a con-man in a misfit outfit, a goldbricking buck private who is outranked by his son, Jim, who acted in a scene or two as a corporal. "I like the role and I liked the picture. And why not," Mitchum noted. "I got $400,000 for working four weeks and had a week off between Christmas and New Year's to go home to the farm."

For a change of pace, he then surprised critics as well as fans playing a sexual psycopath who menaces Polly Bergen and stalks Gregory Peck in *Cape Fear*. Mitchum appeared in cameo roles in Darryl F. Zanuck's World War II epic, *The Longest Day* (portraying Brigadier General Norman Cota) and in John Huston's mystery thriller, *The List of*

Adrian Messenger, and starred opposite Shirley MacLaine in Robert Wise's film version of William Gibson's Broadway hit, *Two for the Seesaw* and again as one of her several husbands in the overblown satire, *What A Way to Go!* He filmed *Rampage* in Hawaii, and played a big-game trapper in a ridiculous jungle *ménage-à-trois*; *Man in the Middle* in England, as the defense attorney in an army court martial; *Mister Moses* in Africa, starring as a fast-talking medicine man and itinerant diamond smuggler in a pseudobiblical parable set in the jungle.

Mitchum then stunned Hollywood by first agreeing to undertake a long publicity junket around the country to promote *Mister Moses* and then deciding to sell his farm in Maryland and move back to the film colony. "After six years, my old lady just didn't like living out there any more—what with me being away so often," Mitchum confided somewhat caustically. "Every time a wasp flew by or a bee stung her on the

Working again with son James on *The Last Time I Saw Archie* (1961).

behind, she'd look at me accusingly as If I had engineered it. So in the end I said, sort of jokingly, 'Okay, sell the joint.'" And she did, while Mitchum was making his first visit to the troops in Vietnam.

Returning to filmmaking, Mitchum then made several of the he-man, buddy-system westerns that teamed him with another screen veteran (or two): Andrew McLaglen's *The Way West* with Kirk Douglas and Richard Widmark, Howard Hawks's *El Dorado* with John Wayne, and Henry Hathaway's *Five Card Stud* with Dean Martin. In the first two, Mitchum's younger brother, John, had small roles as a pioneer and a bartender, respectively. During this time, Dorothy was supervising the family move from the Maryland farm to Hollywood—first to an apartment in Malibu, then to Cole Porter's old house, then into the digs formerly occupied by Ruth Roman, and finally to their present place in Bel Air. Mitchum himself revived his singing career, at his brother John's instigation—out of which came an album re-

On the set of *Two for the Seesaw* (1962) with Shirley MacLaine and director Robert Wise.

With Shirley MacLaine at premiere of *What A Way To Go!* (1964).

During the filming of *El Dorado,* entertaining his mother and the Major (1967).

corded in Nashville for Momument Records. Mitchen even came up with another hit in a ditty called "Little Old Wine Drinker," which he first had urged Dean Martin to record. Dean did— later.

Then followed a second trip to Vietnam to visit the troops in isolated places, traveling by helicopter and truck. The men, of course, always expected him to drink with them as heavily as his public reputation demanded. He later said: "One day we were out there in the boondocks and I must have consumed fourteen or sixteen cans of beer and the greater part of a bottle of whiskey, just to be sociable. I could hardly have orange juice with them, could I? And that was just lunch." When he arrived back in the States, bone-weary after spending up to fifteen hours every day with the front-line troops, Mitchum devoted himself to fulfilling promises he had made to them and called phone number after phone number, assuring parents all over America of their sons' safety.

Following this, it was off to Italy for a war movie (or, rather, an antiwar picture) called *Anzio* for director Edward Dmytryk, with whom Mitchum had worked two decades earlier in *Till the End of Time* and *Crossfire;* next, a trip to Spain to make *Villa Rides!,* a fictitious story about Pancho Villa

Enjoying a break with Dean Martin while filming *Five Card Stud* (1968).

(played by Yul Brynner) with Mitchum as a gun-running American pilot who is pressed into becoming Villa's one-man airforce. Chronologically, *Five Card Stud* came next. It was filmed in Durango, Mexico. From there, he was called in England by Joseph Losey, who offered him ten days work in *Secret Ceremony*. Mitchum accepted, and accepted—to the astonishment of his peers—special below-the-title billing. He disproved the nay-sayers, however, who maintained that once a star agrees to this type of billing, whether his name be boxed far down in the cast list or preceded by such phrases as "special guest star" or "and the extraordinary participation of," that star never again can command important billing. Mitchum's name, listed first, assured the success of many films since, beginning with back-to-back Burt Kennedy westerns, *Young Billy Young* (in which Mitchum acted for the first and only time with his younger son, Chris)* and *The Good Guys and the Bad Guys*, a very underrated cowboy movie spoof. *Young Billy Young* was produced by Max Youngstein, the husband of Mitchum's long-time secretary and business confidant, Reva Frederick (she's the third woman in his life after Dorothy and daughter Trina).

Mitchum spent nearly a full year in the town of Dingle in Ireland filming David Lean's *Ryan's Daughter*, and, according to an unending stream of erroneous press reports, boozing it up with his old collegue hell-raiser, Trevor Howard. Actually, he had cut down as the production dragged on and on, stopping, as he told a reporter, "out of sheer boredom." He also began telling interviewers on the set that he'd been thinking more and more about retirement and that *Ryan's Daughter* would be his last film. How had moviemaking changed over the years, critic William Wolf asked Mitchum on location. "It was an embarrassment then, and it's still an embarrassment," he replied. "There isn't any difference." And what would Mitchum do with his spare time if he made good on his threat to retire? "Goof off. Fool with the horses. I don't think I'd miss the movies. Most of them stink and, for my part, stardom is meaningless. For God's sake, Rin Tin Tin was a star."

When *Ryan's Daughter* was released in late 1970, Mitchum was being touted for an Oscar for his off-beat performance as Rosy Ryan's quiet, bespectacled school-teacher husband. MGM even twisted his arm into doing a publicity tour for the picture, which made a bundle. His retirement

*Chris subsequently has had roles in John Wayne movies like *Chisum, Rio Lobo,* and *Big Jake* and now works primarily in films on the international scene.

With the Mitchum ladies, Dorothy and Trina, at premiere of *Ryan's Daughter* (1970).

lasted a quick eight months. "I took one look at my 1971 taxes and decided I'd better get back to work." So he made *Going Home* for his Talbot Productions, playing a wife-killer who, years later, tries to establish a relationship with his son who had been mentally scarred by witnessing the murder. Next came Ralph Nelson's *The Wrath of God*, in which he starred (again) as a self-styled preacher who lets his guns do his talking for him. Both films were dismissed by the critics, although Mitchum got good personal notices—as usual.

He continues in the seventies as a big movie star and a professional (in the eyes of many dedicated reviewers, a consummate) actor, while grousing that the movie star bit is overblown. "The loot is good," he admits, while claiming he spends half his life figuring out how not to be one. His put-down act, though, fools few. His films of this period had been growing more adventuresome. *Going Home* (1971) was destroyed by MGM's then-chief, James Aubrey, but Mitchum's performance still shines through the wreckage. "We experimented with a new concept," Mitchum has boasted almost grudgingly. "Hopefully it pleased some." And *The Friends of Eddie Coyle* (1973) offered Mitchum in a brilliant study of a tired, small-time hood, just doing his job to keep his wife and kid from going on welfare.

Two abortive projects followed: Otto Preminger's *Rosebud* and Terence Young's (unrealized) *Jackpot*. He signed aboard for the Preminger movie (their third together) with much fanfare in May 1974, and was to have played Larry Martin, the intelligence agent hired to track down the Palestinian terrorists who had kidnapped five rich girls from a luxury yacht. "Otto fired me after three days work," Mitchum has said. "I reported to the set one morning at six o'clock and imitated his German accent and mannerisms for the crew. Old Otto came up to me screaming, 'You've been drinking!' I told him I did my share of drinking, but not at 6 A.M. for God's sake. But he kept yelling. I tried to break the tension on the set by imitating him again, and he almost had a stroke. He flew into a rage. 'You're through! Fired.' " With his customary cool, Mitchum bade Preminger farewell and split.

"I wasn't mad," Mitchum later told UPI's Vernon Scott. "Hell, I think Otto is funny. I don't believe he really wanted to fire me. He just lost his temper and it was too late. I didn't care one way or the other. It's funny. Preminger objects to drinking actors, but he replaced me with Peter O'Toole. Hell, that's like replacing Ray Charles with Helen Keller."

Several months later, *The New York Times* carried an announcement that Mitchum had signed to costar with Richard Burton and Charlotte Rampling in a film called *Jackpot* for director Terence Young. The plot was to revolve around a harried movie actor (Burton), his girlfriend, and a persistent investigator (Mitchum). "The producers made it sound as if I were all signed up, but I insisted on having my salary put in an American bank before I went to Nice to shoot. They wouldn't and I refused. They were still trying to pay Lee Marvin off for their last picture [*The Klansman*]. They conned Burton into it, but not me."

After spending some time in Japan filming Sydney Pollack's distinctive and quite costly *The Yakuza*, one of the most unusual (and enigmatic) action movies of the decade, Robert Mitchum finally had his chance to confim the long-held opinions of countless professional reviewers that he would be the perfect Philip Marlow, starring in the new version of Raymond Chandler's *Farewell, My Lovely*. Among the marvelous tales to come off the set of this production is the one that sounds most like pure Mitchum. Reportedly irked early-on by photographer-turned-director Dick Richards's incessant script-changing, the actor was said to have grumbled: "Listen, Richards, you've got to get your act together. I didn't sign my name on the line to have you change the script every five minutes. I have twelve lawyers outside in the parking lot and they're ready to leap on you if you make me do anything I didn't sign for. So stick to the script."

Mitchum's portrayal of Marlow sparked talk of

a second Oscar nomination three decades after his first. Incredibly, Avco-Embassy, which was releasing the film, removed Mitchum's name (and those of his costars) from its ads, in a pique, apparently, for his lack of cooperation in promoting *Farewell, My Lovely*. Regardless, the critics loved his engaging performance as Marlowe, and, shortly before the Academy Award nominations were announced in early 1976, Mitchum's associates convinced him to abandon his career-long avoidance of filmdom's public activities and assorted Hollywood hoopla. He actually turned up on television as a presenter at such ceremonial spectaculars as the Golden Globe and People's Choice Award affairs.

Since *Farewell, My Lovely*, Mitchum has acted in a cameo role in *Midway*—a one-day job as Admiral "Bull" Halsey, and then played Pat Brady, the Louis B. Mayer/Eddie Mannix character of F. Scott Fitzgerald's unfinished *The Last Tycoon*, "fiinished" for the screen by Harold Pinter. Mitchum said of its producer, Sam Spiegel: "I've seen him twice during the filming. He kissed me on the cheek and patted me on the ass." Subsequently, Mitchum was announced as the male lead opposite Vanessa Redgrave in David Susskind's filming of *The Lonely Passion of Judith Hearne*, for years mentioned as a starring vehicle for Mitchum's good buddy and leading lady, Deborah Kerr. This apparently will be an unrealized Mitchum project. Instead he took the lead in late 1976 in *The Amsterdam Kill*, an European-made film about international dope-smuggling.

Robert Mitchum continues to roll along as the

With Jeanne Moreau and director Elia Kazan during the filming of *The Last Tycoon*.

screen's happy rebel, "more amused than irritated by Hollywood hokum," Vernon Scott has reported. "In truth, he genuinely doesn't give a damn." He still marches to his own drum, parrying with interviews with an economy of words. Does he enjoy being an actor? "It keeps me out of mischief. And it's better than working. I gave work a shot once, and it was no good." Does he ever think about being a director? "I've considered that, but I doubt that I ever will because I'd have to arrive before the actors." Whom does he enjoy working with? "Whoever shows up."

On rare occasions, one can even catch the serious, professional Mitchum off the set—and probably off guard. Then, one is given a thoughtful comment that evidently expresses Mitchum's true feelings about the business of acting. "There's nothing to acting, really, as long as you have the grace that you can translate into human terms, if you're not choked up with self-consciousness, not impeded by technique," he has said. "I care. I'm prepared to be totally sacrificial to a picture. I don't care too much about myself, whether I come off well or badly; those are the breaks of the game. But I am concerned about the whole. That's what I'm hired for, to contribute to the total. I'm a people person and I like the whole togetherness of moviemaking, the ambience, the effort implicit in the manufacture of a film. I care about that . . . I really do."

PART II

The Robert Mitchum Movies

"I got a hundred bucks a week and all the horse manure I could take home."
—Robert Mitchum, 1943

"I like the whole togetherness of moviemaking, the ambiance, the effort implicit in the manufacture of a film. I care about that . . . I really do."
—Robert Mitchum, 1973

1
Border Patrol

United Artists, 1943

THE CAST:

Hopalong Cassidy, WILLIAM BOYD; *California Carlson,* Andy Clyde; *Johnny Travers,* Jay Kirby; *Orestes Krebs,* Russell Simpson; *Inez,* Claudia Drake; *Commandante,* Duncan Renaldo; *Don Enrique,* Cliff Parkinson; *Mexican Officer,* George Reeves; *Henchmen,* Bob Mitchum, Herman Hack, and Pierce Lyden.

Producer, Harry Sherman, *Associate Producer,* Lewis J. Rachmil; *Director,* Lesley Selander; *Screenplay,* Michael Wilson; *Photography,* Russell Harlan; *Music Director,* Irvin Talbot; *Art Director,* Ralph Berger; *Editor,* Sherman A. Rose. Running time: 64 minutes.

The Robert Mitchum saga started rather inauspiciously with a small part as a minor villain in the forty-third entry of the long-running Hopalong Cassidy series. Mitchum appeared in seven of these during 1943 and 1944, and he was billed—if at all—as Bob Mitchum.

There were sixty-six Hopalong Cassidy adventures filmed between 1935 and 1948, all starring William Boyd, who had been one of Cecil B. DeMille's foremost stars during the silent era. Boyd's later falling star was rescued by Harry "Pop" Sherman, an independent producer who,

in the mid-thirties, had obtained the rights to the Hoppy stories from Cassidy's creator, Clarence Edward Mulford. Sherman made himself and Boyd wealthy through the series of well-made, action-filled, black-and-white westerns that, of all the series turned out by Hollywood, was the most enduring Eventually, Boyd bought out Sherman and acquired all the production and television rights to Hoppy, putting himself in complete control of the radio and later television series as well as the last dozen theatrical adventures.

The Hoppy series followed a standard formula, except that its good-guy hero was dressed completely in black, making a striking, if somewhat fatherly figure, astride his all-white horse, Topper. True to the trio form, staple of the B western of the 1930s and 1940s, Hoppy rode with a young, good-looking sidekick (at various times, James Ellison, Russell Hayden, Brad King, Jay Kirby, Jimmy Rogers, and Rand Brooks) and, for comedy relief, a crusty, jack-of-all-trades partner (George "Gabby" Hayes, Britt Wood, and finally Andy Clyde). Usually Hoppy would be found in various locales, to avoid boring his ever-faithful followers, and occasionally he would not be seen as foreman of the Bar 20 Ranch but as the local

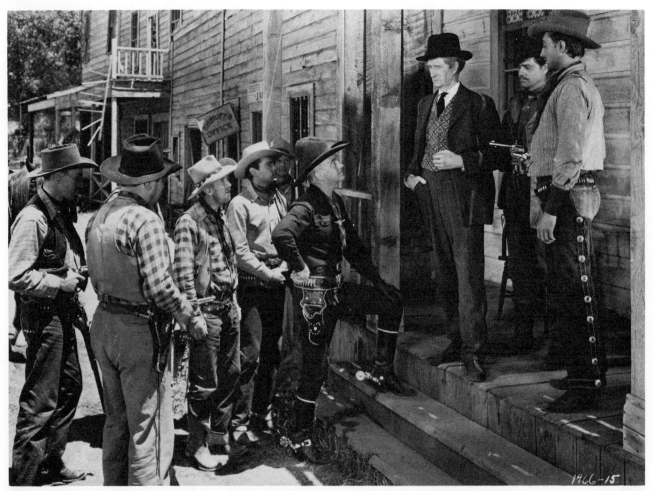

Mitchum (far right) with Andy Clyde (under sign), Jay Kirby, William Boyd, Russell Simpson, and Pierce Lyden in *Border Patrol*.

Mitchum (seated center) with Andy Clyde, Jay Kirby, William Boyd, Russell Simpson (behind bar), Herman Hack (standing under picture), and Pierce Lyden (far right) in *Border Patrol*.

sheriff or riding with the Texas Rangers.

Of all the young actors who gained film experience in the Hoppy stock company, none moved to greater stardom than the laconic, droopy-eyed, two-fisted bad guy (and once-in-a-while hero), Bob Mitchum.

Border Patrol, originally titled *Missing Men*, spotted unbilled Mitchum as a henchman for a ruthless silver-mine operator (Russell Simpson), who has been using Mexicans for slave labor. Hoppy and sidekicks California Carlson (Andy Clyde) and Johnny Travers (Jay Kirby) are Texas Rangers out to bring the villains to justice, but are instead framed for murder and only saved from hanging when a Mexican girl helps them make a getaway in time for the standard blood and thunder finale. George Reeves (later television's "Superman") and Duncan Renaldo (better known as the movies' "Cisco Kid") play Mexican army officers in this outing.

"It's not a slipshod Western," Dorothy Masters wrote in the New York *Daily News,* "but one that has [Boyd's] first rate acting and a believable story. . . . With good production and good acting, *Border Patrol* is a darned good Western."

2
Hoppy Serves a Writ

United Artists, 1943

THE CAST:

Hopalong Cassidy, WILLIAM BOYD; *California Carlson*, Andy Clyde; *Johnny Travers*, Jay Kirby; *Tom Jordan*, Victor Jory; *Steve Jordan*, George Reeves; *Jean Hollister*, Jan Christy; *Greg Jordan*, Hal Taliaferro; *Ben Hollister*, Forbes Murray; *Rigney*, Bob Mitchum; *Danvers (Storekeeper)*, Byron Foulger; *Jim Belnap (Clerk)*, Earle Hodgins; *Tod Colby*, Roy Barcroft; *Card Player*, Ben Corbett.

Producer, Harry Sherman; *Associate Producer*, Lewis J. Rachmil; *Director*, George Archainbaud; *Screenplay*, Gerald Geraghty; *Photography*, Russell Harlan; *Music Director*, Irvin Talbot; *Art Director*, Ralph Berger; *Editor*, Sherman A. Rose. Running time: 67 minutes.

In *Hoppy Serves A Writ*, ninth screen billing went to Bob Mitchum, who again did standard service as a minor villain. This time, as *Variety*, noted, "several wild chases, a lusty barroom fight, and pitched gun battles are included to satisfy action-minded audiences."

While driving a stage to the bank, Hoppy's pal, California Carlson (Andy Clyde), is robbed of $500 by Tom Jordan's gang. Jordan (Victor Jory), a big cattle buyer, actually is a large-scale rustler. California enlists the aid of sheriff Hopalong Cassidy, who decides to go after Jordan alone. Crossing into Oklahoma Territory, Hoppy pretends to be a cattle buyer and is invited into a high-stake card game with Jordan. Provoking a fight, Hoppy finds himself pounced upon by Jordan's henchmen, particularly Rigney (Mitchum).

California and deputy Johnny Travers (Jay Kirby) come to Hoppy's aid and manage to drive off Jordan's men. Then Hoppy comes up with the evidence needed to get the goods on the range boss, and with the help of his sidekicks, manages to lure Jordan and his men across the state line by pretending to steal back the cattle Jordan had conned from a rancher; on Texas soil, Hoppy serves his writ.

"*Hoppy Serves a Writ* shows Hopalong Cassidy doing nothing more or less than chasing crooks,

With William Boyd in *Hoppy Serves A Writ*.

With Jay Kirby, William Boyd, player, and Andy Clyde in *Hoppy Serves A Writ*.

bandits and cattle rustler—the same old thing, but you have to stop and admire the quality in the production," Wanda Hale wrote in the New York *Daily News*. Archer Winsten called the film in the *New York Post* "much fresher than other Westerns of more recent inspiration" and felt that "the hand-to-hand encounters find Boyd struggling through a vast and gratifying amount of shattered furniture . . . the picture adds up as a lively Western, with Boyd at his snowy best."

With Victor Jory and Forbes Murray in *The Leather Burners*.

3
The Leather Burners
United Artists, 1943

THE CAST:

Hopalong Cassidy, WILLIAM BOYD; *California Carlson,* Andy Clyde; *Johnny Travers,* Jay Kirby; *Dan Slack,* Victor Jory; *Sam Bucktoe,* George Givot; *Sharon Longstreet,* Shelley Spencer; *Bobby Longstreet,* Bobby Larson; *Randall,* Bob Mitchum; *Harrison Brooke,* George Reeves, *Lafe,* Hal Taliaferro; *Bart,* Forbes Murray.

Producer, Harry Sherman; *Associate Producer,* Lewis J. Rachmil; *Director,* Joseph Henabery; *Screenplay,* Jo Pagano; *Story,* Bliss Lomax; *Photography,* Russell Harlan; *Music Director,* Irvin Talbot; *Art Director,* Ralph Berger: *Editor,* Carrol Lewis. Running time: 66 minutes.

Mitchum remained on the payroll of dastardly Victor Jory in his third Hopalong Cassidy movie, also filmed in 1942, riding hard and engaging Hoppy in a lengthy, energetic display of fisticuffs. Of the ten actors listed in the cast, however, Mitchum is nowhere to be found.

The Leather Burners finds Hoppy and grizzled old California Carlson called to action by their saddlemate, Johnny Travers, whose ranch is being threatened by rustlers. Riding to Johnny's aid, Hoppy is offered a job by Dan Slack (Jory) and, suspecting that Slack might be involved with the rustlers, he accepts and then secretly sends a wire East inquiring about Slack. The telegrapher, in cahoots with Slack, phonies an answer.

Shortly thereafter, when the telegrapher is found dead, Hoppy and California are framed by Slack for his murder. Johnny asks pretty widow Sharon Longstreet (Shelley Spencer) to help get his pals out of jail. Then, with Hoppy's blessings, her young son Bobby (Bobby Larson) starts some junior sleuthing and follows some cattle trails to a hidden back entrance to a deserted mine. Hoppy's investigation inside the mine leads him to a crazy recluse, Sam Bucktoe (George Givot), who tells Hoppy that Slack and his henchmen (Mitchum, Hal Taliaferro, and Forbes Murray) had turned its passageways into a runway for stolen cattle. Hoppy and his pals soon find themselves in a pitched gun battle inside the mine and, after nearly being trampled in a cattle stampede, spot Bucktoe strangling Slack. Bucktoe, the brains behind the gang, orders his men to kill Hoppy, California, and Johnny, just as young Bobby arrives with the sheriff's posse. Bucktoe is killed, the rustlers are hustled off to the hoosegow, and Johnny decided to resume

With Cliff Parkinson (left), Ted Wells (checkered shirt), Bob Koortman (right), and players in *The Leather Burners.*

riding with Hoppy and California after Sharon decides to marry an Eastern lawyer (George Reeves).

Variety concluded: "To steal from the title, this is another leather burner in the popular Hopalong Cassidy series which appears to maintain a high standard in Western entertainment."

4

The Human Comedy

Metro-Goldwyn-Mayer, 1943

THE CAST:

Homer Macauley, MICKEY ROONEY; *Tom Spangler,* JAMES CRAIG; *Willie Grogan,* FRANK MORGAN; *Mrs. Macauley,* Fay Bainter; *Diana Steed,* Marsha Hunt; *Marcus Macauley,* Van Johnson; *Bess Macauley,* Donna Reed; *Tobey George,* John Craven; *Mary Arena,* Dorothy Morris; *Ulysses Macauley,* Jackie "Butch" Jenkins; *Miss Hicks,* Mary Nash; *Mrs. Steed,* Katharine Alexander; *Matthew Macauley,* Ray Collins; *Charles Steed,* Henry O'Neill; *Lionel,* Darryl Hickman; *Mr. Ara,* S. Z. Sakall; *Brad Stickman,* Alan Baxter; *Fats,* Barry Nelson; *Texas,* Don DeFore; *Horse,* Bob Mitchum; *Mrs. Sandoval,* Ann Ayars; *Negro,* Ernest Whitman; *First Soldier,* Mark Daniels; *Second Soldier,* William Roberts; *Helen Elliott,* Rita Quigley; *Hubert Ackley,* David Holt; *Blenton,* Byron Foulger; *Principal,* Wallis Clark; *Flirt,* Wally Cassell; *Mrs. Beaufrere,* Mary Servoss; *Mr. Beaufrere,* Morris Ankrum; *Daughter,* Lynn Carver; *Augie,* Carl "Alfalfa" Switzer; *Henderson,* Clem Bevans; *Librarian,* Adeline de Walt Reynolds; *Drunk at Bar,* Hobart Cavanaugh; *Policeman,* Emory Parnell; *Dolly,* Con-

nie Gilchrist; *Larry,* Frank Jenks; *Reverend Holly,* Howard Freeman; *Felix,* Jay Ward; *Bartender,* Robert Emmet O'Connor.

Producer/Director, Clarence Brown; *Screenplay,* Howard Estrabrook; *Based on the Novel by* William Saroyan; *Photography,* Harry Stradling; *Music,* Herbert Stothart; *Art Director,* Cedric Gibbons; *Editor,* Conrad A. Nervig. Running time: 118 minutes.

Mitchum's first role in an important film came when producer/director Clarence Brown cast him as a soldier on leave in MGM's unforgettable *The Human Comedy.* Despite twentieth billing, Mitchum has several nice scenes in the sequence

With Dorothy Morris, Don DeFore, Donna Reed, Barry Nelson, and Frank Morgan in *The Human Comedy*.

With Dorothy Morris, Don DeFore, Donna Reed, and Barry Nelson in *The Human Comedy*.

With Barry Nelson, Don DeFore, Dorothy Morris, and Donna Reed in *The Human Comedy*.

in which Donna Reed and Dorothy Morris allow themselves to be picked up on a rainy night by three lonely GIs—Mitchum, Barry Nelson, and Don DeFore.

The Human Comedy, based on William Saroyan's memorable bit of Americana, was stunningly, if somewhat sentimentally, made in the grand Metro-Goldwyn-Mayer manner during the latter part of 1942 with Louis B. Mayer's then-number-one star Mickey Rooney, heading a large cast and playing a teenager who learns the human comedy lived by the residents of the town and is shoved into adulthood when the war forces him to become the family breadwinner. Rooney won a Best Actor nomination from the Academy of Motion Picture Arts and Sciences for his performance.

The film received mixed notices, although it became an important 1943 moral-booster—a faithful translation of Saroyan, though a rambling movie. It tells of the joys and sorrows of the Macauley family and their friends in the atypical American town of Ithaca, California, during the early days of the war. Dead two years, father Matthew is survived by his wife and four children: Marcus, a private in the Army; Bess, a college sophomore; Homer, a high school junior who

works in the local telegraph office; and four-year-old Ulysses.

Those closest to them are Mary Arena, Marcus's girl-next-door; Tom Spangler, who runs the telegraph office with Willie Grogan, the philosophical drunk who often has to be sobered up by Homer and Tobey George, Marcus's army buddy, an orphan with neither home nor family who comes to be one of the Macauleys following Marcus's battlefield death.

Bosley Crowther, in *The New York Times,* wrote that "here, cheek by jowl and overlapping, are set some most charming bits of motion picture expression and some maudlin gobs of cinematic goo. . . . Here in a picture which endeavors to speak such truths about Americans as should be spoken, pop up such artificialities as make one squirm with rank embarrassment. . . . *The Human Comedy* is sentimental showmanship." (Nevertheless, he included the film in the runner-up list among his Ten Best of 1943.)

Time Magazine found that "at its best, *The Human Comedy* is immensely moving. Even its preaching sometimes achieves an eloquence that gives the picture a psychological fifth dimension. The Saroyan touch leaves nothing ordinary; the film is electric with the joy of life."

5
Aerial Gunner
Paramount, 1943

THE CAST:

Foxy Pattis, CHESTER MORRIS; *Ben Davis,* RICHARD ARLEN; *Sandy Lunt,* Jimmy Lydon; *Peggy Lunt,* Lita Ward; *Sgt. Gadget Blaine,* Dick Purcell; *Sgt. Jones,* Keith Richards; *Pvt. Laswell,* Billy Benedict; *Barclay,* Ralph Sanford; *Sergeant,* Bob Mitchum.

A Pine-Thomas Production. *Producers,* William Pine and William Thomas; *Director,* William Pine; *Screenplay,* Maxwell Shane; *Photography,* Fred Jackman, Jr.; *Art Director,* F. Paul Sylos; *Editor,* William Zeigler. Running time: 78 minutes.

Between cowboy assignments with the Hopalong Cassidy stock players, Mitchum put in some

"military" time at Paramount's legendary B unit with the Pine-Thomas players. For producers William H. Pine and William C. Thomas, the famed "Two Dollar Bills," Mitchum fleetingly engaged in wartime heroics in two films. The producers' renowned nickname came from their uncanny talent for turning out action-oriented features for supporting fare on double bills at rock-bottom budgets, with casts of familiar faces headed generally by Chester Morris and/or Richard Arlen. Their adventures followed a strict formula—fast pacing, two-fisted action—and quite often were set against a service background. The two in which Mitchum had roles, unbilled in each, fit the Pine-Thomas mold.

Aerial Gunner marked the directorial debut of William Pine and was somewhat more ambitious than the run-of-the-mill Pine-Thomas efforts. It was filmed "with the cooperation of the U.S. Army Air Corps," giving it the touch of authenticity, and was made at the government aerial gunnery school at Harlingen, Texas. Mitchum can be spotted doing a bit as a cadet in this filler about boyhood enemies (Chester Morris and Richard Arlen) who find themselves training together at gunnery school, with one sacrificing his life for the other during a climactic combat mission.

Although *Variety* found it "one of the best melodramas of precombat training to be wheeled out by any studio," *The New York Times'* Bosley Crowther bemoaned that "never do [the stars] rise above the ceiling prescribed by a normal B-film. This is strictly a picture for the shooting gallery trade . . . heroics for the bumpkins in one-syllable cliches."

6
Follow the Band

Universal, 1943

THE CAST:

Marvin Howe, EDDIE QUILLAN; *Dolly O'Brien,* MARY BETH HUGHES; *Mike O'Brien,* Leon Errol; *Juanita Turnbull,* Anne Rooney; *Pop Turnbull,* Samuel S. Hinds; *Tate Winters,* Bob Mitchum; *Jeremiah K. Barton,* Russell Hicks; *Specialties,* Leo Carrillo, Frances Langford, Ray Eberle, Alvino Rey and The King Sisters, The Kings Men, Skinnay Ennis and The Groove Boys, Hilo Hattie, The Bombardiers; *Cootie,* Bennie Bartlett; *Bert,* Frank Coghlan, Jr.; *Lucille Rose,* Jean Ames; *Peterson,* Irving Bacon; *Mrs. Forbes,* Isabel Randolph; *Brooks,* Frank Faylen; *Seth Cathcart,* Robert Dudley; *Alphonse,* Paul Dubov; *Charlie,* Frank Mitchell; *Mr. Hawkins,* Joe Bernard; *Photographer,* Charles Sherlock.

Associate Producer, Paul Malvern; *Director,* Jean Yarbrough; *Screenplay,* Warren Wilson and Dorothy Bennett; *Story* (as published in *Collier's*), Richard English; *Photography,* Elwood (Woody) Bredell; *Music Director,* Charles Previn; *Art Director,* John B. Goodman; *Editor,* Milton Carruth. Running time: 73 minutes.

With Anne Rooney and Eddie Quillan in *Follow the Band.*

With Anne Rooney and Samuel S. Hinds in *Follow the Band.*

Mitchum's first modern dress role was in *Follow the Band* (originally called *Trombone from Heaven*), and, as the second male lead, nearly got one of the two girls at the finale! This hayseed comedy with music, the epitome of Universal's grade B mini musicals of the era, allowed a threadbare plot that tied together ten or so specialty acts that provided the marquee lure.

Billed sixth in the cast (and nowhere on the ads) and still listed as Bob Mitchum, he was on hand as Eddie Quillan's rival for Anne Rooney, daughter

With Eddie Quillan, Anne Rooney, and Samuel S. Hinds in *Follow the Band.*

of dairyman Samuel S. Hinds. Quillan nominally starred—on the ads, Leo Carrillo received top billing, with Leon Errol second and Mary Beth Hughes third—as a hick who'd rather play his trombone than either milk cows or romance Miss Rooney, and is persuaded by Mitchum to go to New York on a fool's errand. There, through plot contingencies, Quillan meets bandleader Skinnay Ennis, who is impressed by the country boy's trombone technique and gets him a job playing at Leon Errol's restaurant. His success impresses Errol's niece, band singer Mary Beth Hughes, as well as the head of the dairy association (Russell Hicks), who decides to sponsor a radio show headlining Quillan. This new-found fame brings Anne Rooney scurrying to New York, where, to prevent the talented trombonist from following his rural girl back to the farm, Mary Beth Hughes poses as his new girlfriend.

Miss Rooney returns Quillan's ring and goes home to Mitchum, but all ends predictably as Quillan, now an important radio star, goes back to the farm—followed, of course, by the troupe from his program, determined that the show go on—where he convinces Anne to marry him, not Mitchum.

Interspersed among the lightweight proceedings are a series of production numbers, including one of the more memorable tunes of World War II, "Rosie the Riveter," sung by The King Sisters.

7

Colt Comrades

United Artists, 1943

THE CAST:

Hopalong Cassidy, WILLIAM BOYD; *California Carlson*, Andy Clyde; *Johnny Nelson*, Jay Kirby; *Lin Whitlock*, George Reeves; *Lucy Whitlock*, Gayle Lord; *Wildcat Willy*, Earle Hodgins; *Jeb Hardin*, Victor Jory; *Joe Bass*, Douglas Fowley; *Bart*, Bob Mitchum; *Varney*, Herb Rawlinson.

Producer, Harry Sherman; *Associate Producer*, Lewis J. Rachmil; *Director*, Lesley Selander; *Screenplay*, Michael Wilson; *Photography*, Russell Harlan; *Music Director*, Irvin Talbot; *Art Director*, Ralph Berger; *Editor*, Sherman A. Rose. Running time: 67 minutes.

An unbilled Robert Mitchum, henchman once again for Victor Jory, made his fourth Hopalong Cassidy film with most of the Hoppy stock company. "A good entry in the series," *Variety* concluded, "excellently photographed with sufficient action, riding, gunplay to get favorable reaction from western-minded audiences." As in previous outings, the plot boils down to basics: Hoppy versus cattle rustler Jory, with Mitchum helping do the boss' dirty work and taking the punches in the obligatory fight. "I was always being slammed against barroom walls by Hoppy." Mitchum since has boasted.

Colt Comrades finds Hoppy and his sidekicks, California and Johnny, hot on the trail of a hold-up man with $5,000 on his head. The three settle down for a while and buy half interest in a ranch owned by Lin Whitlock (George Reeves), but soon have a run-in with Jeb Hardin (Jory)

With Victor Jory and Douglas Fowley in *Colt Comrades*.

With William Boyd in *Colt Comrades*.

With William Boyd, Andy Clyde, and Jay Kirby in *Colt Comrades*.

56

over water rights. Hardin, it appears, has cut the townspeople off from the local dam so that only *his* cattle can make it to market. When Hoppy tries to organize the ranchers, Hardin has his vigilantes frame the interloper for rustling.

California, meanwhile, is conned into buying an oil derrick from Wildcat Willy (Earle Hodgins), but turns around and forces Willy to do the drilling. The well comes in—not with oil but water, and Willy then volunteers the information that Hardin had stolen deeds belonging to local ranchers. Learning this, Hoppy takes on Hardin and his men (Mitchum, Douglas Fowley, and Herb Rawlinson), recovers the stolen deeds, and then proves his own innocence and Hardin's guilt. Turning his share of the ranch over to Whitlock, Hoppy then rides off with his pals in search of further adventures.

8
Bar 20

United Artists, 1943

THE CAST:

Hopalong Cassidy, WILLIAM BOYD; *California Carlson,* Andy Clyde; *Lin Bradley,* George Reeves; *Marie Stevens,* Dustine Farnum; *Mark Jackson,* Victor Jory; *Slash,* Douglas Fowley; *Mrs. Stevens,* Betty Blythe; *Richard Adams,* Bob Mitchum; *One-Eye,* Francis McDonald; *Tom,* Earle Hodgins.

Producer, Harry Sherman; *Associate Producer,* Lewis J. Rachmil; *Director,* Lesley Selander; *Screenplay,* Morton Grant, Norman Houston, and Michael Wilson; *Photography,* Russell Harlan; *Music Director,* Irvin Talbot; *Art Director,* Ralph Berger; *Editor,* Carrol Lewis. Running time: 54 minutes.

Bar 20 differs from Mitchum's previous Hopalong Cassidy appearances in his being cast as the good guy and romantic lead. He was given eighth billing on the screen, although unlisted on the ads for the film. Also unusual was the casting of George Reeves as Hoppy's sidekick (Jay Kirby had left the company). The villain, as usual, was Victor Jory, while the leading lady was played by Dustine Farnum, daughter of the veteran silent cowboy star, Dustin Farnum.

With Dustine Farnum in *Bar 20.*

With Dustine Farnum and Victor Jory in *Bar 20.*

With Victor Jory in *Bar 20*.

In *Bar 20*, Hoppy, on his way to make a big cattle buy with California and Lin Bradley (Reeves), stumbles upon a stagecoach stickup. The three lose their money but save the lives of Marie Stevens (Miss Farnum), her fiancé, Richard Adams (Mitchum), her mother (Betty Blythe), and cattle baron Mark Jackson (Jory). After accompanying the Stevens ladies to their ranch, Hoppy and Jackson are held up again by the notorious One-Eye (Francis McDonald), who throws suspicion on Adams by leaving a gun with the initials "R.A." at the scene. Adams, meanwhile, has become suspicious of Hoppy's role in the robbery.

Jackson, the real gang leader, then sneaks away and rides to the hideout where he takes Hoppy's cash from One-Eye, planning to buy some of Adams's land with the stolen money. When California later recognizes Hoppy's stolen goldbacks in Adams's hand, he, Hoppy, and Lin follow Adams to a rendevous where the latter is to pay a ransom on jewelry stolen in the holdup. Finding the bandits' hideout, Hoppy and his pals capture One-Eye, but Jackson has One-Eye murdered. Dying, the bandit manages to tell Hoppy the real leader's identity. Hoppy then convinces both Adams and Marie of Jackson's evil machinations and enlists their aid in capturing the cattleman. Adams and Marie are married, and Hoppy and his pals ride off with their new herd of pedigreed cattle.

9
We've Never Been Licked

Universal, 1943

With Danny Jackson, Richard Quine and Noah Beery, Jr., in *We've Never Been Licked.*

THE CAST:

Brad Craig, RICHARD QUINE; *Nina Lambert,* ANNE GWYNNE; *Deedee Dunham,* MARTHA O'DRISCOLL; *Cyanide Jenkins,* NOAH BEERY, JR.; *Nishikawa,* Edgar Barrier; *Fat Man,* William Frawley; *Pop Lambert,* Harry Davenport; *Panhandle Mitchell,* Bob Mitchum; *Col. Jason Craig,* Samuel S. Hines; *Col. J. Armstrong,* Moroni Olsen; *Kubo,* Allen Jung; *Himself,* Bill Stern; *Announcer,* George Putnam; *Chip Goodwin,* Malcolm McTaggart; *Students,* William Blees, Paul Dubov, David Street, Dick Chandlee, Michael Moore, Danny Jackson, Roger Daniel, Dick Morris, Herbert Gunn, Henry Rogers, John Forrest, William Lechner, Bob Lowell, Michael Towne, Bill Nash, Jack Ray, Ward Wood, Jack Edwards, Jr.; *Adams,* Cliff Robertson; *Hank James,* Gordon Wynne; *Shotgun,* Bill Walker; *Captain,* Kenneth MacDonald; *Willie,* Mantan Moreland; *Yoshida,* Frank Tang; *Flight Commander,* John Frazer; *Conductor,* Henry Hall; *Soldier,* Phil Warren; *Deck Officer,* Kendall Bryson; *Italian Mentor,* Franco Corsaro; *German Mentor,* Walter Bonn; *Japanese Mentor,* Beal Fong; *Fortunio Tavares,* Alfredo DeSa; and William Kuhl, Sammy McKim, John James, Dean Benton, Don McGill, Bruce Wong, Alex Havier, Paul Langton, Richard Gunn.

Producer, Walter Wanger; *Director,* John Rawlins; *Screenplay,* Norman Reilly Raine and Nick Grinde; *Story,* Norman Reilly Raine; *Photography,* Milton Krasner; *Music Director,* Charles Previn; *song* "Me For You, Forever," Harry Revel and Paul Francis Webster; *Art Director,* John Goodman; *Editor,* Phil Cahn, Running time: 103 minutes, Reissued in 1949 as *Fighting Command.*

With Allan Jung (with glasses), Paul Dubov, Roland Got, Richard Quine, and players in *We've Never Been Licked.*

Walter Wanger's "tribute" to the Texas Aggies —the tale of a dedicated cadet who is kicked out of school because of his tolerant attitudes toward the Japanese but subsequently clears his name through his wartime heroics—is, as critic Bosley Crowther put it, "a wildly romantic fiction based on the old rah-rah college formula." Wanger's own description to the contrary, the film mixed western and gangster plots, dressing its characters in Army uniforms and throwing in a college cheer and a song or two.

Richard Quine, serviceable leading man of B

movies during the era and subsequently a film and television director, had the hero's role; Anne Gwynne was his sweetheart; Noah Beery, Jr., his roommate at college; and eighth-billed Bob Mitchum one of his cadet friends. When the film was reissued in 1950, it was retitled *Fighting Command,* and now-star Robert Mitchum was accorded sole billing above the title. For those expecting (in vain, it turns out) to view a Mitchum action movie, added enticement was offered by the catch phrase proclaiming it "The savage story of the fightin'est men who rose to glory when all seemed lost!"

Mitchum's lot, though, was to hover rather conspicuously in the background, as Texas A&M

football hero Quine is expelled after turning a secret weapon formula over to a Japanese spy ring, headed by William Frawley. Bitterly, Quine goes to Japan, ostensibly to broadcast propaganda for the enemy, but in reality to use his high Japanese connections to tip the Allies to the forthcoming invasion of the Solomons. Permitted to accompany an enemy bomber squad, Quine kills the pilot and guides a squadron of old Aggie pals (Mitchum among them) to a Jap aircraft carrier. The eyes of Texas are upon him as he dies a hero's death.

While *Variety* felt that "Walter Wanger has built a long but interesting picture around the character of the student," *The New York Times'* Bosley Crowther found that "the spirit of the film is sophomoric and the plotting so artificial that its pretensions to reality are ridiculous." Interestingly, the film did far better in its rerelease under a more positive title and with Mitchum's strong box-office name as the prime come-on.

10
Corvette K-225

Universal, 1943

THE CAST:

Lt. Cmdr. MacClain, RANDOLPH SCOTT; *Sub. Lt. Paul Cartwright,* James Brown; *Joyce Cartwright,* Ella Raines; *Stookey O'Meara,* Barry Fitzgerald; *Walsh,* Andy Devine; *Crickett,* Fuzzy Knight; *Stone,* Noah Beery, Jr.; *Vice-Admiral,* Richard Lane; *Smithy,* Thomas Gomex; *Lt. Rawlins,* David Bruce; *Jones,* Murray Alper; *Lt. Bill Gardner,* James Flavin; *Evans,* Walter Sande; *Merchant Ship Captain,* Oscar O'Shea; *Shephard,* Robert Mitchum; *First Officer,* John Frederick; *Convoy Cmdr. Ramsey,* Holmes Herbert; *Wardroom Steward,* Gene O'Donnell; *Bailey,* John Diggs; *Lt. LeBlanc (navigator),* Edmund Mac Donald; *Rogers,* Matt Willis; *Chief Engineer,* Charles McGraw; *Cmdr. Rowland,* Addison Richards; *Naval Captain,* Jack Wegman; *Steward,* James Todd; *Canadian Captain,* Milburn Stone; *Paymaster Commander,* Ian Wolfe; *British Captain,* Lester Matthews; *Workman,* Frank Faylen; *RAF Pilot,* Guy Kingsford; *Wireless Operator,* George O'Hanlon; *British Naval Officer,* Peter Lawford; *Torpedo Man,* Richard Crane; *Lookout,* Cliff Robertson.

Producer, Howard Hawks; *Director,* Richard Rosson; *Screenplay,* Lt. John Rhodes Sturdy; *Photography,* Tony Gaudio; *Convoy Photography,* Harry Perry; *Music,* David Butolph; *Music Director,* Charles Previn; *Art Directors,* John Goodman and Robert Boyle; *Special Effects,* John Fulton; *Assistant Director,* William Tummel; *Editor,* Edward Curtiss. Running time: 99 minutes.

Corvette K-225 was Universal's patriotic tribute to the British and Canadian navies' fleet of tiny escort warships known as corvettes. A stirring film of dedication and heroism, similar to but

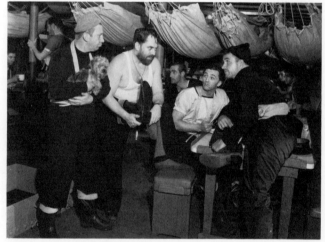

With Fuzzy Knight, Thomas Gomez, and Noah Beery Jr. in *Corvette K-225.*

lacking the scope of Noel Coward's classic *In Which We Serve,* which was released the previous year, *Corvette K-225* was produced by Howard Hawks, who cast the film (the original ads in *Variety* in August of 1942 listed Robert Stack and Patric Knowles as the stars), worked on the script and supervised the shooting. Hawks, though, left the actual directing to Richard Rosson, a minor workhorse from the early talkies. The film became the highlight of Rosson's career.

With Barry Fitzgerald and Thomas Gomez in *Corvette K-225*.

Randolph Scott gives an authoritative performance as the skipper whose first corvette has been shot out from under him. In port, he selects a new ship, oversees its building, romances briefly the sister of his executive officer who had been killed, grooms their brother as his new exec, and shoves off in his new K-225 with a crew including Barry Fitzgerald, Andy Devine, Fuzzy Knight, Thomas Gomez, Noah Beery, Jr. (Universal stock players, good and true), and others—like seventeenth billed Robert Mitchum.

When *Corvette K-225* and another film Mitchum made with Scott, *Gung Ho!*, were rereleased in 1948, Mitchum was elevated to co-star billing. What price stardom for Mitchum—and notoriety via the front-page exposure of his marijuana bust!

11
The Lone Star Trail

Universal, 1943

With Johnny Mack Brown in *The Lone Star Trail*.

THE CAST:

Blaze Barker, JOHNNY MACK BROWN; *Fargo Steele*, TEX RITTER; *Angus MacAngus*, Fuzzy Knight; *Joan Winters*, Jennifer Holt; *Doug Ransom*, George Eldredge; *Ben Slocum*, Bob Mitchum; *Sheriff Waddel*, Harry Strang; *Dan Jason*, Jack Ingram; *Steve Bannister*, Ethan Laidlow; *Jonathan Bentley*, Michael Vallon; *Major Cyrus Jenkins*, Earle Hodgins; *Bartender*, William Desmond; *Stage Passenger*, Billy Engle; *Townsman*, Denver Dixon; *Townsman*, Carl Mathews; *Lynch*, Eddie Parker; *Barfly*, Bob Reeves; *Bank Teller*, Henry Roquemore; *Mitchum's Double*, Tom Steele; and the Jimmy Wakely Trio (Jimmy Wakely, Johnny Bond, and Scotty Harrell).

Associate Producer, Oliver Drake; *Director*, Ray Taylor; *Screenplay*, Oliver Drake; *Story*, Victor Halperin; *Photography*, William Sickner; *Music Director*, H. J. Salter; *Songs*, Oliver Drake, Milton Rosen and Jimmy Wakely; *Art Director*, John Goodman; *Editor*, Roy Snyder. Running time: 57 minutes.

With Johnny Mack Brown, Earle Hodgins, and George Eldredge in *The Lone Star Trail*.

After completing his action roles in the first three Hopalong Cassidy movies in the fall of 1942, big Bob Mitchum grew a mustache and rode over to the back lot at Universal where another henchman role was available in Johnny Mack Brown's last western for that studio. Billed sixth in the cast, Mitchum used his fists and guns on behalf of treacherous George Eldredge, and battled the star in a barroom brawl that still ranks among the very best in the eyes of B-western enthusiasts.

Johnny Mack Brown, considered by movie historian and western authority John Cocchi to be not only one of the most likable and enduring of all western stars but also one of the all-time best movie cowboys (he made 178 films in his career), was joined by his regular screen team—Tex Ritter, Fuzzy Knight, Jennifer Holt, and the Jimmy Wakely Trio—for this latest episode of hard riding and straight shooting. He stars as Blaze Barker, a rancher who returns home to Dead Falls after spending two years in jail, framed by land-grabbers for a bank robbery he

With Tex Ritter, Johnny Mack Brown, Jennifer Holt, Harry Strang, George Eldredge, and Fuzzy Knight in *The Lone Star Trail*.

hadn't committed. Parolled, he cannot wear a gun, but is aided by Fargo Steele (Ritter), a U.S. Marshall, who rescues Blaze from several ugly situations and helps him rope in the quartet of cattle rustlers who had pinned the robbery on him. Lots of action and sharp dialogue added up to, in the opinion of *Film Daily*, "a rip-snorting Western."

12
Cry Havoc
Metro-Goldwyn-Mayer, 1943

THE CAST:

Lieutenant Smith, MARGARET SULLAVAN; *Pat Conlin*, ANN SOTHERN; *Grace Lambert*, JOAN BLONDELL; *Capt. Alice Marsh*, FAY BAINTER; *Flo Norris*, MARSHA HUNT; *Connie Booth*, ELLA RAINES; *Sadie*, Connie Gilchrist; *Andra West*, Heather Angel; *Sue West*, Dorothy Morris; *Stefania "Steve" Polden*, Gloria Grafton; Helen Domeret, Frances Gifford; *Lusita Esperito*, Fely Franquelli; *Nydia Joyce*, Diana Lewis; *Filipino Boy*, Billy Cruz; *Lieutenant Holt*, Allan Byron, *Soldier*, William Bishop; *Man*, Richard Crane; *Chaplain*, Morris Ankrum; *Marine*, Richard Derr; *Nurse*, Anna Q. Nilsson; *Groaning Man*, Bob Mitchum; *Dying Soldier*, Bob Lowell; *Doctor*, Russ Clark.

Producer, Edwin Knopf; *Director*, Richard Thorpe; *Screenplay*, Paul Osborne; *Based on the Play Proof Through the Night by* Allan R. Kenward; *Photography*, Karl Freund; *Music Director*, Daniele Amfitheatrof; *Editor*, Ralph E. Winters. Running time: 97 minutes.

Robert Mitchum had his briefest role in MGM's star-laden dramatic tribute to our nurses in the combat zone of World War II. Seen fleetingly as a dying soldier near the end of the film. Mitchum lies with his head on Ella Raines's lap, groans a few times, recites a word or two of choked dialogue, and becomes another war casualty.

Cry Havoc tells the story of a group of nurses and civilian aides caught up in the Bataan retreat, and features a stellar almost all-girl cast, headed by Margaret Sullavan as the stalwart heroine, Fay Bainter displaying her usual dignity as the girls' commanding officer, Ann Sothern as a wise-cracking, short-tempered former waitress, and Joan Blondell as a flashy ex-stripper. Similar in theme to *So Proudly We Hail*, Paramount's nurse movie released shortly before, *Cry Havoc* dedicated itself to paying homage to the sacrifices women were making in the war.

Actually, *Cry Havoc* had been filmed nearly a year before its release, and sat, for reasons unknown, in MGM's vaults. In chronological listings, therefore this would constitute Mitchum's third movie role. The film was made several months before Allan R. Kenward's source play opened on Broadway (as *Proof Thro' the Night*) on Christmas night, 1942—and closed on New Year's Day.

Newsweek wrote of the film version: "The popularity that *Cry Havoc* should achieve on the screen will stem less from this probably factual record of American nurses starving, sweating and dying in the beleagured Philippine jungle than from the impressive all-woman cast which Metro-Goldwyn-Mayer has rounded up for the historic occasion." Bosley Crowther said in his review in *The New York Times*: "It is moving . . . but it is also another of those pictures which is heavy with theatricality and the affectations of an all-girl cast."

13
False Colors

United Artists, 1943

With Andy Clyde and players in *False Colors*.

THE CAST:

Hopalong Cassidy, WILLIAM BOYD; *California Carlson,* Andy Clyde; *Jimmy,* Jimmy Rogers; *Bud Lawton/Kit Mayer,* Tom Seidel; *Faith Lawton,* Claudia Drake; *Mark Foster,* Douglass Dumbrille; *Rip Austin,* Bob Mitchum; *Sonora,* Glenn Strange; *Lefty,* Pierce Lyden; *Sheriff Clem Martin,* Roy Barcroft; *Judge Stevens,* Sam Flint; *Lawyer Jay Griffin,* Earle Hodgins; *Jed Stevers,* Elmer Jerome; *Townsman,* Tom Landon; *Bar Spectator,* Dan White; *Denton Townsman,* George Morrell.

Producer, Harry Sherman; *Associate Producer,* Lewis J. Rachmil; *Director,* George Archainbaud; *Screenplay,* Bennett Cohen; *Photography,* Russell Harlan; *Music Director,* Irvin Talbot; *Art Director,* Ralph Berger; *Editor,* Fred W. Berger. Running time: 65 minutes.

With Andy Clyde and William Boyd in *False Colors*.

The forty-ninth in the Hopalong Cassidy series, *False Colors* was grade-A Hoppy adventure—a fast-moving hour-plus "extremely long or entertainment," as *Film Daily* concluded. "The story is so packed with violent doings, the kids will work themselves into a dither." Mitchum again was the villain's chief henchman and got some good footage in one of his customary brawls with Hoppy. Notable in *False Colors* was the debut as Hoppy's young sidekick of Will Rogers's son, Jimmy, who used his own name for the character he played. Jimmy Rogers's screen career, unfortunately, never went far (he worked in six films with Hoppy), perhaps the result of *Variety*'s observation in its review of *False Colors:* "Jimmy . . . displays camera fright in his reading of lines."

Hoppy's task in this adventure is to ferret out the killers of the heir to a large cattle ranch. Joined by California Carlson and Jimmy Rogers, as undercover Texas Rangers, he heads for the Lawton ranch when the late owner's daughter, Faith (Claudia Drake), becomes suspicious of her brother's actions. Hoppy soon learns that Bud Lawton, the heir to the spread, has been killed and a lookalike installed in his place by Mark Foster (Douglass Dumbrille), the villainous town

Advertising for the 1950s reissue of the film (along with other Hoppy movies), capitalizing on the subsequent stardom of Mitchum, whose name is now larger than star William Boyd's and whose photo (at right) in modern dress has been "appropriated" from RKO's *Out of the Past* ad campaign.

boss who has been seeking the ranch to gain control of the local water rights.

Foster has his henchmen (Mitchum, Glenn Strange, and Pierce Lyden) keep Hoppy and his sidekicks occupied while he goes about legitimizing his rights to the land. Hoppy, California, and Jimmy manage, however, to outwit Foster's men and, after a series of pitched gun battles and a barroom brawl or two, herd the whole crew into sheriff Roy Barcroft's jail, clearing the way for Faith Lawton to regain her father's ranch.

14
Minesweeper

Paramount, 1943

THE CAST:

Lt. Jim Smith, RICHARD ARLEN; *Mary Smith*, JEAN PARKER; *Elliot*, RUSSELL HAYDEN; *Fixit*, Guinn "Big Boy" Williams; *Moms*, Emma Dunn; *Corney Welch*, Chick Chandler; *Lt. Wells*, Douglas Fowley; *Lt. Gilpin*, Frank Fenton; *Commander*, Charles D. Brown; *Cox*, Ralph Sanford; *Bos'n Helms*, Billy Nelson; *Chuck*, Bob Mitchum.

A Pine-Thomas Production. *Producers*, William Pine and William Thomas; *Director*, William Berke; *Screenplay*, Edward T. Lowe and Maxwell Shane; *Photography*, Fred Jackman, Jr.; *Art Director*, F. Paul Sylos; *Editor*, William Zeigler. Running time: 67 minutes.

Robert Mitchum turns up as a crew member in this Pine-Thomas action filler, made back-to-back with *Aerial Gunner* earlier in 1943 with much of the same cast and production team. And as with *Aerial Gunner*, Mitchum is unbilled and, in most filmographies compiled on him, uncredited.

In this unpretentious, mildly entertaining service melodrama, Jim Smith (Richard Arlen), a former naval lieutenant who had deserted several years before because of gambling debts, rejoins the Navy under a different name after Pearl Harbor. He soon finds a new buddy in the ship's jack-of-all-trades, Fixit (Guinn "Big Boy" Williams), and meets Fixit's daughter, Mary (Jean Parker). Smith makes remarkable progress as a "new" recruit, but finds himself with a rival for Mary in a fellow middie, Elliot (Russell Hayden). Shipped to the combat zone, Smith and Elliot are assigned to a diving operation, and when Smith's air hose becomes entangled, Elliot saves his life. While Smith is resting in the decompression chamber, his superior, Lt. Gilpin (Frank Fenton), discovers that he had been an honor student at Annapolis and quietly starts an investigation to learn the recruit's true identity.

Shortly thereafter, Smith, to win enough money for a ring for Mary, gambles and overstays his leave. Fixit reports in his place and is killed when his ship hits an enemy mine. Contrite, Smith discloses his past to Mary and tells her he intends to desert again. An emergency call sends him back to duty, though, and Gilpin, who had learned that Smith was AWOL, nevertheless permits him to join Elliot on another diving mission to locate a new type of mine in the area. When the two find the explosive, Smith, sensing the danger, uses a ruse to have Elliot pulled to the surface and then begins to defuse the mine, which detonates, killing him. Aboard the diving launch, Gilpin destroys the information revealing Smith's past, and his posthumously awarded Navy Cross is accepted by Mary.

Harrison's Reports found that "except for one or two situations, the film is sorely lacking in excitement . . . the players do their best, but they cannot overcome the weak story material."

15
Beyond the
Last Frontier
Republic, 1943

THE CAST:

John Paul Revere, EDDIE DEW; *Frog Millhouse,* SMILEY BURNETTE; *Susan Cook,* Lorraine Miller; *Sarge Kincaid,* Ernie Adams; *Steve Kincaid,* Richard Clarke; *Trigger Dolan,* Bob Mitchum; *Big Bill Hadley,* Harry Woods; *Major Cook,* Charles Miller; *Clyde Barton,* Kermit Maynard; *Slade,* Jack Kirk; *Doc Jessup,* Wheaton Chambers; *Bartender,* Frank O'Connor; *Stage Driver,* Curley Dresden; *Hadley's Henchmen,* Cactus Mack, Henry Wills, Al Taylor; *Ranger,* Ted Wells.

Associate Producer, Louis Gray; *Director,* Howard Bretherton; *Screenplay,* John K. Butler and Morton Grant; *Photography,* Bud Thackery; *Music,* Mort Glickman; *Art Director,* Russell Kimball; *Editor,* Charles Craft. Running time, 57 minutes.

"A Texas Ranger must shoot like a Tennessean, ride like a Mexican, and fight like the devil!" This credo highlighted the ads that kicked off Republic's new western series about John Paul Revere, a stalwart young Texas Ranger. Unfortunately, the studio had cast in the lead a colorless cowboy actor and dubious hero, Eddie Dew. Republic was unable to drum up much interest in either Dew or "John Paul Revere," and after a second entry replaced Dew with Bob Livingston and then abandoned the whole series shortly thereafter.

In *Beyond the Last Frontier,* Dew is a Ranger who works undercover to get the goods on Harry Woods' gang of gunrunners, and fourth-billed Bob Mitchum is one of Woods's henchmen who becomes rehabilitated. Mitchum outacted everyone else in the film.

Posing as a nefarious outlaw, Revere (Eddie Dew) infiltrates the smuggling operation of Big Bill Hadley (Woods), spies on the gang, and sneaks off at night to report to the Rangers through his pal, Frog Millhouse (Smiley Burnette). Suspicious when the Rangers too often interfere with his plans, Hadley plants his own man, mean eyed Trigger Dolan (Mitchum), among them. Beneath his swagger, Trigger soon becomes a disgruntled spy after being impressed by the fair treatment he receives from "the enemy." Meanwhile, Hadley forces a showdown with the Rangers, and in the dead of night, he has his gang overpower Revere's sidekick, Frog, who has been guarding the illegal arms the Rangers have taken from Hadley. After seizing the weapons, the gang sets fire to a stable, leaving Frog to die in the flames. Sickened by this, Trigger returns to the burning building and risks his life to save the old Ranger. Revere rushes in and rescues both Trigger and Frog before the flaming roof falls in, and then, with Trigger's help, he takes care of Hadley and his gang. Trigger is promised that after a brief jail sentence a spot will be waiting for him with the Texas Rangers.

With Eddie Dew in *Beyond the Last Frontier.*

In *Beyond the Last Frontier*.

16
The Dancing Masters

20th Century-Fox, 1943

THE CAST:

Stan, STAN LAUREL; *Oliver*, OLIVER HARDY; *Trudy Harlan*, Trudy Marshall; *Grant Lawrence*, Robert Bailey; *Wentworth Harlan*, Matt Briggs; *Louise Harlan*, Margaret Dumont; *George Worthing*, Allan Lane; *Mickey*, Bob Mitchum; *Silvio*, Nestor Paiva; *Jasper*, George Lloyd; *Reservations Clerk*, Edward Earle; *Butler*, Charles Rogers; *Dentist*, Sperry Hall; *Pianist*, Sam Ash; *Truck Driver*, William Haade; *Director*, Arthur Space; *Mother*, Daphne Pollard; *Mr. Featherstone*, Emory Parnell; *Vegetable Man*, Hank Mann; *Bus Driver*, Chick Collins; *Auctioneer*, Robert Emmett Keane; *Dowager*, Florence Shirley; *Man on Crutches*, Harry Tyler; *Gangster*, George Tyne; *Barker*, Hallam Cooley; *Stage Driver*, Jay Wilsey (Buffalo Bill, Jr.).

Producer, Lee Marcus; *Director*, Malcolm St. Clair; *Screenplay*, W. Scott Darling; *Story*, George Bricker; *Photography*, Norbert F. Brodine; *Misic*, Arthur Lange; *Music Director*, Emil Newman; *Art Director*, James Basevi; *Editor*, Norman Colbert. Running time: 63 minutes.

Tying his horse to a hitching post and hanging up his cowboy duds, Mitchum donned a suit, tie, top coat, and soft hat to play a comic villain in a minor Laurel and Hardy romp at 20th Century-Fox. "I was now a character actor," Mitchum has recalled wryly, "I played just about everything: Chinese laundrymen, midgets, Irish washerwomen, faggots. I even played a journalist once. I don't know what I was like. I never *saw* the pictures. But I got overtime, and I'd live on my overtimes and save my basic salary." The next time Mitchum was to set foot on the Fox lot, he would be a major star, working opposite (and billed above) Marilyn Monroe.

In *The Dancing Masters*, he and George Lloyd are strong-arm men for Nestor Paiva's protection racket, and in one or two scenes, "encourage" Oliver Hardy into taking out an accident policy on his pal, Stan Laurel, operators of the floundering Arthur Hurry School of Dancing. One of Stan and Ollie's pupils, Trudy Harlan (Trudy Marshall) is in love with Grant Lawrence (Robert Bailey), a young inventor working in her father's war materiel plant. Grant has developed a revolutionary new laser gun but is fired from his job before he can demonstrate it to Mr. Harlan (Matt Briggs).

Realizing that Grant needs backing for his invention, Trudy talks Stan and Ollie into volunteering to conduct a laser demonstration in the garden on the Harlan estate. It is a flaming success, although it gets out of hand and sets the Harlan house ablaze. Vowing to replace Grant's destroyed laser, Ollie recalls the accident policy he had taken out on Stan, and arranges a series of mishaps on which he can collect the needed insurance money. These "accidents" lead the boys to adventures on a runaway bus, which somehow finds its was to an amusement park and onto the rollercoaster tracks. The result is that Ollie only manages to break his own leg and land in the hospital.

With George Lloyd, Oliver Hardy, and Stan Laurel in
The Dancing Masters.

Nevertheless, right finally prevails, with Trudy and Grant reunited at Ollie's bedside and Harlan agreeing to finance Grant's invention. Most Laurel and Hardy authorities rate this vehicle among the team's lesser works. In his book, *The Films of Laurel and Hardy,* cinema historian William K. Everson wrote: "*The Dancing Masters* remains an amusing comedy, fast-paced despite its excess of plot. . . . Laurel, however, was now getting rather too old to continue to be amusing in his dame masquerade, especially when clad in ballet skirt and tights." And in *The New York Times,* critic Theodore Strauss felt: "*The Dancing Masters*

is a better bargain than their recent full-length excursions. . . . [It] is neither original nor under-stated but its slow-motion insanity does manage to be funny sometimes." Less kind was the reviewer for the New York *Daily News,* who awarded the film a negligible one-half star, and the critic for *Variety* agreed, feeling that: "It's strictly for the duals [double bills]," and complaining that "the pair go through their usual slapdash stuff."

For Robert Mitchum, in any case, a job was a job, and as an up-and-coming young player, any role provided needed screen exposure as well as invaluable experience.

17
Doughboys in Ireland

Columbia Pictures, 1943

THE CAST:

Danny O'Keefe, KENNY BAKER; *Molly Callahan,* JEFF DONNELL; *Gloria Gold,* LYNN MERRICK; *Chuck Hayers,* Guy Bonham; *Corny Smith,* Red Latham; *Tiny Johnson,* Wamp Carlson; *Ernie Jones,* Bob Mitchum; *Jimmy Martin,* Buddy Yarus; *Mickey Callahan,* Harry Shannon; *Mrs. Callahan,* Dorothy Vaughan; *Captain,* Larry Thompson; *Sergeant,* Syd Saylor; *Larry Kent,* Herbert Rawlinson, *Medical Captain,* Neil Reagan; *Miss Wood,* Constance Wood, *Soldier,* Harry Anderson; *Sentry,* James Carpenter; *Corporal,* Craig Woods; *Nick Greco,* Muni Seroff.

Producer, Jack Fier; *Director,* Lew Landers; *Screenplay,* Howard J. Green and Monte Brice; *Photography,* L. W. O'Connell; *Music Director,* Morris Stoloff; *Art Director,* Lionel Banks; *Set Decoration,* Frank Tuttle; *Editor,* Mel Thorsen. Running time: 61 minutes.

In this minor-league musical from Columbia, which wastes the singing talents of tenor Kenny Baker and wavers between farce comedy and heavy dramatics, Robert Mitchum turns up as one of the hero's buddies. On the ads, he was billed seventh—after The Jesters (a popular radio and club singing group of the era).

Doughboys in Ireland is formula program material turned out during the war to fill out theater bills. In this one, Danny O'Keefe (Kenny Baker), a club bandleader and vocalist, is inducted into the army, but before leaving, gets his girl, Gloria Gold (Lynn Merrick), the band's singer, to promise she'll wait for him. Stationed in Ireland, Danny spends the days waiting for mail from Gloria, but she is an ambitious girl and takes up with a Broadway producer when he lands her a show.

On guard duty, Danny meets a local colleen, Molly Callahan (Jeff Donnell), after her dad (Harry Shannon) and the other Callahans take on the army in a local brawl over her. In order to avoid another set-to, Danny pretends he's in love

with Molly, although his heart still belongs to Gloria, who turns up as special USO entertainer. Molly resigns herself to giving up Danny, but her mother (Dorothy Vaughan) sends her back to win him over. Finding him hospitalized after being seriously wounded, she nurses him back to health and proves that she is the girl for him.

"Even Kenny Baker's superb ballading fails to save *Doughboys in Ireland* from being a lightweight supporting feature," wrote *Variety.* "Why Baker's valuable singing voice should be wasted on this trite vehicle is difficult to understand . . . the picture moans for a couple of outstanding thespians." Also difficult to comprehend is the name "doughboys" in the title—a term that went out with World War I!

With Jeff Donnell, Kenny Baker, and players in *Doughboys in Ireland.*

Mitchum and players, plus The Jesters, Kenny Baker (on cot), and Buddy Yarus in *Doughboys in Ireland.*

18
Riders of the Deadline

United Artists, 1943

With William Boyd and Anthony Warde in *Riders of the Deadline*.

THE CAST:

Hopalong Cassidy, WILLIAM BOYD; *California Carlson,* Andy Clyde; *Jimmy,* Jimmy Rogers; *Tim Mason,* Richard Crane; *Sue,* Frances Woodward; *Crandall,* William Halligan; *Madigan,* Tony Warde; *Drago,* Bob Mitchum; *Tex,* Jim Bannon; *Martin,* Hugh Prosser; *Captain Jennings,* Herb Rawlinson; *Calhoun,* Montie Montana; *Sourdough,* Earle Hodgins; *Kilroy,* Bill Beckford; *Sanders,* Pierce Lyden; *Tom,* Herman Hack.

Producer, Harry Sherman; *Associate Producer,* Lewis J. Rachmil; *Director,* Lesley Selander; *Screenplay,* Bennett Cohen; *Photography,* Russell Harlan; *Music Director,* Irvin Talbot; *Art Director,* Ralph Berger; *Editor,* Walter Hanneman. Running time: 68 minutes.

With Herman Hack, William Boyd and Jack Rockwell in *Riders of the Deadline*.

Bob Mitchum (as he still was being cast) played his last B-western villain in *Riders of the Deadline.* For a change, he apparently was noticed enough to be singled out by *Variety,* which wrote: "Bob Mitchum is a tough customer who continually tangles with Boyd."

In this outing, Hoppy and his sidekicks, California and Jimmy, are trying to track down a band of gun smugglers. When a tough character named Madigan (Tony Warde), thought to be involved in the smuggling racket, has Hoppy's Texas Ranger buddy, Tim Mason (Richard Crane), killed, Hoppy pretends to turn outlaw and lets Madigan's gang use his Bar 20 ranch as a hideout. His ploy to gain Madigan's confidence is successful, but he soon realizes that he still doesn't have the top man in the organization. Elbowing aside the boss' henchmen (Mitchum, Herman Hack, and Pierce Lyden) to become Madigan's right-hand man, he finally breaks the case after some hard riding and a barrage of .45s, unmasking Crandall (William Halligan), the town banker, as the brains behind the gang.

"The yarn is strictly formula and oft-told," *Variety* wrote, "with only the familiar characters of

With William Boyd and William Halligan in *Riders of the Deadline*.

the series and background exteriors holding the feature up for more than passing attention." Archer Winsten of the *New York Post,* found: "Same people, same troubles, same end. You might reply: 'Sighted Western; sunk by same.'" He then noted that "the picture has one special source of interest. Bill Boyd's fisticuffs fascinate

because he is so stiff. There's always the possibility that he might break his own arm."

And in the *Daily News,* Wanda Hale called it "a typical Bill Boyd Western, well made, fast moving, less brutal than most, and just right for Western fans."

19
Gung Ho!
Universal, 1943

THE CAST:

Colonel Thorwald, RANDOLPH SCOTT; *Kathleen Corrigan,* GRACE MacDONALD; *John Harbison,* ALAN CURTIS; *Kurt Richter,* Noah Beery, Jr.; *Lt. Christoforos,* J. Carrol Naish; *Larry O'Ryan,* David Bruce; *Kozzarowski,* Peter Coe; *Pigiron Mathews,* Bob Mitchum; *Rube Tedrow,* Rod Cameron; *Lt. Roland Browning,* Louis-Jean Heydt; *Captain Dunphy,* Richard Lane; *Commander Blade,* Milburn Stone; *Transport,* Sam Levene; *Frankie Montana,* Harold Landon; *Buddy Andrews,* John James; *Gunner McBride,* Walter Sande; *Sgt. Jim Corrigan,* Harry Strang; *Waiter,* Irving Bacon; *Singing Marine,* Joe Hayworth; *Marine on Sub,* Carl Varnell; *Sub Officer,* Robert Kent; *Narrator,* Chet Huntley.

Producer, Walter Wanger; *Director,* Ray Enright; *Screenplay,* Lucien Hubbard; *Based on a Factual Story by* Capt. W. S. LeFrancois, U.S.M.C.; *Photography,* Milton Krasner; *Music,* Frank Skinner; *Music Director,* H. J. Salter; *Art Directors,* John B. Goodman and Alexander Golitzen; *Special Effects,* John P. Fulton; *Editor,* Milton Carruth. Running time: 88 minutes.

Mitchum's prolific screen activity during 1943 started paying off handsomely, with the increasing amount of film footage he began obtaining. In Walter Wanger's flag-waving *Gung Ho!,* a fairly factual re-creation of the celebrated August 1942 assault on Japanese-held Mackin Island by Colonel Evans Carlson's raiders (forerunners of the Green Berets), Mitchum appears the archetypal leatherneck in his second consecutive war movie—as well made as the one that preceded it was bush league. The top-budget audience

rouser, an almost all-male film, graphically demonstrated the wartime pulling power of star Randolph Scott who, like John Wayne and Errol Flynn, showed how easily (if energetically) he won it all for our side. (Scott and Mitchum shared equal co-star billing in the advertising when this film and *Corvette K-225* were reissued both together and separately several years later.)

In *Gung Ho!,* Scott is Colonel Carlson's fictional counterpart, tough and unsmiling Colonel Thorwald. J. Carrol Naish, cast as the fictional Lt. Christoforos, is on hand to chronicle the raid (the character is based on Capt. W. S. LeFrancois,

With John James and Harold Landon in *Gung Ho!*

With John James and Randolph Scott in *Gung Ho!*

With J. Carrol Naish and players in *Gung Ho!*

author of the source material), while most of the others in Scott's outfit are Hollywood's stock leatherneck types: Rod Cameron is the obligatory oversized hillbilly; Alan Curtos the minister; Harold Landon the big-city toughie; John James the Jap hater; Peter Coe the standard Polish bruiser; and Mitchum the ex-boxer who is wounded in action. In his big scene, Mitchum, lying on a stretcher in a rear evacuation area after being shot in the throat, spots a Japanese sniper taking a bead on one of the medics. Unable to shout a warning, he struggles to a sitting position, flings a knife at the sniper, and falls back exhausted—all in true gung ho style!

Bosley Crowther observed in *The New York Times*: "Mr. Enright has directed for good tension and pyrotechnic display, the settings are true, and the fighting on the island is as hot and lurid as any that we've seen. . . . *Gung Ho!* is for folks with strong stomachs and a taste for the sub-machine gun."

20
Mr. Winkle Goes to War
Columbia Pictures, 1944

THE CAST:

Wilbert Winkle, EDWARD G. ROBINSON; *Amy Winkle*, Ruth Warrick: *Barry*, Ted Donaldson; *Jack Pettigrew*, Bob Haymes: *Sergeant "Alphabet,"* Richard Lane; *Joe Tinker*, Robert Armstrong; *Ralph Wescott*, Richard Gaines; *Plummer*, Walter Baldwin; *McDavid*, Art Smith; *Martha Pettigrew*, Ann Shoemaker; *A. B. Simkins*, Paul Stanton; *Johnson*, Buddy Yarus; *Captain*, William Forrest; *Gladys*, Bernadene Hayes; *Hostess*, Jeff Donnell; *Mayor*, Howard Freeman; *Sergeant #1*, James Flavin; *Corporal*, Bob Mitchum; *Doctor*, Herbert Hayes; *Sergeant #2*, Fred Kohler, Jr.; *Draftees*, Fred Lord, Cecil Ballerino, Ted Holley; and Ben Taggart, Sam Flint, Nelson Leigh, Forrest Murray, Ernest Hilliard, Les Sketchley, Nancy Evans, Ann Loos, Larry Thompson, Earl Cantrell, Warren Ashe, Ed Jenkins, Paul Stupin, Terry Frost, Hugh Beaumont, Dennis Moore, Emmett Vogan, Tommy Cook.

Producer, Jack Moss: *Associate Producer*, Norman Deming; *Director*, Alfred E. Green; *Screenplay*, Waldo Salt, George Corey, and Louis Solomon; *Based on the Novel by* Theodore Pratt; *Photography*, Joseph Walker; *Music Score*, Carmen Dragon and Paul Sawtell; *Music Director*, M. W. Stoloff; *Assistant Director*, Earl Bellamy; *Art Directors*, Lionel Banks and Rudolph Sternad; *Editor*, Richard Fantl. Running time: 80 minutes.

In uniform again, Mitchum makes a fleeting appearance as a corporal in this mild comedy that starred Edward G. Robinson as a middle-aged bank clerk who gets drafted. In his autobiography, Robinson admitted that the film was trivial. "Yet deep in my heart," he wrote, "I was grateful that anyone would find a role for a fifty-one-year-old man."

Wilbert George Winkle, a bank clerk for fourteen years, builds himself a fixit shop next to his home, where he finds satisfaction in doing odd jobs—enough, apparently, to quit the bank, to the dismay of his wife, Amy (Ruth Warrick), who gives him an ultimatum: return to the bank or move into the shop. Winkle chooses the latter. When a draft notice arrives in the mail, Winkle is astounded. Although the country is still drafting men up to age of forty-five, forty-four-year-old Winkle does not believe he will be inducted, but he is wrong, and accompanied by neighbor Jack Pettigrew (Bob Haymes), he is off to basic training camp. (One of their instructors, seen briefly, is Mitchum.)

Winkle manages to survive basic training and is shipped to the South Pacific with Pettigrew and "older" buddies Joe Tinker (Robert Armstrong) and Alphabet (Richard Lane). Sent to repair a bulldozer during an enemy attack, Winkle drives it toward a sniper's foxhole and plows the gunner under. Wounded, he later learns that both Tinker and Alphabet had been killed. He is given a medal and sent home, but he by-passes the hometown celebration awaiting his arrival and goes directly to his old fixit shop. There he is reconciled with Amy.

"The erstwhile Little Caesar does everything within his power to give a comic situation of a Casper Milquetoast turned G.I., and some of his flashes of bewilderment are briefly amusing,"

critic Bosley Crowther thought. But Howard Barnes of the *New York Herald Tribune* felt "The truth remains that he merely walks through his role, leaving a trail of tiny, tiresome situations behind him . . . Robinson swaggers through most of the sequences, not quite sure whether he is Little Caesar or a timid bookkeeper."

Of stock player Mitchum's blink-of-the-eye appearance, nothing was noted in print.

21
Girl Rush

RKO Radio, 1944

With Frances Langford in *Girl Rush*.

THE CAST:

Jerry Miles, WALLY BROWN; *Mike Strager*, ALAN CARNEY; *Flo Daniels*, FRANCES LANGFORD; *Suzie Banks*, Vera Vague; *Jimmy Smith*, Robert Mitchum; *Muley*, Paul Hurst; *Claire*, Patti Brill; *Emma*, Sarah Padden; *Barlan*, Cy Kendall; *Scully*, John Merton; *Martha*, Diana King; *Prospector*, Michael Vallon; *Monk*, Sherry Hall; *Bartender*, Kernan Cripps; *Dealer*, Wheaton Chambers; *Dave*, Ernie Adams; *Mac*, Lee Phelps; *Oscar*, Byron Foulger; *Girl*, Chili Williams; *Members of Troupe*, Rita Corday, Elaine Riley, Rosemary LaPlanche, Daun Kennedy, and Virginia Belmont.

Producer, John Auer; *Director*, Gordon Douglas; *Screenplay*, Robert E. Kent; *Story*, Laszlo Vadney and Aladar Laszlo; *Photography*, Nicholas Musuraca; *Music*, Gene Rose; *Music Director*, C. Bakaleinikoff; *Songs*, Lew Pollack and Harry Harris; *Musical Numbers* staged by Charles O'Curran; *Art Directors*, Albert S. D'Agostino and Walter Keller; *Special Effects*, Vernon L. Walker; *Editor*, Duncan Mansfield, Running time: 65 minutes.

Robert Mitchum began his lengthy tenure at RKO as he had as a free-lancer—in cowboy duds. Assigned to Sid Rogell's B unit, he first was cast in a frontier musical in support of RKO's house comics, Wally Brown and Alan Carney. Director Gordon Douglas wanted him for the role but the front office, it seems, hadn't really pictured Mitchum as a "romantic" leading man, just a possible action star.

Girl Rush turned out a better than average B about a couple of second-rate vaudevillians during the Gold Rush, and Mitchum a young, footloose miner who gets mixed up with them. The plot: Barbary Coast saloon comics Jerry Miles (Brown) and Mike Strager (Carney), stranded when gold is discovered Sutter's Mill, in desperation try prospecting to hold their troupe together—singer Flo Daniels (Frances Langford), lady stooge Suzie Banks (Vera Vague), and eight dancing girls. Unsuccessful as miners, the boys then drift on to Red Creek, a boom town, where they get into trouble working their crooked shell game at the local gambling place.

Learning that the pair had a troupe of girls back in San Francisco, the miners agree to stake the show to Red Creek where the girls can become prospective brides. The boys plan to take off for New York with the miners' money, but are finessed when Jimmy Smith (Mitchum) and Muley (Paul Hurst) are sent with them to make

With Wally Brown, Paul Hurst, and Alan Carney in *Girl Rush*.

With Sarah Padden, Paul Hurst, Vera Vague, Frances Langford, Wally Brown, and Alan Carney in *Girl Rush*.

sure that everyone comes back to Red Creek. En route, the stage is ambushed by crooked miner Barlan (Cy Kendall) and his men, but Jimmy and Muley hold off the outlaws after instructing their passengers to go on to San Francisco. There, Jerry and Mike prepare to skip with the girls, but Jimmy and Muley turn up too soon, and Flo, attracted to Jimmy, persuades then all to return to Red Creek.

As the troupe reaches the outskirts of town, Jimmy finds that Barlan's men now intend to kill the men and kidnap the girls, and he devises a plan to outwit the villains, convincing Jerry, Mike, and Muley to join him disguised as women. They then take on the outlaws in a knock-down fight. Jerry and Mike are now free to stage their show before a packed house, which immediately empties when news arrives of a new gold strike, leaving the company to play to empty seats as it had when the story began.

"Robert Mitchum," *Variety* reported, "catches attention with a smooth performance and a likeable personality." That likeable personality together with a virile image convinced RKO that

Mitchum would be perfect as the star of its newly planned Zane Grey cycle of B westerns.

22
Johnny Doesn't Live Here Anymore

Monogram, 1944

With James Ellison and William Terry in *Johnny Doesn't Live Here Anymore*.

THE CAST:

Kathi Aumont, SIMONE SIMON; *Mike O'Brien*, JAMES ELLISON; *Johnny Moore*, WILLIAM TERRY; *Mrs. Collins*, Minna Gombell; *Jack*, Chick Chandler; *Judge*, Alan Dinehart; *Sally*, Gladys Blake; *CPO Jeff Daniels*, Robert Mitchum; *Irene*, Dorothy Granger; *Georgie*, Grady Sutton; *Mr. Collins*, Chester Clute; *The Shrew*, Fern Emmett; *B. O. Rumplestiltskin (The Gremlin)*, Jerry Maren; *The Iceman*, Joe Devlin; *Gladys*, Janet Shaw; *Court Recorder*, Charles Williams; *Rudy*, Douglas Fowley; *David (neighbor)*, Harry Depp; *Cab Driver*, Duke York; *Cab Passengers*, Emmett Lynn and Pat Gleason; *Conductor*, Milton Kibbee; *Recruit*, Sid Melton; *Charlie Miller (silk stocking salesman)*, George Chandler; *Marine Sergeant*, Dick Rich; *Chauffeur*, Frank Scannell; *B. Graves (undertaker)*, Rondo Hatton; *Florist*, Mike Vallon; *Subscription Lady*, Mary Field; *Grocer*, George Humbert.

A King Brothers Production. *Producer*, Maurice King; *Associate Producer*, Frank King; *Director*, Joe May; *Screenplay*, Philip Yordan and John H. Kafka; *Story*, Alice Means Reeve; *Photography*, Ira Morgan; *Music Director*, W. Franke Harling; *Art Directors*, Paul Palmentola and George Moskov; *Special Effects*, Ray Mercer; *Technical Advisor*, Herman King; *Editor*, Martin G. Cohn. Running time: 77 minutes.

Robert Mitchum's agent wangled a deal for his client with King Brothers Productions that was a notch or two above the Pine-Thomas operation as a budget B independent. The King Brothers, however, released through Monogram Pictures, a poverty row company, while Pine-Thomas at least had the prestigious Paramount behind them.

Mitchum was truly scraping bottom in the

minor league comedy, *Johnny Doesn't Live Here Anymore*—an innocent little bedroom romp about a sweet young thing who gets mixed up with a gremlin, manages to talk a newly drafted Marine into letting her use his vacant Washington apartment while he's on duty, and then discovers that all of his buddies have keys to the place. Mitchum turns up near the end as a navy chief petty officer ("a tough guy who looks like a movie star," one of the characters comments, "this guy's dynamite!") who rents the apartment for the night from one of the keyholders. Most of the film's scant charm exuded from Simone Simon, the French émigré whose talents were ill used in American movies—ranging from the lead opposite James Stewart in *Seventh Heaven* and starring roles in *The Cat People* and *Curse of the Cat People* to a series of increasingly less distinguished B features.

Here she attractively carried off the undemanding role of a young defense-plant worker who is forced to choose between the handsome Marine (William Terry) who has leased her his apartment and the Marine's sailor buddy (James Ellison), while fending off a steady stream of keyholders who turn the apartment into Grand

In *Johnny Doesn't Live Here Anymore.*

Central Station. By the time Mitchum shows up, the place has turned into a shambles and the whole affair ends up in police court, where the harried judge (Alan Dinehart) orders the girl to choose between her Marine and her sailor. The film ends with a twist by having the put-upon young lady run off with the judge.

Reviewing the movie, *Harrison's Reports* observed that "with a little bit more care, it might have turned into an hilarious comedy. . . . Chief flaw in the film is the unintelligible dialogue spoken by Simone Simon, because of her accent and of her mumbling way of speaking her lines."

To cash in on Mitchum's subsequent popularity, *Johnny Doesn't Live Here Anymore* was reissued several years later, renamed *And So They Were Married* (not to be confused with the 1936 Columbia movie of the same title). Mitchum was advanced to above-the-title billing alongside Miss Simon—originally, his name had been buried far below the title in eighth place—but his fans undoubtedly were disappointed to discover that their hero's part was limited merely to the final reel or so.

23
Nevada
RKO Radio, 1944

With Richard Martin in *Nevada*.

THE CAST:

Jim "Nevada" Lacy, ROBERT MITCHUM; *Julie Dexter*, ANNE JEFFREYS; *Dusty*, Guinn "Big Boy" Williams; *Hattie Ide*, Nancy Gates; *Chito Rafferty*, Richard Martin; *Cash Burridge*, Craig Reynolds; *Joe Powell*, Harry Woods; *Ed Nelson*, Edmund Glover; *William Brewer*, Alan Ward; *Marvie Ide*, Harry McKim; *Ben Ide*, Larry Wheat; *Red Berry*, Jack Overman; *Comstock*, Emmett Lynn; *Dr. Darien*, Wheaton Chambers; *Ed Nolan*, Philip Morris; *Henchman*, Russ Hopton; *Bartender*, Sammy Blum.

Producers, Sid Rogell and Herman Scholm; *Director*, Edward Killy, *Screenplay*, Norman Houston; *Story*, Zane Grey; *Photography*, Harry J. Wald; *Music*, Paul Sawtell; *Music Director*, C. Bakaleinikoff; *Editor*, Roland Gross. Running time: 62 minutes.

With Nancy Gates in *Nevada*.

In RKO's initial entry in its Zane Grey cycle, Robert Mitchum had his first lead and brought into sharper focus the screen persona that would identify him for the next three decades—the image of the tough but laconic hero, sleepy-eyed, mouth set in a semileer, a man who prefers to let his fist and sometimes his guns do his talking when interlopers disrupt his lackadaisical routine, a character on which Mitchum has since played countless variations.

Nevada had been filmed twice previously by Paramount: as a silent in 1927 with Gary Cooper and again in 1935 with Larry "Buster" Crabbe. The third version, with Mitchum, elaborated on the original Grey tale, adding two important characters: a second leading lady (played by Anne Jeffreys) and a sidekick in the person of Chito Gonzales Jose Bustamonte Rafferty (Richard Martin). Martin played Chito in both Zane Grey movies that starred Mitchum, in those of Mitchum's successor, James Warren, and in the later ones made with Tim Holt.

As the footloose cowpoke named Nevada, Mitchum arrives in the mining town of Gold Hill just in time to stumble onto a claim-jumping swindle involving huge deposits of blue clay, thought to be worthless but actually rich in silver.

With Anne Jeffreys in *Nevada*.

Knowing this, Cash Burridge (Craig Reynolds), the town's leading citizen, plans to buy the miners' claims at low prices, and learning that miner Ben Ide (Larry Wheat) is to have his clay assayed, Burridge and his henchman, Joe Powell (Harry Woods), ambush Ide. Nevada discovers the body just outside of town as the sheriff's posse arrives. Burridge stirs up the miners to lynch Nevada, but the latter's pals, Chito (Martin) and Dusty (Guinn "Big Boy" Williams) ride in to rescue him. Then, at the urging of Ben Ide's daughter, Hattie (Nancy Gates), Nevada goes after the real killer and tries to drag a confession from Powell. Fearing that Powell will talk, Burridge has him killed and implicates Nevada once again. Meanwhile, Nevada discovers the truth about the blue clay and how Burridge had tricked Hattie Ide into selling her property to him. Learning that Burridge is on his way to Carson City to legalize his claims, Nevada, Chito, and Dusty go in pursuit and capture him after a pitched gun battle.

Burridge goes to jail and Nevada goes off with Hattie Ide.

Mitchum's performance in the title role impressed moviegoers as well as RKO's front-office personnel. Here was an actor well on his way to becoming a star—with or without molding by the studio. *Film Daily* wrote in its review of *Nevada*: "Bob Mitchum for the first time is presented as the star of a Western. The actor certainly justifies the faith placed in him, delivering a performance that is smack in the groove. The fellow does himself pretty, dishing out the heroic stuff."

Harrison's Reports observed of *Nevada*: "It should please those who enjoy this type of entertainment, for it has exciting horse riding, a few good fist fights, and some comedy."

Mitchum then was rushed into a second Zane Grey western. It would be his last role before being elevated to stardom with the big studio push behind him.

24
When Strangers Marry
(also called *Betrayed*)
Monogram, 1944

With Kim Hunter in *When Strangers Marry*.

THE CAST:

Paul Dean, DEAN JAGGER; *Millie*, KIM HUNTER; *Fred*, Robert Mitchum; *Detective Blake*, Neil Hamilton; *Hamilton*, Lon Lubin; *Charlie*, Milt Kibbee; *Newstand Man*, Dewey Robinson; *Middle-aged Woman*, Claire Whitney; *Middle-aged Man*, Edward Keane; *Chambermaid*, Virginia Sale; *Prescott*, Dick Elliott; *Old Man*, Lee "Lassus" White; *Landlady*, Minerva Urecal; *Baby's Mother*, Marta Mitrovitch; *Girl on Train*, Rhonda Fleming; and George Lloyd, Billy Nelson, Weldon Heyburn, Sam McDaniel.

A King Brothers Production. *Producer*, Maurice King; *Associate Producer*, Frank King; *Director*, William Castle; *Screenplay*, Philip Yordan and Dennis Cooper; *Story*, George Moscov; *Photography*, Ira Morgan; *Music Director*, Dimitri Tiomkin; *Art Director*, F. Paul Sylos; *Technical Advisor*, Herman King; *Editor*, Martin G. Cohn. Running time: 67 minutes.

With Kim Hunter, Neil Hamilton, and Weldon Heyburn in *When Strangers Marry*.

With Kim Hunter in *When Strangers Marry*.

The King Brothers next gave Mitchum his first important role, second male lead, in William Castle's trim little mystery thriller, *When Strangers Marry* (originally called *I Married a Stranger* and subsequently known as *Betrayed*). A psychological drama, shot in just ten days, the film has become a model of a budget thriller, and movie historian Don Miller calls it "unquestionably the finest 'B' film made." Quickly attaining "sleeper" status, it is the common tale (uncommonly filmed) of a small-town waitress (Kim Hunter) who arrives in New York City to meet her new husband (Dean Jagger), only to discover that she not only married a stranger but a possible murderer. Mitchum is her former boyfriend to whom she turns in an effort to help her husband clear himself.

Worried when her new husband, Paul, forces her to go into hiding with him, Millie Dean is further frightened when her loyalty makes her flee with him from the law. Police detective Blake (Neil Hamilton), involved in the case, becomes suspicious of Millie's ex-boyfriend, Fred, and decides that he knows more of the crime than he has divulged. Discovered and arrested, Paul admits that he was at a bar in Philadelphia where the murdered man was last seen alive. Nagging suspicions soon lead Millie to believe that Fred might be involved in the crime, and with Blake's help, she catches Fred in the act of mailing an envelope containing the exact amount stolen in the murder. Fred confesses, and Paul is released, leaving with Millie on a long-postponed honeymoon.

"A superior thriller with a misleading title," is how *Variety* described it, noting that "Robert Mitchum has a breezy quality to fit his role of the boyfriend." The movie had no Manhattan opening (its local premiere was at the Brooklyn Strand), and none of the New York critics saw fit to make note of the restrained acting, William Castle's thoughtful direction, or Dimitri Tiomkin's creative music score.

Mitchum, billed as Robert on the credits, Bob on the ads, not only was top-billed when the film later was reissued as *Betrayed* but also concedes that his work in it probably was instrumental in landing him his long-term RKO contract in June 1944.

25
Thirty Seconds Over Tokyo

Metro-Goldwyn-Mayer, 1944

THE CAST:

Capt. Ted W. Lawson, VAN JOHNSON; *David Thatcher*, ROBERT WALKER; *Ellen Jones Lawson*, PHYLLIS THAXTER; *Lt. Col. James H. Doolittle*, SPENCER TRACY; *Dean Davenport*, Tim Murdock; *Davey Jones*, Scott McKay; *Bob Clever*, Gordon McDonald; *Charles McClure*, Don DeFore; *Bob Gray*, Robert Mitchum; *Shorty Manch*, John R. Reilly; *Doc White*, Horace (Stephen) McNally; *Lt. Randall*, Donald Curtis; *Lt. Miller*, Louis-Jean Heydt; *Don Smith*, William "Bill" Phillips; *Brick Holstron*, Douglas Cowan; *Capt. "Ski" York*, Paul Langton; *Lt. Jurika*, Leon Ames; *General*, Moroni Olsen; *Captain Halsey*, Morris Ankrum; *Mrs. Jones*, Selena Royle; *Young Chung*, Benson Fong; *Old Chung*, Dr. Hsin Kung Chan Chi; *Girls at Officers' Club*, Myrna Dell, Peggy Maley, Hazel Brooks, Elaine Shepard, and Kay Williams; *Jane*, Dorothy Ruth Morris; *Mrs. Parker*, Ann Shoemaker; *Mr. Parker*, Alan Napier; *Foo Ling*, Wah Lee; *Guerrilla Charlie*, Chin Wah Lee; *Emmy York*, Jacqueline White; *Dick Joyce*, Jack McClendon; *Pilot*, John Kellogg; *Spike Henderson*, Peter Varney; *M.P.*, Steve Brodie; *Judge*, Harry Hayden; *Second Officer*, Blake Edwards; *Hoss Wyler*, Will Walls; *Hallmark*, Jay Norris; *Jig White*, Robert Bice; *Bud Felton*, Bill Williams; *Sailor*, Wally Cassell.

Producer, Sam Zimbalist; *Director*, Mervyn LeRoy; *Screenplay*, Dalton Trumbo; *Novel* Capt. Ted W. Lawson and Robert Considine; *Photography*, Harold Rosson and Robert Surtees; *Music Director*, Herbert Stothart; *Art Directors*, Cedric Gibbons and Paul Groesse; *Editor*, Frank Sullivan. Running time: 139 minutes.

With Van Johnson in *Thirty Seconds Over Tokyo*.

Robert Mitchum played his last minor character role in MGM's exciting tribute to the men who flew the first bomber raid over Japan. Director Mervyn LeRoy, alerted to that interesting young actor just signed by RKO, had Mitchum test for a small role in *Thirty Seconds Over Tokyo*. LeRoy was said to have later told Mitchum: "You're either the lousiest actor in the world or the best. I can't make up my mind which." In any event, he gave Mitchum a brief part as a crewman aboard Van Johnson's plane in the re-creation of the heroic April 1942 Doolittle raid on Japan, which LeRoy, using Dalton Trumbo's documentary-style adap-

With Douglas Cowan, Don DeFore, Van Johnson, and
John R. Reilly in *Thirty Seconds Over Tokyo*.

With Don DeFore (on cot), John R. Reilly (pointing),
Douglas Cowan, William "Bill" Philips (standing rear),
Van Johnson, and Gordon McDonald in *Thirty Seconds
Over Tokyo*.

tation of the best seller by Captain Ted Lawson and Bob Considine, turned into "certainly a most stimulating and emotionally satisfying film" (Bosley Crowther, *The New York Times*).

As one of the crew of "The Ruptured Duck," Mitchum flew alongside then-Lieutenant Lawson (Van Johnson, in *his* first important dramatic role) and co-pilot Tim Murdock, navigator Don DeFore, gunner-mechanic Robert Walker, and bombardier Gordon McDonald. Others on the mission: Scott McKay, William "Bill" Phillips, John R. Reilly, and Horace (later Stephen) McNally. Phyllis Thaxter made an impressive screen debut as Ellen Lawson, and Spencer Tracy was recruited to do a cameo as Lieutenant Colonel James H. Doolittle.

As with so many of the Mitchum films of the 1940s, *Thirty Seconds Over Tokyo* went into subsequent re-release (in 1955) with Mitchum now receiving equal above-the-title billing with Spencer Tracy and Van Johnson, taking the spot originally assigned to the now-deceased Robert Walker.

26
West of the Pecos
RKO Radio, 1945

With Thurston Hall, Barbara Hale, Russell Hopton, and Bruce Edwards in *West of the Pecos*.

THE CAST:

Pecos Smith, ROBERT MITCHUM; *Rill Lambeth*, BARBARA HALE; *Chito Rafferty*, Richard Martin; *Col. Lambeth*, Thurston Hall; *Suzanne*, Rita Corday; *Jeff Stinger*, Russell Hopton; *Tex Evans*, Bill Williams; *Brad Sawtelle*, Harry Woods; *Clyde Morgan*, Bruce Edwards; *Sam Sawtelle*, Perc Landers; *Doc Howard*, Bryant Washburn; *Marshal*, Philip Morris; *Don Manuel*, Martin Garralaga; *Gambler*, Sammy Blum; *Gambler*, Robert Anderson; *Dancer*, Italia DeNubila; *Lookout*, Ethan Laidlaw; *Groupier*, Jack Gargan; *Butler*, Larry Wheat.

Executive Producer, Sid Rogell; *Producer*, Herman Schlom; *Director*, Edward Killy; *Screenplay*, Norman Houston; *Based on the Novel by* Zane Grey; *Photography*, Harry J. Wild; *Music*, Paul Sawtell; *Music Director*, C. Bakaleinikoff; *Art Directors*, Albert S. D'Agostino and Lucius Croxton; *Editor*, Roland Gross. Running time: 66 minutes.

Robert Mitchum's portrayal of Pecos Smith in his second Zane Grey western (filmed previously by RKO in 1934 with Richard Dix) confirmed his two-fisted good-guy image and established him as a popular outdoor hero. *West of the Pecos*, spiced with the right combination of hard riding, blazing guns, humor, and romance, has Mitchum as a happy-go-lucky cowpuncher who becomes involved in an unlikely romance with a Chicago debutante. As the film begins, Pecos (Mitchum) and his pal Chito Rafferty (Richard Martin) meet Rill Lambeth (Barbara Hale), her father, the Colonel (Thurston Hall), a wealthy meatpacker, and her French maid, Suzanne (Rita Corday),

With Barbara Hale and Thurston Hall in *West of the Pecos.*

With Thurston Hall and Barbara Hale in *West of the Pecos.*

shortly after their rude introduction to the West. Their stagecoach had been held up on the trip to Lambeth's Texas ranch, and Rill has decided to masquerade as a boy when, accosted by two gamblers in town after reporting the holdup, she feels that a pretty girl isn't safe in these parts. In this guise, she bumps into cowpoke Pecos Smith, who orders her to fetch his horse. When she doesn't obey, he gives her a swift kick in the rear and rides away.

Later, when Rill, the Colonel, and Suzanne lose their way in the desert, Pecos and Chito find them and accept the Colonel's offer of jobs on his spread. Still disguised as a young boy, Rill finds herself falling for Pecos, while Chito strikes up a romance with the vivacious Suzanne. On the way to the ranch, the party is bushwacked by town boss Brad Sawtelle (Harry Woods) and his men. The quickshooting Pecos and Chito manage to repel the attack. Afterwards, Pecos discovers that the young tenderfoot he had been ordering around is actually a girl, when, while fording a river, he playfully pushes her into the water.

Following another unsuccessful attempt on the Lambeth's at their ranch, Sawtelle has Pecos framed for the stage holdup, but the cowpoke and his sidekick capture the stagecoach driver and learn who had persuaded him to lie. Another attack on the ranch is thwarted by the arrival of the sheriff's posse as Pecos and Chito take off after Sawtelle and help bring law and order west of the Pecos. Rill decides to marry her easy-going hero while Chito decides to settle down with Suzanne.

In the New York *Daily News,* critic Kate Cameron gave the western three stars and advised her readers: "Remember Mitchum's name, for you are going to hear it again and again after the release of *G.I. Joe,* in which he plays a leading role. He's in the Army now, but is destined for stardom." Of the film, she found: "It is packed with the type of action that makes a well-made Western such good escapist entertainment." *Film Daily* wrote: "Mitchum plays the hero extremely well," while reviewer Howard Barnes, in the *New York Herald Tribune,* concluded: "A run of the mill horse opera has been given some pleasant comic overtones. . . . Robert Mitchum is angular and tough as the fellow who fights a gang of badmen single-handed."

And this from *Variety:* "For fans of the great outdoors who like their Zane Grey without too many frills, this picture is a natural. . . . Robert Mitchum, with the help of Richard Martin, does the riders of the range proud."

27
The Story of G.I. Joe

United Artists, 1945

With Freddie Steele and Burgess Meredith in *The Story of G.I. Joe.*

THE CAST:

Ernie Pyle, BURGESS MEREDITH; *Lt. Walker,* ROBERT MITCHUM; *Sgt. Warnicki,* Freddie Steele; *Private Dondaro,* Wally Cassell; *Private Spencer,* Jimmy Lloyd; *Private Murphy,* Jack Reilly; *Private Mew,* Bill Murphy; *Cookie Henderson,* William Self; *Sergeant at Showers,* Dick Rich; *Whitey,* Billy Benedict; *Lopez,* Tito Renaldo; *Sergeant,* Michael Browne; *Amelia,* Yolanda Lacca; *Nurse,* Dorothy Coonan; and the Combat Veterans of the Africa, Italy, and Sicily Campaigns.

Producer, Lester Cowan; *Associate Producer,* David Hall; *Director,* William A. Wellman; *Screenplay,* Leopold Atlas, Guy Endore, and Philip Stevenson; *Based on the Novel by* Ernie Pyle; *Photography,* Russell Metty; *Music Director,* Louis Forbes; *Music Score,* Ann Ronell and Louise Applebaum; *Assistant Director,* Robert Aldrich; *Art Director,* James Sullivan; *Editor* Otho Lovering. Running time: 108 minutes. (Reissued in 1949 by Eagle-Lion Films.)

While negotiating a new contract with Mitchum's agent, RKO loaned him out to producer Lester Cowan for a war movie based on Ernie Pyle's writings. Cowan had badgered director William Wellman into joining the project, and Wellman, who had seen Mitchum in some of his westerns, decided he'd like the young actor to test for the role of the human infantry officer in the film. Overcoming Mitchum's skepticism ("Everyone's after that role," Mitchum was said to have told Wellman, "Gary Cooper and all the rest. Why me?"), Wellman convinced him to make the test. "I very foolishly made the test of one of the most important scenes in the picture," the director later wrote, "the scene where he was the tired officer writing letters to the mothers of kids who'd been killed. It was my big mistake. Really, for I saw something so wonderful, so completely compelling, that I was mad at myself for not having built the set before so that I could have made the test the *actual* scene that came out in the picture." Wellman insisted that Cowan borrow Mitchum from RKO.

With Burgess Meredith and player in *The Story of G.I. Joe.*

The Story of G.I. Joe emerged as one of the great films of World War II, an honest tribute to the slogging foot-soldier and his grim determination to fight well under an officer he respected. Mitchum is the battle-hardened C.O. of Infantry Company C, whom correspondent Ernie Pyle (Burgess Meredith) befriends. "Meredith is remarkably good as the gray-haired correspondent," critic Howard Barnes wrote. "Even better is Robert Mitchum as the lieutenant who becomes a captain and leads his company, bitterly and steadfastly."

The film opens in Africa where Charlie Company is bivouacked for the night. As several members of a squad idle the time away in conversation, Ernie Pyle wanders onto the scene.

In *The Story of G.I. Joe.*

At dawn, squad commander Lt. Walker (Mitchum) hustles his men into a truck and tells Pyle to climb aboard if he wants to get to the front. By nightfall, the company arrives within the sound of battle. Fighting their way painfully into Italy, the men of Company C are soon in the thick of the bombardment of San Vittorio. With them, as usual, is Pyle. The streets of the war-wracked town are a mass of rubble, and, with bullets whizzing about, a few of the dog-tired G.I.s, crouching in a ruined café, manage time out for a little innocent romance with some terrified barmaids. Orders come from Eisenhower to bomb the monastery at Cassino, but the resisting Germans delay an Allied victory until after a bitter struggle. Sergeant Warnicki (Freddie Steele) breaks under the strain and is turned over to the medics. As Pyle notes the number of casualties, the men of Charlie Company silently watch the approach of a line of mules bearing the bodies of the fallen. On the final mule is Walker, whom Pyle had come to know personally, sharing food and drink on occasions when Walker bitterly went through the motions of sending final word to dead soldiers' next of kin. One by one, the G.I.s came closer to say goodbye to Walker, and then move wearily down the road to the next battle.

Newsweek said: "Robert Mitchum, hitherto limited chiefly to Westerns, gives a fine performance as the officer in command of Pyle's favorite outfit," and *Daily News* reviewer Kate Cameron raved that Mitchum "plays the role of Lt. Walker with an authority that gives the film power and glory. It is, insofar as this reviewer is concerned, the best performance of the year."

Nearly three decades later, Andrew Sarris assessed Mitchum's performance in *The Village Voice* and called it "extraordinarily haunting," writing that "Mitchum provides an emotional and metaphysical climax of the movie simply by being slung over a mule as a corpse, and led down the hill to the periphery of his platoon, and there in death dangling in silent communion with his living comrade. . . . The scene is still a convulsive emotional experience not because of any lingering idolatry of a dead G.I., but because Mitchum's exquisite stillness in death is the result of his expressive stoicism in life."

Mitchum received his first (and to date only) Academy Award nomination as Best Supporting Actor, losing at Oscar time to James Dunn (for *A Tree Grows in Brooklyn*. Nevertheless, major stardom awaited him on his return from the Army. For the 1949 reissue of *The Story of G.I. Joe*, a complete new advertising compaign was created, focusing on Mitchum. "Mitchum plays his greatest role in the mightiest action drama ever filmed!" it shouted, and he was now billed over Burgess Meredith, with his bearded likeness, machine-gun in hand (in true Errol Flynn style) dominating the ads. What price glory!

28
Till the End of Time

RKO Radio, 1946

THE CAST:

Pat Ruscomb, DOROTHY McGUIRE; *Cliff Harper*, GUY MADISON; *William Tabeshaw*, ROBERT MITCHUM; *Perry Kincheloe*, BILL WILLIAMS; *C. W. Harper*, Tom Tully; *Sgt. Gunny Watrous*, William Gargan; *Helen Ingersoll*, Jean Porter; *Tommy Hendricks*, Johnny Sands; *Pinky*, Loren Tindall; *Amy Harper*, Ruth Nelson; *Scuffy*, Harry Von Zell; *Mrs. Kincheloe*, Selena Royle; *The Boy from Idaho*, Richard Benedict; *Jimmy Kincheloe*, Dickie Tyler; *Capt. Jack Winthrop*, Stan Johnson; *Warrant Officer*, Billy Newell; *Burton*, Lee Slater; *Epstein*, Robert Lowell; *Franks*, Peter Varney; *Gilman*, George Burnett; *Jackson*, Bill Barnum; *Captain*, Richard Slattery; *Ed Tomkins*, Harry Hayden; *Mrs. Tomkins*, Mary Worth; *Steve Sumpter*, Tim Ryan; *Mrs. Sumpter*, Ellen Corby; *Mrs. Ingersoll*, Margaret Wells; *Zeke Ingersoll*, Fred Howard; *Freddie Stewart*, Teddy Infuhr; *Foreman*, Blake Edwards.

Producer, Dore Schary; *Director*, Edward Dmytryk; *Screenplay*, Allen Rivkin; *Based on the Novel They Dream of Home* by Niven Busch; *Photography*, Harry J. Wild; *Music*, Leigh Harline; *Music Director*, C. Bakaleinikoff; *Art Directors*, Albert S. D'Agostino and Jack Okey; *Editor*, Harry Gerstad. Running time: 105 minutes.

Returning from the Army, Mitchum found his new contract divided his services between Dore

With Guy Madison in *Till the End of Time*.

With Dorothy McGuire and Guy Madison in *Till the End of Time.*

With Jean Porter and Guy Madison in *Till the End of Time.*

Schary, now head of RKO, and David O. Selznick, Schary's former boss. Mitchum's first postwar film, *Till the End of Time,* reintroduced him as Hollywood's new hearthrob, along with Selznick newcomer Guy Madison and young Bill Williams, recently elevated from RKO's B unit. (Of the three, only Mitchum lived up to and surpassed his promise.)

A somewhat less ambitious attempt at *The Best Years of Our Lives* (released the same year by RKO), *Till the End of Time* was based on a novel called *They Dream of Home,* which Niven Busch had written for his wife, Teresa Wright. Selznick acquired the screen rights and sold part interest in the project to RKO when his protégé Dore Schary became executive vice-president in charge of production. Selznick insisted that his own star, Dorothy McGuire, be cast in the lead, and she, Mitchum and Madison appeared "through the courtesy of David O. Selznick." (Although Selznick owned fifty percent of Mitchum, this was the only film the actor ever did for him.)

Allen Rivkin's soppy/sentimental script, Leigh Harline's score, which interpolated Chopin's "Polonaise" (newly rediscovered by pop music fans through Perry Como's recording of it as *Till the End of Time*), and the participation of the three "new" leading men combined to make the film a smashing success. Madison, Mitchum, and Williams are three ex-combat Marines trying to adjust to civilian life. Madison is the small-town boy seeking to find himself in the postwar world, Mitchum is his ex-broncobuster buddy drowning himself in drink to ease the pain from the steel plate in his head, and Williams is a paraplegic now only able to dream of those prewar days when he was an up-and-coming boxer.

Virtually nagged out of his house by his parents (Tom Tully and Ruth Nelson) who want him to get a job, and dogged by Helen Ingersoll (Jean Porter), his amorous teenaged neighbor, Cliff Harper (Madison) goes off on an extended binge with his pal, Bill Tabeshaw (Mitchum). Eventually Cliff ends up with Pat Ruscomb (Dorothy McGuire), a girl he had fallen for when they were earlier introduced, and at her urging, he finally takes a job. She even gets him to stick with it after he battles with his foreman, but she rejects his marriage proposal until he agrees to settle down. Cliff runs into Bill again in a bar. Sick and broke, his steel plate is giving him increasing trouble but he resists going to the hospital. Their buddy Perry Kincheloe (Bill Williams), now on artificial legs, tries to help Cliff straighten out Bill, but the three get into a brawl with a group of racial bigots. At the hospital where the three are being patched up, Cliff learns that his parents really do understand and sympathize with him, and making certain that Bill can get back to his ranch in New Mexico, he returns to his factory job and to Pat.

"Mitchum's portrayal of an alternately tough-and-tender cowpuncher lassos top acting honors," *Newsweek* said. Thomas M. Pryor, in *The New York Times,* wrote that "with the exception of Dorothy McGuire's characterization of the moody girl and Robert Mitchum's portrayal of a breezy cowboy, there is nothing exceptional about the performances." And in the *Daily News,* critic Kate Cameron commented: "Robert Mitchum, who will be remembered for his outstanding work in *G. I. Joe,* comes through with another fine characterization as a wounded vet."

29
Undercurrent
Metro-Goldwyn-Mayer, 1946

THE CAST:

Ann Hamilton, KATHARINE HEPBURN; *Alan Garroway*, ROBERT TAYLOR; *Michael Garroway*, ROBERT MITCHUM; *Professor "Dink" Hamilton*, Edmund Gwenn; *Lucy*, Marjorie Main; *Sylvia Lea Burton*, Jayne Meadows; *Mr. Warmsley*, Clinton Sundberg; *Professor Herbert Bangs*, Dan Tobin; *Mrs. Foster*, Kathryn Card; *George*, Leigh Whipper; *Justice Putnam*, Charles Trowbridge; *Henry Gilson*, James Westerfield; *Uncle Ben*, Billy McLain; *Julia Donnegan*, Bess Flowers; *Cora*, Sarah Edwards; *Gwen*, Ellen Ross, *Saleslady*, Betty Blythe; *Minister*, Milton Kibbee; *Mrs. Davenport*, Jean Adren; *Senator Edwards*, Forbes Murray; *Proprietor*, Wheaton Chambers; *Attendant*, Hank Worden; *Station Master*, Robert Emmet O'Connor.

Producer, Pandro S. Berman; *Director*, Vincente Minnelli; *Screenplay*, Edward Chodorov; *Based on the Story* "You Were There" *by* Thelma Stradel; *Photography*, Karl Freund; *Music*, Herbert Stothart; *Art Director*, Cedric Gibbons; *Editor*, Ferris Webster. Running time: 114 minutes.

With Katharine Hepburn in *Undercurrent*.

RKO next loaned Mitchum to MGM for two films. The first, *Undercurrent*, marked his debut in a "prestige" movie and co-starred him with Katharine Hepburn and Robert Taylor (in *his* "welcome back" film for MGM after naval service).

A moody piece directed by Vincente Minnelli and photographed with the proper amount of menacing shadows by Karl Freund, *Undercurrent* is glossy melodrama about the dowdy small-town daughter (Miss Hepburn) of a noted scientist (Edmund Gwenn) who marries a wealthy industrialist (Robert Taylor) and becomes enmeshed in various evil doings her husband has been trying to hide. Third-billed Mitchum plays the mysterious Taylor's equally mysterious brother, with whom Hepburn runs off after learning of her psychopathic husband's attempt on her life. Mitchum had little to do and, as the saying goes, he did it well.

"Pan [producer Pandro Berman] and I decided Mitchum would play the brother," Minnelli recalled in his autobiography, *I Remember It Well*. "Bob Mitchum feels it was fiscal collusion between the

With Katharine Hepburn in *Undercurrent*.

With Katharine Hepburn in *Undercurrent*.

afternoon. On top of this, Bob was working at night on *The Locket* for RKO. 'I worked the three pictures for twenty-six straight days,' Bob remembers. 'We'd shoot all night at RKO, then I'd report for *Undercurrent* from seven in the morning until noon, when I'd be flown to Monterey to work all afternoon on the picture with Greer Garson.' No wonder he became famous for his sleepy eyes."

Mitchum was as miscast in *Undercurrent* as was Taylor, who was forced to play the cold, cruel husband, a curious assignment from a studio trying to reestablish its foremost leading man's postwar career. Manny Farber, critic for *The New Republic,* called the whole affair "a two-hour waste of high-priced Hollywood talent," and *Time,* using similar terms, asked "How can such a wealth of high-priced Hollywood talent add up to such a poor movie?" John McCarten wrote in *The New Yorker:* "Miss Hepburn employs all her celebrated mannerisms, Mr. Taylor is as handsome as ever with his geometrically perfect widow's peak, and Mr. Mitchum is gloomy and earnest." Best of the relatively few favorable notices went to Mitchum and are summed up by critic Howard Barnes's comment that "Mitchum plays it straight, which is quite proper for his assignment."

studio and David Selznick, to whom he was under contract, that brought him the part. For he admits he was never comfortable in the role of the sensitive Michael. But Bob didn't need the later-developed Mitchum swagger to convey his innate strength. He's always underestimated his ability." Minnelli then said: "Selznick was being paid $25,000 a week to loan out Bob for my picture, and getting the same amount for a second Metro picture, *Desire Me,* which Bob was shooting in the

30
The Locket

RKO Radio, 1946

THE CAST:

Nancy Monks, LARAINE DAY; *Dr. Blair,* BRIAN AHERNE; *Norman Clyde,* ROBERT MITCHUM; *John Willis,* Gene Raymond; *Nancy (age 10),* Sharyn Moffett; *Mr. Bonner,* Ricardo Cortez; *Lord Wyndham,* Henry Stephenson; *Mrs. Willis,* Katherine Emery; *Mr. Wendell,* Reginald Denny; *Mrs. Bonner,* Fay Helm; *Mrs. Monks,* Helene Thimig; *Mrs. Wendell,* Nella Walker; *Woman Singer,* Queenie Leonard; *Lady Wyndham,* Lilian Fontaine; *Thelma,* Myrna Dell; *Donald,* Johnny Clark; *Mrs. Donovan,* Vivien Oakland; *Miss Wyatt,* Nancy Saunders; and George Humbert, Trina Varella, Nick Thompson, Connie Leon, Sam Flint, Wyndham Standing, Ellen Corby, Gloria Donovan, Martha Hyer, Mari Aldon, Charles Flynn, Broderick O'Farrell.

Executive Producer, Jack L. Gross; *Producer,* Bert Granet, *Director,* John Brahm; *Screenplay,* Sheridan Gibney; *Photography,* Nicholas Musuraca; *Music,* Roy Webb; *Music Director,* C. Bakaleinikoff; *Art Directors,* Albert S. D'Agostino and Alfred Herman; *Editor,* J. R. Whittredge. Running time: 86 minutes.

Next for Mitchum, back on his home lot, was another pseudopsychological piece, *The Locket* (originally titled *What Nancy Wanted),* directed by

John Brahm from an original Sheridan Gibney screenplay. Cast as a moody Greenwich Village artist, Mitchum is one of three leading men in support of the lady star—in this case, Laraine Day, playing an inveterate kleptomaniac who destroys the lives of her various lovers.

The Locket hold a special place among film buffs as the most flashback-obsessed movie of all time. On the eve of his marriage to Nancy Monks (Miss Day), wealthy John Willis (Gene Raymond) is visited by Dr. Blair (Brian Aherne), a psychiatrist. Blair informs him that he had been married to Nancy for five years and warns Willis against going through with the wedding. He relates that Norman Clyde (Mitchum), a former fiancé of Nancy's, had once discovered a stolen bracelet in her handbag and was told that, as a child, she had been falsely accused of stealing a locket, an experience that had left her with a guilt complex and an uncontrollable urge to steal. Although Norman had extracted a promise from her that she never again would steal, Nancy was later arrested in a robbery/murder. She was able to supply an alibi, and the victim's valet was convicted instead. A distraut Norman went to Blair, Nancy's psychiatrist, and pleaded with him to induce Nancy to clear the valet. Instead, Blair believed Nancy's denials, the valet was executed, and Norman committed suicide.

Several years later, Blair, now married to Nancy, discovered a hoard of jewels stolen from their friends. When she blithely denied any knowledge of them, Blair divorced her. Unconvinced, Willis summons Nancy, who convinces her new fiancé that Blair is suffering from delusions. Willis decides to go ahead with the wedding. As Nancy starts the march to the altar, she receives a gift from Willis's mother (Katherine Emery): a

With Laraine Day and Brian Aherne in *The Locket*.

With Brian Aherne in *The Locket*.

With Laraine Day in *The Locket*.

locket, which Nancy recognizes as the one she had been accused of stealing as a child. Realizing that Mrs. Willis had been her childhood oppressor, Nancy is stirred by a myriad of youthful memories and has a complete mental collapse. The story ends with her confinement in an institution.

In *The New York Times*, Thomas M. Pryor felt that "neither Laraine Day nor Robert Mitchum displays any discernible understanding of the characters they play. . . . Mitchum gives a completely monotonous and inexpressive performance. There is not the slightest hint about his rigid face of the temperament of an artist, even granting that the fellow he is representing is a broody sort." On the other hand, fellow critic Howard Barnes, of the *New York Herald Tribune* thought that "Robert Mitchum gives a forceful portrayal." *Time* called the film "a dull blend of two of Hollywood's hardest worn current themes—psychiatry and vicious womanhood, with Laraine Day a sweet-faced wanton who lies, cheats, steals and murders her way through the ruination of three remarkably gullible leading men."

RKO apparently heard from Mitchum's fans that they'd rather not see him doing psychological melodramas. The studio got the word, and its rising star was given (generally) tough, two-fisted roles for the remainder of his term as a contract player.

31
Crossfire

RKO Radio, 1947

THE CAST:

Captain Finlay, ROBERT YOUNG; *Sgt. Peter Keeley,* ROBERT MITCHUM; *Monty Montgomery,* ROBERT RYAN; *Ginny Tremaine,* Gloria Grahame; *The Man,* Paul Kelly; *Joseph Samuels,* Sam Levene; *Mary Mitchell,* Jacqueline White; *Floyd Bowers,* Steve Brodie; *Arthur Mitchell,* George Cooper; *Bill Williams,* Richard Benedict; *Detective,* Richard Powers (Tom Keene); *Leroy,* William Phipps; *Harry,* Lex Barker; *Miss Lewis,* Marlo Dwyer; *Tenant,* Harry Harvey; *Deputy,* Carl Faulkner; *1st M.P.,* Jay Norris; *2nd M.P.,* Robert Bray; *3rd M.P.,* George Turner; *Police Sergeant,* Philip Morris; *Major,* Kenneth MacDonald; *Soldier,* Allen Ray; *4th M.P.,* Don Cadell; *Waiter,* Bill Nind; *Police Surgeon,* George Meader.

A Dore Schary Presentation. *Producer,* Adrian Scott; *Director,* Edward Dmytryk; *Screenplay,* John Paxton; *Based on the Novel The Brick Foxhole by* Richard Brooks; *Photography,* J. Roy Hunt; *Music,* Roy Webb; *Music Director,* C. Bakaleinikoff; *Art Directors,* Albert S. D'Agostino and Alfred Herman; *Special Effects,* Richard Cully; *Assistant Director,* Nate Levinson; *Editor,* Harry Gerstad. Running time, 86 minutes.

The landmark movie about anti-Semitism, *Crossfire* is remembered fondly by cinemaddicts as the film that starred the three Bobs—Young, Mitchum, and Ryan. Dore Schary won the race with Darryl F. Zanuck by bringing in *Crossfire,* adapted by John Paxton from Richard Brooks's novel, *The Brick Foxhole,* several months ahead of 20th Century-Fox's *Gentleman's Agreement.* The Schary film, shot in just twenty-three days on

With Robert Young in *Crossfire.*

a miniscule ($500,000) budget, remains the high water mark of director Edward Dmytryk's career—and his last major work before he and *Crossfire* producer Adrian Scott were caught up in the Hollywood witchhunt of the budding McCarthy Era.

With anti-Semitism substituted for the homosexuality angle of Brooks's original, *Crossfire* exploded as a savage, off-beat melodrama of the investigation into the murder of a Jewish war veteran. Robert Ryan, whom Dmytryk had discovered in the late thirties at the Pasadena Playhouse, plays the sadistic killer, and Robert Mitchum, who had worked under Dmytryk in *Till the End of Time,* is, in the words of critic Otis L. Guernsey, "perfect as a tough-minded, good-hearted sergeant who helps solve the crime." The film begins with police captain Finlay (Robert Young) looking into the slaying of ex-G.I. Joseph Samuels (Sam Levene) in a sleezy hotel room. Reconstructing the case, Finlay finds that Samuels had been seen earlier in a local bar with B-girl Ginny Tremaine (Gloria Grahame) and

With Steve Brodie and Richard Benedict in *Crossfire*.

With George Cooper in *Crossfire*.

three soldiers—soft-spoken Monty Montgomery (Ryan) and his buddies, Floyd Bowers (Steve Brodie) and Arthur Mitchell (George Cooper). Mitchell's wallet had been found beside Samuels's body, but before Finlay can pick him up, the soldier's sergeant, Keeley (Mitchum), whisks him away.

Mitchell convinces Keeley of his innocence. Meanwhile, Montgomery is urging Bowers to stick to the story that Samuels had still been alive when all three left the bar. Learning that the cops have broken Bowers's story, though, Montgomery later returns and strangles him. Discovering the second killing, Finlay and Mitchell's wife (Jacqueline White) prevail upon Keeley to surrender Mitchell in order to trap the real killer. Finlay finally locates Ginny to corroborate Mitchell's alibi, and with Keeley's aid, the police captain lures Montgomery into a trap. There, in a lengthy exchange with Finlay, Montgomery reveals an inflamed racial prejudice bordering on the psychopathic that led him to murder both Samuels and Bowers. Montgomery then tries to escape, and Finlay is forced to shoot him down.

Taut and fast-moving despite the long dissertation on prejudice in the final reel, *Crossfire* remains one of the great films of the 1940s. *The New York Times* listed it among the year's Ten Best, and critic Bosley Crowther wrote that "Edward Dmytryk has handled most excellently a superlative cast." *Time* found that "Robert Mitchum has a great deal of laconic authority as the sergeant who holds the harassed soldiers together," and Alton

Cook, reviewing in the *New York World-Telegram*, decided that "Mitchum adds another shrewd cynic to his gallery in his effective deadpan style."

Director Edward Dmytryk has confessed to wishing the part given Mitchum had been a stronger one, explaining that he had asked RKO for the star because of the box-office value of his name. "On the surface," Dmytryk has said, "Mitchum is irresponsible and vague—and wacky. Underneath, he knows the score as few men in Hollywood do."

32
Pursued

Warner Bros., 1947

With Lane Chandler, Teresa Wright, Norman Jolley, and Jack Montgomery in *Pursued*.

THE CAST:

Thorley Callum, TERESA WRIGHT; *Jeb Rand,* ROBERT MITCHUM; *Medora Callum,* Judith Anderson; *Grant Callum,* Dean Jagger; *Jake Dingle,* Alan Hale; *Prentice McComber,* Harry Carey, Jr.; *Adam Callum,* John Rodney; *The Sergeant,* Clifton Young; *Jeb (at age 8),* Ernest Severn, *Adam (at age 10),* Charles Bates; *Thorley (at age 8),* Peggy Miller, *The Callums,* Norman Jolley, Lane Chandler, Elmer Ellingwood, Jack Montgomery, and Ian MacDonald; *Army Captain,* Ray Teal; *Coroner,* Ian Wolfe; *Woman at Wedding,* Virginia Brissac; and Kathy Jeanne Johnson, Mickey Little, Scotty Hugenberg, Eddy Waller, Russ Clark, Crane Whitley, Lester Dorr, Harry Lamont, Tom Fadden.

A United States Picture. *Producer,* Milton Sperling; *Director,* Raoul Walsh; *Screenplay,* Niven Busch; *Photography,* James Wong Howe; *Music,* Max Steiner; *Music Director,* Leo F. Forbstein; *Art Director,* Ted Smith; *Special Effects,* William McGann and Willard Van Elger; *Editor,* Christian Nyby. Running time: 101 minutes.

Raoul Walsh's rugged *Pursued* pioneered the genre known as the "adult" western, with an involved plot structure encompassing flashbacks and Freudian overtones. An intellectual, original work, it was written for the screen by Niven Busch for his wife, Teresa Wright, who was billed ahead of Mitchum—on loanout once again from RKO, for the final time. The film, magnificently photographed by James Wong Howe in Monument

With Teresa Wright in *Pursued*.

With Teresa Wright and Judith Anderson in *Pursued*.

Valley, John Ford's favorite backdrop, opened the way for the psychological western on the screen and was followed in the next few years by equally acclaimed and more popular movies like *The Gunfighter* and *High Noon*.

Pursued opens in an abandoned ranch house in turn-of-the-century New Mexico. Waiting in the shadows for a lynch mob is Jeb Rand (Mitchum), who, in flashback, recalls his childhood, the murder of his father, and his adoption by Medora Callum (Judith Anderson), who had raised Jeb with her own children, Adam (John Rodney) and Thorley (Teresa Wright). Jeb's enigmatic adoptive father, Grant (Dean Jagger), was a rugged individualist who insisted that either of the two boys enlist in the Spanish-American War. Thorley flips a coin, and Jeb loses, declaring his love for her as he goes. Returning a war hero, Jeb again weighs his future on the toss of a coin, giving up his share of the Callum ranch to Adam after a violent quarrel.

When Jeb tries to return later with a fortune won at gambling, he is ambushed by Adam. In self-defense, Jeb kills his brother, is acquitted for the crime, but is still seen as guilty by Medora and Grant. Thorley then agrees to marry him, telling Medora that she will kill him instead. Her shot misses on their wedding night, and she grows to love Jeb.

Grant continues to track Jeb and forces him to flee to the abandoned ranch; there Thorley reveals the cause of the Callum's hatred: as a child Adam had come upon his mother with Jeb's real father together one night and the scene had scarred his mind. Grant arrives with a lynch mob, and Jeb, in order to save Thorley, agrees to surrender. Medora, though, saves him from hanging by shooting the avenging Grant, and releases Thorley and Jeb to their future.

Many of the critical notices were raves. *Newsweek* called *Pursued* "a horse opera with a difference—and with most of the difference in its favor . . . an intelligent and refreshing departure from the regulation sage-brush saga . . . the characterizations—particularly those of Teresa Wright, Judith Anderson and Robert Mitchum—are superior to those performances usually associated with gunplay and the great open spaces." In the same vein, critic Howard Barnes said, "Mitchum gives a modulated characterization of the man pursued by fugitive memories and very real enemies," and called the film "a novel, vastly effective Western."

On the negative side, *Time* felt: "Apparently everyone involved in this independent produc-

tion had the laudable hope of making a Western with a difference, but perhaps too many differences for one picture, and none of them is very interesting." Bosley Crowther, in agreement, observed that "it is . . . hard to work up any sympathy for the hero, who seems bored by all his woes. That may be because Robert Mitchum, who plays the latter, is a very rigid gent and gives off no more animation than a Frigidaire turned to 'defrost.' "

Pursued was a praise-worthy failure. Its true status and importance were to take many future years to be recognized.

33
Desire Me
Metro-Goldwyn-Mayer, 1947

THE CAST:

Marise Aubert, GREER GARSON; *Paul Aubert,* ROBERT MITCHUM; *Jean Renaud,* RICHARD HART; *Hector Martin,* Morris Ankrum; *Father Donnard,* George Zucco; *Dr. Andre Leclair,* Cecil Humphreys; *Alex (Postman),* David Hoffman; *Dr. Poulin,* Max Williams; *Salesman,* Clinton Sundberg; and Tony Carson, Mitchell Lewis, Fernanda Eliscu, Sid D'Albrook, David Leonard, Edward Keane, Belle Mitchell, Hans Schumm, Fredric Brunn, William Yetter, John Maxwell Hayes, Lew Mason, Josephine Victor, Jean Del Val, Stanley Andrews, Harry Wood, Sam Ash, Earle Hodgins, Gil Perkins, Max Cutler, Albert Petit.

Producer, Arthur Hornblow, Jr.; *Directors,* George Cukor and Mervyn LeRoy;* *Screenplay,* Marguerite Roberts and Zoe Akins; *Based on the Novel Karl and Anna by* Leonhard Frank; *Adaptation,* Casey Robinson; *Photography,* Joseph Ruttenberg; *Music,* Herbert Stothart; *Art Directors,* Cedric Gibbons and Uric McCleary; *Editor,* Joseph Dervin. Running time: 91 minutes.

Mitchum made *Desire Me* in early 1946, back-to-back with *Undercurrent* while on loan to MGM. Filming on the project, a remake of the German *Homecoming* (Ufa, 1928), began under George Cukor, and had Mitchum co-starring with Greer Garson and Robert Montgomery. It then was

*No official screen credit given at their request.

In *Desire Me.*

With Richard Hart in *Desire Me*.

entitled *A Woman of His Own*; subsequently it became *Sacred and Profane*. Production soon bogged down in rewrites, Montgomery was pulled off for another project, newcomer Richard Hart was brought in to replace him, Mitchum moved up to second billing, director Cukor departed, and Jack Conway began reshooting, only to step aside for Mervyn LeRoy. Cukor has admitted that he shot *Desire Me* "from a script that didn't really make sense, and when it was finished I was just removed from the picture, and another director reshot a good deal of it with the understanding that his name wouldn't appear on the credits. Since very little of the final footage was mine, I wouldn't allow my name to be on the picture either." *Desire Me* remains one of the very few major films to go into release with no director credited.

And no wonder. With Queen Greer, Mitchum, and Hart all vainly struggling to portray French-

men in an American adaptation of a German story, few intelligible scenes emerged from the befuddled melodrama despite the customary MGM gloss and the ad-line that trumpeted: "Greer Garson and Robert Mitchum ... excitingly together for the first time!" *Desire Me* sat in an MGM vault for more than eighteen months. The ponderous tale with its "Enoch Arden" theme tells of Marise Aubert (Greer Garson), desperately in love with her husband, Paul (Mitchum), but unable to bring herself to live with him. In flashback, she tells a psychiatrist (Cecil Humphreys) how she had seen her fisherman husband off to war and remained faithful to him, even after the official news of his death at the hands of the Nazis.

A stranger, Jean Renaud (Richard Hart), tells her that he had been in prison camp with Paul, had become obsessed with Paul's tales of Marise, and had thus left Paul to die of bullet wounds

With Greer Garson in *Desire Me*.

after they had escaped together. Drawn by Renaud's loneliness, Marise had permitted him to remain in her cottage and had eventually fallen in love with him.

Intercepting a letter from the still-alive Paul, Renaud persuades Marise to sell Paul's business and go away with him immediately. Paul returns prematurely, though, and Marise is heartsick because she realizes that his faith in her has received a mortal shock. Paul causes Renaud's death in a desperate fight on a cliff, but while her husband's love is strong enough to forget the past, Marise cannot overcome her sense of tragedy and guilt until the psychiatrist gives her the courage to return to him.

"Robert Mitchum tries a Gaelic gesture now and then, but most of the time he just looks sleepy, and no audience will blame him much for that," wrote *Time*. Howard Barnes observed in the *New York Herald Tribune* that "the brief appearance of Mitchum is extremely welcome in the tedious doings. He gives a lot of melodramatic impact to the fight scene, but he might well have kept his name off the credits, too, so far as this film will advance his career."

Newsweek thought: "In *Desire Me*, Robert Mitchum's back and Greer Garson's got him—unfortunately, because Mitchum deserves better than an inconsequential role in a tear-jerker that is phony from stumbling start to maudlin finish." And *Variety* commented on "the growing b.o. [box-office] importance of Robert Mitchum" in helping put over the film, while feeling that "Mitchum has too little footage as the husband, appearing briefly in the beginning during a prison camp sequence and again in the final reel, but he makes every scene count."

34
Out of the Past

RKO Radio, 1947

With Jane Greer in *Out of the Past*.

THE CAST:

Jeff Bailey, ROBERT MITCHUM; *Kathi Moffat*, JANE GREER; *Whit Sterling*, Kirk Douglas; *Meta Carson*, Rhonda Fleming; *Jim*, Richard Webb; *Fisher*, Steve Brodie; *Ann Miller*, Virginia Huston; *Joe Stefanos*, Paul Valentine; *The Kid*, Dickie Moore; *Leonard Eels*, Ken Miles; *Sheriff Douglas*, Frank Wilcox; *Marney*, Mary Field; *Canby Miller*, Harry Hayden; *Mrs. Miller*, Adda Gleason; and Jose Portugal, Jess Escobar, Hubert Brill, Brooks Benedict, Primo Lopez, Caleb Peterson, Theresa Harris, Wesley Bly, Michael Branden (Archie Twitchell), Philip Morris.

Executive Producer, Robert Sparks; *Producer*, Warren Duff; *Director*, Jacques Tourneur; *Screenplay*, Geoffrey Homes (Daniel Mainwaring) (and, uncredited, James M. Cain and Frank Fenton); *Based on the novel Build My Gallows High by* Geoffrey Homes; *Photography*, Nicholas Musuraca; *Music*, Roy Webb; *Music Director*, C. Bakaleinikoff; *Art Directors*, Albert S. D'Agostino and Jack Okey; *Editor*, Samuel E. Beetley. Running time: 97 minutes.

With Kirk Douglas in *Out of the Past*.

Out of the Past gave Robert Mitchum his first chance to carry a film. RKO built its selling campaign around his name—"It's like lightning kissing thunder when Mitchum makes love to a girl with a gun!" the ad-line screamed, and there, dominating the ad, was big Bob in full head shot, his sleepy eyes squinting dreamily from under a low brimmed hat, a cigarette dangling lazily from his mouth. A second shot of him had him in a clinch with seductive Jane Greer, introducing them subliminally as RKO's version of Bogart and Bacall: Mitchum the trench-coated, hard-boiled, chain-smoking shamus; Jane the ice-cold, sloe-eyed femme fatale holding the smoking gun. And true to the RKO formula, a second tough guy, young Kirk Douglas on loan from Paramount, was added to fill out the top of the cast.

At the suggestion of writer Daniel Mainwaring, executive producer Robert Sparks tried to talk studio head Dore Schary into prying Bogart loose from Warner Bros. for the lead, but Schary chose

With Paul Valentine and Kirk Douglas in *Out of the Past*.

to go with his RKO contract players instead. Mainwaring had come to RKO as part of the deal when the studio bought the rights to his book, *Build My Gallows High,* and he became one of the studio's house scriptwriters, frequently using the pseudonym Geoffrey Homes. *Build My Gallows High* was kept as the film's title until (as with virtually every RKO Mitchum movie), it became *Out of the Past* on the eve of its release. Writer Mainwaring subsequently said: "I wrote the first draft and then went on to something else. Producer Warren Duff put Jim [James M.] Cain on it, and Cain threw away my script and wrote a completely new one. They paid him twenty or thirty thousand and it had nothing to do with my novel or anything. He took it out of the country and set the whole thing in the city. Duff didn't like it and called me back, and I made some changes and did the final. That's the way things used to work." On Dore Schary, Mainwaring confessed: "He didn't like anything that was in progress at the studio when he got there. He tried to get rid of them all. He just threw them out without any decent publicity."

Though completely identifiable as an RKO movie, *Out of the Past* emerged, in the hands of director Jacques Tourneur (late of Val Lewton's remarkable horror unit on the lot), as a complex, episodic crime melodrama that has been elevated in the years since to cult status. In it, the archetypal Mitchum character was molded—the mercenary tough guy whose "macho" presence belies his laconic, take-it-or-leave-it attitude with the RKO dames and his two-fisted brawn. Ironically, *Out of the Past* provided Mitchum with his only private eye role until his Philip Marlowe of *Farewell, My Lovely* nearly thirty years later.

Hard-boiled characters, forceful performances, and crisp direction cleverly masked the film's confusing story line and many improbabilities, as Tourneur moves his tale from Los Angeles to Mexico to San Francisco to Lake Tahoe. Hiding out in a small, peaceful town, retired detective Jeff Bailey (Mitchum) learns that a figure from his past, gambler Whit Sterling (Douglas), wants to see him again. Bailey recalls how he had first been summoned by Sterling to go after his mistress, Kathi Moffat (Jane Greer), and get back $40,000 she had stolen from him. Finding her in Acapulco, Bailey succumbs to her charms and decides to settle down with her. But the two are tracked down in San Francisco by Bailey's former partner, Fisher (Steve Brodie), who tries to get a cut of Sterling's money in exchange for his silence on their whereabouts.

Bailey orders him out, and in the ensuing fight, Kathi shoots him and takes off with the money. Disgusted at being played the fool, Bailey decides to retire after hiding Fisher's body, and tries to seek anonymity with girlfriend Ann Miller (Virginia Huston).

When Bailey reluctantly goes to see Sterling, he finds Kathi had worked her way back into the gambler's affections. Sterling offers to forget Bailey's double-cross if he will steal some incriminating records from Leonard Eels (Ken Miles), a San Francisco lawyer who is blackmailing Sterling. Bailey agrees, but finds Eels mysteriously murdered and realizes that he has stepped into a frameup. Wanted now for the murders of both Eels and Fisher, Bailey traces everything back to Kathi, whom he finds standing gun in hand over the body of Sterling in the latter's Lake Tahoe estate.

Now in charge, Kathi orders Bailey to run away with her. With all hope of clearing himself gone, Bailey is trapped, but finds an opportunity to call the police. Fleeing, the two quickly run into a police roadblock, and Kathi realizes what Bailey has done. She shoots him and then dies herself in a fusillade of machine-gun fire.

The *New York Herald Tribune's* Otis L. Guernsey, Jr., found that "Robert Mitchum is ideally suited to his role . . . he can fling a line of dialogue to an arrogant gunman or brush off an unwanted dame with the best of them, and he gives the two-dimensional melodrama exactly what it requires—personality rather than character." Bosley Crowther's view in *The New York Times* was that "Robert Mitchum is magnificently cheeky and self-assured as the tangled private-eye, consuming an astronomical number of cigarettes in displaying his nonchalance." And *Newsweek* concluded: "Mitchum is particularly effective as the cryptic, casual sleuth who mixes business with pleasure and isn't afraid to pay for it."

Time commented: "When he performs with other men—most memorably in *The Story of G.I. Joe,* Robert Mitchum is a believable actor. But it seems to be a mistake to let him tangle—as a hero, anyhow—with the ladies. In love scenes, his curious languor, which suggests Bing Crosby supersaturated with barbiturates, becomes a brand of sexual complacency that is not endearing."

And what was Daniel Mainwaring's opinion of Mitchum as the Jeff Bailey of his novel: "He was fine, but he looks a little fat."

35
Rachel and the Stranger

RKO Radio, 1948

THE CAST:

Rachel, LORETTA YOUNG; *Big Davey Harvey,* WILLIAM HOLDEN; *Jim Fairways,* ROBERT MITCHUM; *Little Davey,* Gary Gray; *Parson Jackson,* Tom Tully; *Mrs. Jackson,* Sara Haden; *Mr. Green,* Frank Ferguson; *Gallus,* Walter Baldwin; *Mrs. Green,* Regina Wallace; *Jebez,* Frank Conlan.

Executive Producer, Jack L. Gross; *Producer,* Richard H. Berger; *Director,* Norman Foster; *Screenplay,* Martin Rackin; *Based on the Novel Rachel by* Howard Fast; *Photography,* Maury Gertsman; *Music,* Roy Webb; *Music Director,* C. Bakaleinikoff; *Songs,* Roy Webb and Waldo Salt; *Art Directors,* Albert S. D'Agostino and Walter E. Keller; *Editor,* Les Milbrook. Running time: 92 minutes.

With William Holden in *Rachel and the Stranger.*

"Robert Mitchum is well cast as a guitar-playing hunter," critic Otis L. Guernsey, Jr., wrote in his appraisal of *Rachel and the Stranger,* "a little too 'woodsy' for the taste of a settled farmer, but a better judge of women that his twice-married friend." Mitchum's headline making drug-bust prompted RKO to rush this agreeable, unpretentious, frontier comedy/drama into quick release to take advantage (and test the waters) of its star's sudden notoriety. Those front-page stories, RKO soon learned, did not harm Mitchum's box-office attraction, and undoubtedly helped *Rachel* bring a more sheckels into the till than the studio had any right to expect.

The homey little tale, adapted by Waldo Salt from Howard Fast's story and directed in a leisurely, low-key style by Norman Foster, combined humor, pathos, comedy, human appeal, several songs sung by Mitchum, and a slam-bang Indian raid at the climax for the type of good family entertainment now recalled by many with a warm glow. Set in the Northwest Frontier

With Loretta Young in *Rachel and the Stranger.*

With William Holden, Gary Gray, and Loretta Young
in *Rachel and the Stranger*.

country of the early 1800s, the film deals with widower, Big Davey Harvey (William Holden), who, shortly after his wife's death, decides his young son (Gary Gray) needs a woman's care and goes to the nearest settlement where he buys a bondswoman, Rachel (Loretta Young), for twenty-two dollars and marries her for propriety. Back at the cabin, Big Davey, still in love with his dead wife, treats Rachel simply as a servant, while his son refuses to accept her as a substitute mother, despite her quiet efforts to please them both.

Into Rachel's cold and cheerless existence comes Big Davey's old friend, Jim Fairways (Mitchum), who notices her unappreciated status and sets out to charm her, awakening Big Davey's jealousy. The situation comes to a head a short time later when Big Davey suggests that Jim has overstayed his welcome. It is then that Jim offers to buy Rachel from his friend, precipitating a fight between the men. When Rachel learns of their quarrel, she scornfully puts them in their place

and then heads back to the settlement. The two men and the boy follow her, with Big Davey and Jim each trying to outwit the other to make peace with Rachel. A sudden glow in the night alerts them to an Indian attack and the four rush back to the cabin and manage to stave off a full assault until a relief party comes to the rescue.

The following morning, Jim, seeing that Big Davey and his son have at last realized their true love for Rachel, decides to resume his roving life and moves on.

Time wrote that "in its own terms, *Rachel* is an engaging piece and an unpretentious show . . . a better piece of history than most, with pleasant work by Loretta Young and Robert Mitchum, and a skillful comic, notably engaging performance by William Holden."

This film, Dore Schary's last for RKO before departing for MGM, introduced Mitchum the singer and guitar player as the footloose frontier Ishmael. A singing Mitchum was to prove a screen rarity.

36
Blood on the
Moon
RKO Radio, 1948

With Robert Preston in *Blood on the Moon.*

THE CAST:

Jimmy Garry, ROBERT MITCHUM; *Amy Lufton,* BARBARA BEL GEDDES; *Tate Riling,* ROBERT PRESTON; *Kris Barden,* Walter Brennan; *Carol Lufton,* Phyllis Thaxter; *Jack Pindalest,* Frank Faylen; *John Lufton,* Tom Tully; *Milo Sweet,* Charles McGraw; *Joe Shotten,* Clifton Young; *Frank Reardan,* Tom Tyler; *Fritz Barden,* George Cooper; *Ted Elser,* Richard Powers (Tom Keene); *Cap Willis,* Bud Osborne; *Nels Titterton,* Zon Murray; *Bart Daniels,* Robert Bray; *Chet Avery,* Al Ferguson; *Mitch Moten,* Ben Corbett; and Joe Devlin, Erville Alderson, Robert Malcolm, Chris-Pin Martin, Ruth Brennan, Harry Carey, Jr., Hal Taliaferro, Al Murphy, Iron Eyes Cody.

Producers, Sid Rogell and Theron Warth; *Director,* Robert Wise; *Screenplay,* Lillie Hayward; *Based on the Novel Gunman's Choice by* Luke Short; *Adaptation,* Harold Shumate; *Photography,* Nicolas Musuraca; *Music,* Roy Webb; *Music Director,* C. Bakaleinikoff; *Art Directors,* Albert S. D'Agostino and Walter E. Keller; *Editor,* Samuel E. Beetley. Running time: 88 minutes.

"Where there's Blood on the Moon . . . death lurks in the shadows!" That ad-line highlighted RKO's big sell for Robert Mitchum's first "A" western, rushed, like *Rachel and the Stranger,* into release to cash in on the publicity from its star's narcotics arrest. Taking the familiar cattlemen versus homesteaders theme, *Blood on the Moon* became, under the even hand of director Robert Wise (his eighth film) and a good cast, a superior outdoor drama. Mitchum plays quiet gunfighter Jim Garry, who gets involved in a range war over grazing rights. On one side is gentlemanly Tate Riling (Robert Preston), who has secretly been rustling cattle while romancing Carol (Phyllis Thaxter), daughter of cattle baron Jim Lufton (Tom Tully), in his plan to obtain the Lufton

spread. Rilling talks Garry into helping pressure Lufton and Carol's tough-minded sister, Amy (Barbara Bel Geddes), to selling off their lucrative range land. He also needs Garry's skills with a gun in the coming battle of homesteaders against Lufton's cowhands.

After Rilling leads the homesteaders in a clash with Lufton's men—during which the son of Kris Barden (Walter Brennan), one of the leaders of the homesteaders, is killed—and two of Rilling's hands try to murder Lufton, Garry decides that he's on the wrong side and leaves after beating up Rilling and one of his henchmen. Garry then rides to Lufton's ranch and suggests a counter-scheme to foil Rilling's plan to force Lufton off of government range lands with the aid of Jack Pindalest (Frank Faylen), a crooked federal agent. Amy persuades her father to go along with Garry, who kidnaps Pindalest while Lufton convinces the homesteaders that Rilling had been using them. Rilling tracks down Garry and, in the ensuing gun battle, is shot dead along with Pindalest. The homesteaders make peace with Lufton, while Amy plans her future with Garry.

"In *Blood on the Moon,*" director Robert Wise has recalled, "we tried to do something for the first time in a western: a barroom fight that was at least realistic. We said, let's have these men go at it all the way, as hard as they can, and let's have them exhausted at the end, which they would be.

With Barbara Bel Geddes and Tom Tully in *Blood on the Moon*.

With Frank Faylen in *Blood on the Moon*.

And I think it worked. Mitchum and Preston liked the idea very much, and I think it's the most distinctive scene in the whole film."

In its review of the film, *Newsweek* felt that "the only thing that distinguishes it from the 'gallop and gun-belt' sort of thing is the presence of Robert Mitchum in the cast. But that makes a considerable difference. Afoot or on horseback, the slow-voiced, sad-faced RKO star moves with the feline grace of a mountain lion, and despite his appealing diffidence, belongs to that rare breed of Hollywood cowhand—he not only acts tough but looks as though he really could use his rifle or six-shooter if necessary [and] is equal to the task of making even the preposterous circumstances that lead up to [the climax] convincing."

Thomas M. Pryor, critic for *The New York Times*, wrote: "This picture has a sound, sensible story to tell and, besides, it is well acted. Robert Mitchum carries the burden of the film and his acting is superior all the way."

37
The Red Pony
Republic, 1948

THE CAST:

Alice Tiflin, MYRNA LOY; *Billy Buck*, ROBERT MITCHUM; *Grandpa*, Louis Calhern; *Fred Tiflin*, Shepperd Strudwick; *Tom Tiflin*, Peter Miles; *Teacher*, Margaret Hamilton; *Jinx Ingals*, Patty King; *Jackie*, Jackie Jackson; *Beau*, Beau Bridges; *Nino*, Nino Tempo; *Dale*, Tommy Sheridan; *Himself*, Little Brown Jug; *Truck Driver*, Wee Willie Davis; *Charlie*, George Tyne; *Clown*, Poodles Hanneford; *Circus Performers*, Grace Hanneford and Eddie Borden; *Bartender*, Max Wagner; *Telegrapher*, Alvin Hammer; *Gert*, Dolores Castle; *Ben*, William Quinlan.

A Lewis Milestone/Charles K. Feldman Group Production. *Producer/Director*, Lewis Milestone; *Associate Producer*, Norman Lloyd; *Screenplay*, John Steinbeck from his novel; *Photography*, Tony Gaudio; *Music*, Aaron Copland; *Art Director*, Victor Greene; *Special Effects*, Howard and Theodore Lydecker; *Editor*, Harry Keller. Technicolor. Running time: 89 minutes.

In the screen version of *The Red Pony*, Mitchum was ideally cast for the role of Billy Buck, the easy-going handyman. Independent producer Charles K. Feldman arranged with Howard Hughes for Mitchum's services, and the actor came to a production top-heavy with major

With Peter Miles in *The Red Pony*.

With Myrna Loy and Peter Miles in *The Red Pony*.

With Myrna Loy in *The Red Pony*.

talent—Myrna Loy, deglamorized to play the mother; Old Guard director Lewis Milestone to supervise the performances; Aaron Copland to provide one of his rare film scores; John Steinbeck to write his own screenplay; and veteran Warner Bros. cameraman Tony Gaudio (in his last assignment) to lovingly photograph the film in Technicolor—it was the first color movie for both Mitchum and Milestone.

Mitchum, taking second billing to Myrna Loy, personified Billy Buck, playing his stalwart, man-of-few-words self. The character part was expanded considerably from the Steinbeck original—actually he appears only in the third part of the trilogy ("The Gift," "The Leader of the People," and "The Promise") that comprises *The Red Pony*. In the 1972 television version with Maureen O'Hara and Henry Fonda, the Billy Buck figure was eliminated entirely. Working for Fred Tiflin (Shepperd Strudwick) and his wife Alice (Myrna Loy), Billy Buck is the jack-of-all-

trades in the ranch and the idol of nine-year-old Tom* (Peter Miles), helping the boy train his small red pony, Gablian. Fred, a former schoolteacher and ill-at-ease on the ranch, resents the fact that his son has turned to Billy Buck for guidance, and he vents most of his resentment on his elderly father-in-law (Louis Calhern), a pioneer of the plains who lives in the daydream world of a romantic past.

Sensing his parents' domestic problems, Tom turns his world to his pony and cares for it lovingly under Billy Buck's tutelege. While Fred is away in San Jose, the pony is injured after breaking out of its corral during a storm. Tom blames Billy Buck for Gablian's condition, and Alice sends for Fred, whose confidence is boosted by the fact that he is needed during a family emergency.

*Jody in the book, but changed presumably to avoid confusion with *The Yearling*.

When the pony dies, an inconsolable Tom holds Billy Buck responsible, so the handyman, impressing on the boy some of the cruelties of nature, promises Tom a colt that his prize mare is about to foal. Fortunately, the colt is born without complications, and Billy Buck proudly presents him to Tom, restoring the boy's faith both in him and in his father, who had come back when Tom needed him.

The Red Pony, wrote *Newsweek,* "is rooted in an honest tenderness that refreshes a familiar theme.... With the exception of Robert Mitchum, who plays the understanding Billy Buck with his customary ease and persuasion, the other actors are handicapped by adult concerns that are suggested only fragmentarily as they impinge on Tom's small, private world." Robert Hatch, critic for the *New Republic,* thought: "The picture is played in a key of uneasy emotionalism that never quite escapes being maudlin.... Of the adult supporting cast, Robert Mitchum, as the ranch hand, is at least at ease in his part."

"In directing the picture," Bosley Crowther said in *The New York Times,* "Mr. Milestone had adopted a frankly casual style which further invests the proceedings with a languid quality.... Robert Mitchum is strangely laconic—too much so—as the hired man." And *Time* felt: "In the movie version, adapted by author Steinbeck, many of the facts and most of the mystery have been lost.... Hollywood, with scripter Steinbeck's connivance, has sold author Steinbeck and his story down the river."

A fragile, gossamer tale of the caliber of *The Red Pony* naturally requires careful nurturing in order to find a mass audience. Adding handicaps: its distributor, Republic Pictures, was out of its element in handling "prestige" films and only half-heartedly devoted itself to their merchandising; and the Mitchum marijuana bust had hit the headlines before the film's release. Notwithstanding, producer Feldman apparently recovered his initial costs on *The Red Pony* and reissued it in 1957 on the strength of the Mitchum name.

38
The Big Steal

RKO Radio, 1949

THE CAST:

Lt. Duke Halliday, ROBERT MITCHUM; *Joan "Chiquita" Graham,* JANE GREER; *Capt. Vincent Blake,* WILLIAM BENDIX; *Jim Fiske,* Patric Knowles; *Colonel Ortega,* Ramon Navarro; *Lieutenant Ruiz,* Don Alvarado; *Julius Seton,* John Qualen; *Manuel,* Pasqual Garcia Pena; and Henry Carr, Alfonso Dubois, Frank Hagney, Ted Jacques, Carl Sklover, Virginia Farmer, Bing Conley, Nacho Galindo, Tony Roux, Felipe Turich, Pat O'Malley, Juan Duval, Rodolfo Hoyas.

Executive Producer, Sid Rogell; *Producer,* Jack J. Gross; *Director,* Don Siegel; *Screenplay,* Geoffrey Holmes (Daniel Mainwaring) and Gerald Drayson Adams; *Based on the Story* "The Road to Carmichael's" (*Saturday Evening Post*) by Richard Wormser; *Photography,* Harry J. Wild; *Music,* Leigh Harline; *Music Director,* C. Bakaleinikoff; *Art Directors,* Albert S. D'Agostino and Ralph Berger; *Editor,* Samuel E. Beetley. Running time: 71 minutes.

With Don Alvarado, Ramon Navarro, and Jane Greer in *The Big Steal.*

The saga of *The Big Steal,* director Don Siegel's third feature film, is in itself nearly as convoluted as the movie. "It was an excuse to get Robert Mitchum out of jail," Siegel has said. Howard Hughes, now head of RKO, dragged the script off the shelf ("it was incredibly bad," Siegel wrote of the story) to prove to the court that the studio and many innocent people were suffering because production was set to roll but the star was unavailable. (Actually, according to an item in the

With William Bendix in *The Big Steal*.

With Jane Greer in *The Big Steal*.

New York Herald Tribune dated 12/23/48, George Raft had been signed to star in *The Big Steal* opposite Claire Trevor. Raft then was shoved to another project and Mitchum was cast. His co-star was to have been Lizabeth Scott, who suddenly was called "home" by Hal Wallis and replaced on the Siegel film by Jane Greer.)

Mitchum began filming *The Big Steal* while out on bail, prior to his grand jury hearing, then left to do his time in the country jail, and returned two months later to complete his assignment. Siegel did the film's entire chase sequence without his star, then patched in Mitchum later. "The whole picture was done tongue-in-cheek," Siegel had admitted, "and none of us took it very seriously, least of all Mitchum and Siegel."

The film opens with a steamer docking at Vera Cruz. On shipboard, Duke Halliday (Mitchum), an Army lieutenant, is confronted by Captain Vincent Blake (William Bendix), his superior. Blake attempts to arrest Halliday, but Halliday knocks him out and steals his I.D. papers, and then leisurely saunters ashore with pretty fellow passenger Joan Graham (Jane Greer). In Vera Cruz, Halliday goes to see Jim Fiske (Patric Knowles). Fiske had robbed him of a $300,000 army payroll, and Halliday wants it back. Pretending to be Blake, he gets into Fiske's room to find only Joan there. Learning that Fiske had headed for the interior, Halliday and Joan go on his trail, with the local police and Blake himself taking up the chase as well.

Nearing Fiske's hideout in Tehuacan, Halliday and Joan are captured and taken to the ranch where Fiske is about to turn the money over to Julius Seton (John Qualen), an international crook. When Blake suddenly shows up, Halliday realizes it was Blake and Fiske who had planned the payroll heist together. Blake shoots Fiske, but Joan then distracts him long enough for Halliday to overpower him. With the payroll recovered and his reputation cleared, Halliday prepares to return to the States with Joan.

Various tough-sounding ads alerted the moviegoing public to *The Big Steal*. "Mitchum is mad . . . Bendix is bad . . . Greer is gorgeous!" went the alliterative line of one ad. "A man of ice—a woman of fire—a guy with a gun . . . and a deadly goal!" shouted another. *Variety* felt that "the star trio is good, each polishing the meller antics with a breezy lightness under Siegel's smooth direction." The *Newsweek* review said that "even when the actors stand still long enough to catch their breath and start shooting at each other, the plot doesn't make much sense. What is clear is that the producers have set out to stage a movie chase to end all movie chases. They come very close to doing it."

Robert Hatch, in *The New Republic*, decided that "no cautious reviewer is going to come right out and say that *The Big Steal* is a ludicrous miscarriage of an adventure picture, because there is an outside chance that RKO meant it that way. What *seems* to be happening on the screen is a wooden, implausible, humorless melodrama." Of Mitchum, critic Howard Barnes wrote in the *New York Herald Tribune:* "[He] acquits himself ably in the violent sequences. He is not so successful as a great lover."

39
Holiday Affair

RKO Radio, 1949

THE CAST:

Steve Mason, ROBERT MITCHUM; *Connie Ennis,* JANET LEIGH; *Carl Davis,* WENDELL COREY; *Timmy Ennis,* Gordon Gebert; *Mrs. Ennis,* Griff Barnett; *Mrs. Ennis,* Esther Dale; *Mr. Crowley,* Henry O'Neill; *Police Lieutenant,* Henry (Harry) Morgan; *Johnson (Plainclothes Officer),* Larry J. Blake; *Floorwalker,* James Griffith; *Emily,* Helen Brown; *Mary (Housekeeper),* Frances Morris; *Mr. Gow,* Allen Mathews; *Santa Claus,* Frank Johnson; and Al Murphy, Mame Henderson, Pat Hall, Bill Henry, Jim Hawkins, Robert Lyden, Jack Chete, Don Dillaway, Joe Ray, Mary Stewart, Frank Mills, Philip Morris, Chick Chandler.

Producer/Director, Don Hartman; *Screenplay,* Isobel Lennart; *Based on the Story* "Christmas Gift" *by* John D. Weaver; *Photography,* Milton R. Krasner; *Music,* Roy Webb; *Music Director,* C. Bakaleinikoff; *Art Directors,* Albert S. D'Agostino and Carroll Clark; *Editor,* Harry Marker. Running time: 87 minutes.

RKO tried a new Mitchum image in his next film, giving his fans the opportunity to see him doing romantic comedy. His surprisingly breezy manner in an offbeat role turned this sentimental little Christmas picture into a rather unlikely but likable attraction. Based on *The Man Who Played Santa Claus,* a novelette by John D. Weaver, the confection (originally called *Christmas Gift*) begins when war widow Connie Evans (Janet Leigh), a comparison shopper for a department store chain, buys an expensive electric train set from Steve Mason (Mitchum), an easy-going sales clerk in a rival store. He spots her as a comparison shopper but nevertheless sells her the train, and when she returns it the following day, he refunds her money and is fired for failing to report her to his superiors.

Afterwards, Steve invites Connie to lunch, spends a hectic day helping her shop, and then loses her in the crowd. At her apartment later, he meets her young son, Timmy (Gordon Gebert), and her fiancé, Carl Davis (Wendell Corey), a stuffy, prosperous lawyer. Timmy takes to Steve at once; Carl does not. On Christmas morning, Timmy gets a shiny new train from Steve, and

Connie, aware that Steve really could not afford it, tries to reimburse him. He finally accepts a tie, giving the one he's wearing to a Central Park vagrant, who reciprocates by presenting Steve with a stolen salt shaker set. Within minutes, Steve is under arrest. With the reluctant assistance of Carl, Connie convinces the police of Steve's innocence, and then invites him to Christmas dinner.

Learning of Carl and Connie's upcoming wedding, Steve shocks everyone by first congratulating Carl and then telling Connie that she's marrying the wrong man. In the days that follow, Carl comes to the same conclusion and bows out gracefully, as Connie races to catch up with Steve on a train to Chicago.

The ad campaign for *Holiday Affair* offered the moviegoer somewhat more than the film delivered. The shot of a surprisingly wide-eyed Mitchum ogling a Saran-wrapped Miss Leigh and commenting "Baby, you're just what I want for Christmas" hinted rather strongly if erroneously that his fans were in for a sex comedy. A second campaign was hastily devised, with the tag line changed to "When Mitchum kisses 'em, they hear bells . . . wedding bells!"

Most critics were caught up in the Christmas spirit and had nice things to say about the film and/or Mitchum. Howard Barnes, in the *New York Herald Tribune,* called it "a slick and appropriate holiday film . . . as smooth as parfait and about as substantial. . . . Mitchum is really working out of his usual territory in handling comedy. He does extremely well with the role of the frank suitor who understands children." *Variety* enthused: "Mitchum does somewhat of a type switch and it comes out as one of his best acting stints. However the departure isn't far enough to lose the virile personality that is his best stock-in-trade, so his fans will be pleased." And *Newsweek* felt that "Don Hartman directed Mitchum in a role that allows him to vary his customary tough, laconic characterization with humor and—precariously—a mite of whimsy. This the actor carries off with easy assurance, whether he is helping a lady carry her bundles, doubling as a child psychologist, or feeding the seals in Central Park.

The New York Times' Bosley Crowther observed: "Robert Mitchum, the sleepy-eyed young man with a drawl . . . is directed to ramble around blandly and is quite as mechanical with his charm as is that swank electric train."

Despite Mitchum's critical and personal success in light comedy, Howard Hughes apparently saw him only as a two-fisted tough guy who could swap provocative banter with the broads, and allowed him to be cast in a comedy only once again—on the eve of Mitchum's departure from the studio.

With Janet Leigh in *Holiday Affair*.

With Janet Leigh in *Holiday Affair*.

With Janet Leigh in *Holiday Affair*.

40
Where Danger Lives

RKO Radio, 1950

With Faith Domergue in *Where Danger Lives*.

THE CAST:

Jeff Cameron, ROBERT MITCHUM; *Margo Lannington*, FAITH DOMERGUE; *Lannington*, Claude Rains; *Julie*, Maureen O'Sullivan; *Police Chief*, Charles Kemper; *Klauber*, Ralph Dumke; *Mr. Bogardus*, Billy House; *Dr. Maynard*, Harry Shannon; *Milo de Long*, Philip Van Zandt; *Dr. Mullenback*, Jack Kelly; *Mrs. Bogardus*, Lillian West; *Nurse Collins*, Ruth Lewis; *Nurse Seymour*, Julia Faye; *Nurse Clark*, Dorothy Abbott; *Nurse Bates*, Elaine Riley; *Dr. Mathews*, Stanley Andrews; *Casey*, Jack Kruschen; *Cop*, Gaylord (Steve) Pendleton; *Honest Hal*, Tol Avery; *Girl in Iron Lung*, Sherry Jackson; *Joe Bordeen*, Ray Teal; *Asst. Police Chief*, Lester Dorr; *Desk Clerk*, Herschel Daugherty.

A John Farrow Production. *Producer*, Irving Cummings, Jr.; *Associate Producer*, Irwin Allen; *Director*, John Farrow; *Screenplay*, Charles Bennett; *Story*, Leo Rosten; *Photography*, Nicholas Musuraca; *Music*, Roy Webb; *Music Director*, C. Bakaleinikoff; *Art Directors*, Albert S. D'Agostino and Ralph Berger; *Editor*, Eda Warren. Running time: 84 minutes.

With Claude Rains and Faith Domergue in *Where Danger Lives*.

Few films better exemplify the type of sex-laden potboiler that had become standard RKO fare under Howard Hughes than John Farrow's *Where Danger Lives* (nee *White Rose for Julie*). The melodrama was written to formula as a vehicle for Hughes's top male star and Faith Domergue, "the latest graduate of Hughes' straining bodice school of dramatic art," as *Time* described her.

"MITCHUM IN ACTION" is what RKO promised in its screaming headline ads, and that's what his fans got, although he had to expend most of his energy in a losing struggle with an incredible script about a doctor who dumps his fiancée for a seductive patient, fails to recognize her as a whacko, and gets dragged into a murder and the life of a fugitive.

After young doctor Jeff Cameron (Mitchum) saves socialite Margo Lannington (Faith Domergue) from suicide, he finds himself falling for her, unaware of her mental instability. But only after breaking off with his girlfriend, Julie (Maureen

O'Sullivan), does Jeff learn that Margo's "father" (Claude Rains) actually is her husband. By this time, Jeff is too much in love with Margo to end the relationship. Refusing to believe that Margo is a mental case, Jeff knocks down the older man in a fight and collapses with a concussion. He later awakens to find Lannington's body beside him, and Margo leads him to believe that he had killed her husband, smothering him with a pillow. Jeff lets Margo persuade him to flee with her to Mexico.

With the police on their trail, Jeff at last learns the truth about Margo's sanity, but before he can act, she smothers him and then goes out to keep a date with the men who will smuggle her across the border. Jeff regains consciousness and struggles to intercept her at the International Gate. Margo maniacally tries to shoot him but is cut

With Ralph Dumke and Faith Domergue in *Where Danger Lives*.

down by border guards. Dying, she clears Jeff of Lannington's death, allowing him to return to Julie.

Newsweek wrote: "Lurid as his predicament becomes, Mitchum succeeds in making the doctor's agony of cranium and spirit look grimly genuine. And despite the fact that Faith Domergue turns out to be a monster of incredible proportions, she remains outwardly unblemished to the end. To the more romantically inclined, this should be sufficient to justify the awful prose Mitchum was willing to pay for her."

Bosley Crowther's review in *The New York Times* noted that "in this solemn demonstration, Mr. Mitchum does a fairly credible job as a man operating in a vacuum and beset by unfortunate circumstances," while Joe Pihodna, Crowther's colleague at the *New York Herald Tribune*, found that "*Where Danger Lives* is a decidedly minor film. Mitchum's fans will see plenty of the star, but not necessarily at advantage." Four words summed up the review in Britain's *Monthly Film Bulletin:* "Robert Mitchum performs somnambulistically."

41
My Forbidden Past

RKO Radio, 1951

THE CAST:

Dr. Mark Lucas, ROBERT MITCHUM; *Barbara*, AVA GARDNER; *Paul Beaurevel*, MELVYN DOUGLAS; *Aunt Eula*, Lucile Watson; *Corinne*, Janis Carter; *Clay Duchesne*, Gordon Oliver; *Dean Cazzley*, Basil Ruysdael; *Pompey*, Clarence Muse; *Coroner*, Walter Kingsford; *Cousin Phillippe*, Jack Briggs; *Luther Tuplady*, Will Wright; *Hotel Clerk*, Watson Downs; *Horse Vendor*, Cliff Clark; *Fishmonger*, John B. Williams; and Louis Payne, Johnny Lee, George Douglas, Ken MacDonald, Everett Glass, Barry Brooks, Daniel de Laurentis.

Producers, Robert Sparks and Polan Banks; *Director*, Robert Stevenson; *Screenplay*, Marion Parsonnet; *Based on the novel Carriage Entrance by* Polan Banks; *Adaptation*, Leopold Atlas; *Photography*, Harry J. Wild; *Music*, Frederick Hollander; *Music Director*, C. Bakaleinikoff; *Art Directors*, Albert S. D'Agostino and Alfred Herman; *Editor*, George Shrader. Running time: 70 minutes.

With Janis Carter and Ava Gardner in *My Forbidden Past*.

"Fires of love fanned by the fury of a woman scorned!" So went the enticing promise of the ads for RKO's *My Forbidden Past*, which Howard Hughes had had made in August of 1949 but not released until the spring of 1951. A stoic, heavy-lidded Robert Mitchum was pictured gazing rather unenthusiastically at a decolleté Ava Gardner.

A somewhat offbeat item for RKO, the film was a period soap opera, based on Polan Banks's best-selling 1947 novel, *Carriage Entrance*. Originally it was to have starred Ann Sheridan and Robert Young, but when Hughes dragged his feet in starting production, Miss Sheridan sued for $350,000. Her role subsequently was given to Ava Gardner, borrowed from MGM, and Mitchum was brought in to play the penniless Yankee doctor. To round out the cast, Melvyn Douglas took the part of Ava's ne'er-do-well cousin and was allowed to chew the scenery. A curiously wooden, lurid melodrama set in New

With Ava Gardner in *My Forbidden Past*.

With Ava Gardner and Melvyn Douglas in *My Forbidden Past.*

Orleans of the gaslight era, *My Forbidden Past* stands as an unpleasant tale with stilted dialogue and lacking the slightest human interest touch. It is cast with unpleasant characters, all of whom are either unscrupulous or immoral.

The plot: New Orleans socialite Barbara Beaurevel (Ava Gardner) remains in constant fear of the revelation that her dead grandmother had been a "notorious" woman. Even her boyfriend, Mark Lucas (Mitchum), a young doctor from the North, is unaware of Barbara's "forbidden past," and she hopes to keep the secret from him until she can get him to marry her. To bolster the family's depleted coffers, though, Barbara's scheming cousin, Paul (Melvyn Douglas), persuades her to announce her engagement to wealthy Clay Duchesne (Gordon Oliver). Clay destroys a note explaining the situation to Mark, who, on the rebound, marries an old girlfriend, Corinne (Janis Carter).

Shortly thereafter, Barbara inherits her grandmother's tainted fortune and accepts it over the stern protests of her haughty old Aunt Eula (Lucile Watson). When Mark returns to New Orleans with his new bride, Barbara is stunned to learn of the marriage, only to find that it had been her cousin who had broken up her romance. Vainly she pleads with Mark to divorce Corinne. Rebuffed, Barbara then bribes Paul to destroy Mark's marriage. Paul arranges a tryst with Corinne at a deserted boathouse where Mark's bride is accidentally killed. Mark believes Barbara is involved in the killing but says nothing at the inquest, causing the finger of suspicion to point to him. Shocked by this, Barbara comes forward with the truth at the last minute, implicating Paul and clearing Mark. Now convinced of Barbara's love, Mark decides to marry her.

"Mitchum," *Variety* observed, "is required only to deliver a wooden performance, but his personality does give it some lift." A. H. Weiler, reviewing for *The New York Times*, called the film "a cloyingly saccharine saga" and noted that "as the Yankee 'germ detective,' Robert Mitchum's characterization is somewhat wooden." And Joe Pihodna wrote in the *New York Herald Tribune:* "Robert Mitchum is really living in *My Forbidden Past*. . . . the actor not only has Ava Gardner infatuated with him but Janis Carter plays his wife. Between the girls, Mitchum has a time of it in a screenplay that is hardly distinguished by originality."

Most of the interest of the film's New York opening in April 1951, at the Paramount focused on the hardly coincidental combination of Ava Gardner on the screen and a between-careers Frank Sinatra headlining the stage show.

42
His Kind of Woman

RKO Radio, 1951

THE CAST:

Dan Miller, ROBERT MITCHUM; *Lenore Brent*, JANE RUSSELL; *Mark Cardigan*, Vincent Price; *Bill Lusk*, Tim Holt; *Thompson*, Charles McGraw; *Helen Cardigan*, Marjorie Reynolds; *Nick Ferraro*, Raymond Burr; *Jennie Stone*, Leslye Banning; *Myron Winston*, Jim Backus; *Gerald Hobson*, Carlton Young; *Jose Morro*, Philip Van Zandt; *Martin Kraft*, John Mylong; *Estaban*, Erno Verebes; *Tex Kearns*, Dan White; *Milton Stone*, Richard Berggren; *Harry*, Stacy Harris; *Hernandez*, Robert Cornthwaite; *Corey*, Paul Frees; and Jim Burke, Joe Granby, Daniel de Laurentis, John Sheehan, Sally Yarnell, Anthony Caruso, Robert Rose, Tol Avery, Paul Pierro, Mickey Simpson, Joey Ray, Joan Olander (Mamie Van Doren), Joy Windsor, Jerri Jordan, Dan Borzage, Dorothy Abbott, Mike Lally, Peter Brocco, Ralph Gomez, Alberto Morin.

Executive Producer, Howard Hughes; *Producer*, Robert Sparks; *Director*, John Farrow; *Screenplay*, Frank Fenton and Jack Leonard; *Photography*, Harry J. Wild; *Music*, Leigh Harline; *Music Director*, C. Bakaleinikoff; *Songs* "Five Little Miles from San Berdoo" by Sam Coslow and "You'll Know" by Harold Adamson and Jimmy McHugh; *Art Director*, Albert S. D'Agostino; *Editors*, Eda Warren and Frederic Knudston. Running time: 120 minutes.

Robert Mitchum, the king of the RKO lot, met Jane Russell, the studio's queen, in *His Kind of Woman,* a tough melodrama spiced with light-hearted sex, though a more improbable set of characters and situations would be difficult to conjure up and place against the full backdrop of RKO's cutrate production values—a gambler down on his luck who irons things when he's bored; a golddigging mystery woman who manages to find singing jobs despite her three note vocal range; a burly gangster who wants to look like Robert Mitchum; a psychotic plastic surgeon; an inexcusably careless immigration agent; a hammy matinee idol who dreams of being a real-life hero; et al.

His Kind of Woman had been filmed early in 1950 by John Farrow, back to back with the previous Farrow/Mitchum project, *Where Danger Lives.* Under its original title, *Smiler with a Gun,* Howard Hughes had relegated it—and nearly two dozen other completed films—to the vaults until he could catch up on his personal reediting. When Hughes hired Warner Bros.' wunderkind producing team, Jerry Wald and Norman Krasna, he gave them a contract for sixty films in five years for fifty million dollars (actually they made only four). Wald and Krasna then took on the job of doctoring the movies the studio had shelved. "The Wald-Krasna improvements," *Newsweek* wrote of *His Kind of Woman,* "explain why the eccentric Hughes, whose whims become company policy under his one-man rule, finally decided to release the film . . . editing could not have been one of the Wald-Krasna changes, for the melodrama still runs too long [and] it never is quite clear what the makers had uppermost in mind: suspense, comedy or action."

Helping RKO reap a small fortune from the film was the ad campaign that simply carried the Louella Parsons endorsement; "The hottest combination that ever hit the screen!" A hugh closeup of la Russell and big Bob, obviously in a horizontal position, added to the illusion that dynamite screen magic was being offered. The movie opens in a small Mexican airport café, into which saunters Dan Milner (Mitchum), a professional gambler. There, his sleepy eyes first behold the fantastic figure of sultry Lenore Brent (Russell), a petulant singer. Missing no detail of her expansive geography, Dan moves in on her the moment she finished her song, and then discovers that they're both headed for the same resort lodge somewhere south of Nogales, where Lenore makes a bee-line for Mark Cardigan (Vincent Price, in a truly hilarious performance), an egocentric movie star who is trying to dodge his wife (Marjorie Reynolds). At the resort, Dan learns that he has been hired to drop out of sight so that Nick Ferraro (Raymond Burr), a Lucky Luciano-type gangster, can take Dan's identity to reenter the States. He soon becomes aware that Thompson (Charles McGraw), a shady character hanging around the lodge, is one of Ferraro's henchmen, and that playboy Bill Lusk (Tim Holt) is really an immigration agent trying to keep an eye on Ferraro. Lusk tips Dan to the gangster's plan—that a plastic surgeon is going to remake Ferraro's face to match Dan's, after which Dan is to be killed.

When Lusk turns up dead, Dan decides to call off the deal, but Thompson forces him at gunpoint to accept Ferraro's long-standing invitation

With Jane Russell in *His Kind of Woman.*

With Daniel DeLaurentis and Jane Russell in *His Kind of Woman.*

With Peter Brocco, Charles McGraw, and Mike Lally in *His Kind of Woman.*

for a yacht trip. Observing Dan's rather reluctant departure, Lenore rushes to Cardigan for help, and the actor, seeing a chance to prove himself a real hero, organizes a party to go to Dan's aid. On the yacht, meanwhile, Dan is stripped to the waist and mauled by Ferraro's henchmen. Before being turned over to Ferraro's plastic surgeon, anxious to test an experimental drug he had developed for the Nazis during the war, Dan manages to overpower Thompson and then take on Ferraro, as Cardigan, in a grandiose raid, leads a Wild West rescue squad of bewildered Mexican police. At the fade-out, Lenore sashays insinuatingly into Dan's hotel room where she finds him ironing his money ("I always do a little ironing when I'm bored," he confesses). She, of course, relieves him of the iron and coaxes him into a steamy clinch.

Reviewing for the *New York Herald Tribune,* James S. Barstow, Jr. observed: "RKO, heretofore a reasonably conservative studio, has gone hog wild with a cockeyed mixture of hokum and violence . . . the cast, headed by Robert Mitchum and Jane Russell, and director John Farrow are forced to play this nonsensical melodramatic hodgepodge with a straight face. It must have been as painful an experience as watching the result." Howard Thompson wrote in *The New York Times:* "In addition to being one of the worst Hollywood pictures in years, it is probably the only one since the advent of Vitaphone that needs sub-titles. . . . The stars are more to be pitied than censured—or, for that matter, censored. Mr. Mitchum blinks sleepily into space and Miss Russell, strategically sheathed in some opulent gowns, merely and understandably arches her upper lip as though she were smelling something awful."

Less harsh was Manny Farber, the critic for *The Nation,* who called the movie "good, coarse, romantic, adventure nonsense, exploiting the expressive deadpans of Robert Mitchum and Jane Russell . . . who would probably enjoy doing in real life what they do here for RKO." The word on the film's hero from *Time,* however, was that "Mitchum manages his undemanding part with an air of static resignation."

43
The Racket

RKO Radio, 1951

THE CAST:

Capt. Thomas McQuigg, ROBERT MITCHUM; *Irene Hayes*, LIZABETH SCOTT; *Nick Scanlon*, ROBERT RYAN; *Johnson*, William Talman; *Welch*, Ray Collins; *Mary McQuigg*, Joyce MacKenzie; *Dave Ames*, Robert Hutton; *Lucy Johnson*, Virginia Huston; *Sgt. Turck*, William Conrad; *Delaney*, Walter Sande; *Chief Harry Craig*, Les Tremayne; *Connolly*, Don Porter; *Sullivan*, Walter Baldwin; *Higgins*, Howland Chamberlain; *Joe Scanlon*, Brett King; *Enright*, Richard Karlan; *Tony*, Tito Vuolo; *Governor's Aide*, William Forrest; *Governor*, Howard Petrie; *Durko*, Max Wagner; *Davis*, Ralph Peters; *Sadie*, Iris Adrian; and Jane Hazzard, Claudia Constant, Jack Shea, Joey Ray, Milburn Stone, Don Beddoe, Herb Vigran, Harry Lauter, Ed Parker, Gregg Barton.

A Howard Hughes Production. *Producer*, Edmund Grainger; *Director*, John Cromwell; *Screenplay*, W. R. Burnett and William Wister Haines; *Based on the Play by* Bartlett Cormack; *Photography*, George E. Diskant; *Music*, Paul Sawtell and Roy Webb; *Music Director*, C. Bakaleinikoff; *Art Directors*, Albert S. D'Agostino and Jack Okey; *Editor*, Sherman Todd. Running time: 89 minutes.

To get the most mileage out of the ongoing Kefauver crime hearings of the early 1950s, Howard Hughes dusted off the old Bartlett Cormack play, *The Racket*, a screen property that he had filmed previously as a silent movie in 1928. John Cromwell, who had starred opposite Edward G. Robinson in the original play, was assigned to direct Robert Mitchum, as the incorruptible police captain, and Robert Ryan, as the sydicate payoff man. Between them, in standard RKO two-tough-guys-and-sultry-babe formula, Lizabeth Scott was cast as a hard-looking nightclub thrush.

Under Cromwell, *The Racket* turned out to be a somber black-and-white study of big city corruption, teeming with police brutalities and syndicate vengeance. However, the plot line not only lacked originality but the potentiality for hard-hitting action—especially with strong actors like Mitchum and Ryan—was diffused by director Cromwell's lethargic pacing. He has confessed that the original "was the forerunner of all the good gangster things. It was the first . . . but by this time [the early fifties], the material had been used and resued and kicked around. It was so old hat that I couldn't arouse much interest in it at all."

The tale of a tough cop's fight against crooked politicians unfolds in a typical big city of filmdom: the metropolis under the thumb of an unseen crime czar who uses a long-time mobster-turned-quasi-respectable as his front man. The racketeer, Nick Scanlon (Ryan), defies orders from the syndicate, though, and orders his henchmen to kill a political candidate suspected of talking to the crime commission. A young cop named Johnson (William Talman) has spotted the fleeing killers and is assigned to the case by police captain Thomas McQuigg (Mitchum). Assistant state's attorney Welch (Ray Collins) and his investigator, Sergeant Turck (William Conrad),

With Lizabeth Scott in *The Racket*.

With Virginia Huston in *The Racket*.

With Walter Sande, Stephen Roberts, Robert Ryan, and Pat Flaherty in *The Racket*.

at the urging of the syndicate, try to talk McQuigg out of pursuing the case, but he stubbornly refuses to lay off his investigation.

Suspecting that Nick Scanlon, his long-time nemesis, is involved, McQuigg finds that the racketeer's weak spot is his kid brother, Joe (Brett King). McQuigg has Joe arrested for carrying an unlicensed gun, and than has Joe's girlfriend, singer Irene Hayes (Lizabeth Scott), brought in as a material witness. When Irene offers to talk, Scanlon tries to have her silenced.

Officer Johnson, meanwhile, sets a trap for the hit men, is forced to shoot them in self-defense, and is slain later in the police station by Scanlon. McQuigg goes after Scanlon and nabs him after a rooftop shootout. At the station, the gangster is provoked into a confession by Irene, who had witness the original killing. Although the syndicate wants Scanlon to stay behind bars until after

the upcoming elections, he forces its hand and is bailed out. He is given a chance to run, and then a contract is put out on his life. Having anticipated this double-cross, McQuigg has arranged for crime commission investigators to nab Welch and Turck at the station house while the syndicate is taking care of Scanlon.

Time called *The Racket* "the trashiest major production of the year . . . not to be outdone by the truth, producer Edmund Grainger now strikes a blow for the moviemakers by offering a big-city crime fable as outlandish as oversimplification and exaggeration can make it." Joe Pihodna, in the *New York Herald Tribune*, felt that "Mitchum ably portrays a police captain in the same grim stony-faced manner with which he plays roles of underworld characters. His is the sort of part that dominates the screen and helps make the picture seem better than it really is."

44
Macao
RKO Radio, 1952

With Jane Russell in *Macao*.

THE CAST:

Nick Cochran, ROBERT MITCHUM; *Julie Benton*, JANE RUSSELL; *Lawrence Trumble*, WILLIAM BENDIX; *Lt. Sebastian*, Thomas Gomez; *Margie*, Gloria Grahame; *Vincent Halloran*, Brad Dexter; *Martin Stewart*, Edward Ashley; *Itzumi*, Philip Ahn; *Kwan Sum Tang*, Vladimir Sokoloff; *Gimpy*, Don Zelaya; *Ship Captain*, Emory Parnell; *Customs Official*, Philip Van Zandt; and George Chan, Nacho Galindo, Sheldon Jett, Genevieve Bell, Tommy Lee, Alex Montoya, Spencer Chan, Trevor Bardett, Michael Visaroff, W. T. Chang, Manuel Parig, James Leong.

A Howard Hughes Presentation. *Executive Producer*, Samuel Bischoff; *Producer*, Alex Gottlieb; *Director*, Josef von Sternberg (and uncredited Nicholas Ray); *Screenplay*, Bernard C. Schoenfield and Stanley Rubin (and uncredited Walter Newman); *story*, Bob Williams; *Photography*, Harry J. Wild; *Music*, Anthony Collins; *Music Director*, C. Bakaleinikoff; *Art Directors*, Albert S. D'Agostino and Ralph Berger; *Editor*, Samuel E. Beetley. Running time: 80 minutes.

With William Bendix in *Macao*.

For their second screen teaming, Howard Hughes dropped Robert Mitchum and Jane Russell in the teeming (back-lot set) colony of Macao, and stranded them there with an incredible script that took one from column A and one from column B of his action-thriller copybook. As the ad-line read: "Mitchum—a man from nowhere . . . Russell—a woman with nowhere to go . . . together trying forget their pasts in exotic, exciting MACAO, port of sin and shady dealings!"

To direct *Macao* (made between August and October of 1950 and then shelved until the spring of 1952), Hughes assigned Josef von Sternberg, hot off Hughes's disastrous *Jet Pilot*, to work his assumed magic on Jane Russell as he had done two decades earlier with Marlene Dietrich. In his autobiography, von Sternberg confessed: "After *Jet Pilot*, I made one more film in accordance with the RKO contract I had foolishly accepted. This was made under the supervision of six different men in charge. It was called *Macao*, and instead of fingers in that pie, half a dozen clowns immersed

With Gloria Grahame in *Macao*.

various parts of their anatomy in it. Their names do not appear in the list of credits." Nor does that of director Nicholas Ray, who "doctored" *Macao* and several other impossible productions. "I shot about 50% of it," Ray later admitted. "Never for any publicity for working on it until Jo von Sternberg began to get some accolades and recognition and the film began to make some money."

Strictly formula RKO melodrama—generous slices of cheesecake, doses of salty dialogue, a steady stream of confusing chases, and the standard Hughes ploy of splitting up two pals with wine, money, and a dame—*Macao* opens with the arrival by steamer of three Americans: Nick Cochran (Mitchum), an ex-GI on the run; Julie Benton (Russell), a cynical, wise-cracking cabaret singer; and Lawrence Trumble (William Bendix), a New York City detective, trying to bring gambling kingpin Vincent Halloran (Brad Dexter) back to the States. Nick saves Julie from the advances of a drunken passenger on board the ship, and she reciprocates by stealing Nick's wallet. In Macao, Lieutenant Sebastian (Thomas Gomez), a corrupt local gendarme, suspects Nick of being a cop and reports this to Halloran, who tries to bribe Nick to leave the colony. Nick, though, would rather remain to woo Julie, who already has lined up a singing job at Halloran's casino. Halloran, too, makes a play for Julie, much to the annoyance of Margie (Gloria Grahame), his girlfriend and gambling croupier.

Learning of Halloran's bribe, Trumble involves Nick in a diamond-smuggling scheme to lure Halloran out beyond the three-mile limit where he can legally be arrested. Suspecting a trap, however, Halloran has Nick beaten up by his henchmen and then convinces Julie that Nick is a cop who was only using her to get to him (Halloran), and urges her to join him aboard his yacht on a trip to Hong Kong. Accidentally knifed by one of Halloran's men, Trumble tells Nick that he has arranged with the U.S. authorities for Nick to be cleared if he brings in Halloran. Nick makes his way to Halloran's yacht and takes the wheel as the gambler is boarding with Julie. He guides the boat beyond the three-mile limit and then delivers the gambler to Interpol police. Now he is free to make plans with Julie to go back to the States.

To beef up the plot, several additional enticements were inserted among the incredible proceedings. Foremost was one sequence showing Jane Russell encased in a twenty-six-pound gold-silver-mesh lame dress, adjusted (so the publicity noted) with pliers instead of needle and thread. Mitchum, too, showed off his firm frame in his seemingly obligatory beefcake scenes. Russell also got to sing the Johnny Mercer/Harold Arlen standard "One for My Baby" and a pair of new songs by Jule Styne and Leo Robin, "Ocean Breeze" and "You Kill Me." And not to be forgotten is one of the all-time great dialogue exchanges in film history, as Jane catches Bob ogling her strategically exposed superstructure and asks: "Enjoying the view?" To which Mitchum drawls: "It ain't the Taj Mahal or the Hanging Gardens of Babylon, but it'll do."

Calling *Macao* "an amalgam of corn and cleavage [that] has been handsomely directed by Josef von Sternberg as if it matters," *Time* noted that "Jane sings . . . and clinches with Mitchum on a sampan, a yacht and a bed . . . and rolls her eyes at intervals and effectively registers two moods: petulance and boredom. Meanwhile, Mitchum maintains his sleepy-eyed deadpan."

Bosley Crowther observed in *The New York Times:* "*Macao* is a flimflam and no more . . . the show is between Miss Russell and Mr. Mitchum as they brazenly parade their irresistible persons back and forth across the screen and in various haphazard poses designed to reveal their charms." Critic Otis L. Guernsey, meanwhile, called the film "a mysterious East drama with Robert Mitchum and Jane Russell playing games among sampans and slant-eyed killers . . . directed by Josef von Sternberg, it is a dull arrangement of sultry poses and rugged pretensions."

45
One Minute to Zero

RKO Radio, 1952

With Ann Blyth in *One Minute to Zero.*

THE CAST:

Col. Steve Janowski, ROBERT MITCHUM; *Linda Day,* ANN BLYTH; *Col. John Parker,* William Talman; *Sgt. Baker,* Charles McGraw; *Mary Parker,* Margaret Sheridan; *Capt. Ralston,* Richard Egan; *Dr. Gustav Engstrand,* Eduard Franz; *Major Davis,* Robert Osterloh; *Major Carter,* Robert Gist; *Lt. Stevens,* Eddie Firestone; *General Thomas,* Roy Roberts; *Sgt. Cook,* Tom Irish; *Chico Mendoza,* Lalo Rios, *Pvt. Means,* Wally Cassell; and Peter Thompson, Steve Flagg, Ted Ryan, Larry Stewart, Tom Carr, Hal Baylor, Al Murphy, Alvin Greenman, Buddy Swan, Maurice Marsac, William Forrest, Tyler McVey, Dorothy Granger, Robert Bray, Karen Hale, Ray Montgomery, Stuart Whitman.

A Howard Hughes Presentation. *Producer,* Edmund Grainger; *Director,* Tay Garnett; *Screenplay,* Milton Krims and William Wister Haines; *Photography,* William E. Snyder; *Music,* Victor Young; *Music Director,* C. Bakaleinikoff; *Art Directors,* Albert S. D'Agostino and Jack Okey; *Editors,* Robert Belcher and Frank McWhorter. Running time: 105 minutes.

One Minute to Zero, Mitchum's first war movie since *The Story of G.I. Joe,* was one of the first major Hollywood productions about the Korean War. Originally it was to have co-starred Claudette Colbert and been called *The Korean Story.* Instead, Ann Blyth was recruited as Mitchum's somewhat unlikely love interest, and even less was delivered than promised in the ads, which called *One Minute to Zero* a sizzling action film "produced at a cost of millions . . . to bring you a million THRILLS!"

What it did deliver was a standard war movie with formula heroics and stereotyped dialogue. The action takes place during the early days of the war. Steve Janowski (Mitchum), an Army colonel and military observer in Seoul, is ordered to evacuate all Americans to Japan, and in the process, meets Linda Day (Ann Blyth), a pretty war widow with the U.N. Commission. After saving her life twice, he bundles her aboard the last flight out against her wishes. Steve subsequently is wounded in battle and flown back to

With Charles McGraw in *One Minute to Zero.*

With Charles McGraw and Alvin Greenman in *One Minute to Zero.*

Japan, where he meets Linda once again. The two fall in love during his convalescence (to the romantic strains of Victor Young's memorable ballad and subsequent standard, "When I Fall in Love"). Eventually Steve is sent back to Korea and Linda gets herself assigned to a front-line field hospital.

Escaping Red guerrillas when the hospital is overrun, Linda arrives in Steve's sector as he is giving orders to shell a refugee column in which enemy soldiers are hiding out. After learning the truth, she apologizes for upbraiding Steve over his battlefield decision. Steve then takes his unit on a vital mission and finds his men cut off by the enemy. With heavy losses, he manages to lead the unit through to the U.N. forces that have been consolidated for the Inchon invasion. For his heroism, Steve is promoted to general, and after a short leave in Japan with Linda, he is returned to his command.

In *Saturday Review,* Arthur Knight categorized the film as "a cheap, routine affair produced to cash in on current headlines but contributing

nothing to an understanding of them." Knight then complained that "the better part of two hours is given over to [Mitchum and Blyth's] off-again on-again love affair with occasional interruptions while Mitchum goes out to be heroic." *Variety* thought that "Mitchum makes the character acceptable with his specialized style of laconic heroics."

Bosley Crowther reported in *The New York Times*: "Plainly, *One Minute To Zero* is a ripely synthetic affair, arranged to arouse emotions with the most easy and obvious cliches . . . neither the story nor the performances of the actors, including Miss Blyth and Mr. Mitchum, rings true. Here is another war picture that smells of grease paint and studios."

Of interest is the word that the Defense Department tried to pressure RKO into eliminating the sequence in which Mitchum orders the shelling of the civilian refugees. As *Time* wrote: "The producers refused to eliminate the scene, and it remains the only unusual feature in a formula film."

46
The Lusty Men
RKO Radio, 1952

With Susan Hayward in *The Lusty Men.*

THE CAST:

Louise Merritt, SUSAN HAYWARD; *Jeff McCloud,* ROBERT MITCHUM; *Wes Merritt,* ARTHUR KENNEDY; *Booker Davis,* Arthur Hunnicutt; *Al Dawson,* Frank Faylen; *Buster Burgess,* Walter Coy; *Rusty Davis,* Carol Nugent; *Rosemary Maddox,* Maria Hart; *Grace Burgess,* Lorna Thayer; *Jeremiah,* Burt Mustin; *Ginny Logan,* Karen King; *Red Logan,* Jimmy Dodd; *Babs,* Eleanor Todd; and Sam Flint, Riley Hill, Robert Bray, Sheb Wooley, Marshall Reed, Paul E. Burns, Dennis Moore, George Wallace, Chuck Robertson, Mike Ragan, Edward McNally, Mike Lally, Dick Crockett, Les Sanborn, Hazel (Sonny) Boyne, Chili Williams, Richard Reeves, Roy Glenn, Emmett Lynn, Glenn Strange, Denver Plye, Frank Matts, Wally Russell, George Sherwood, Lane Chandler.

A Wald/Krasna Production. *Producers,* Jerry Wald and Norman Krasna; *Director,* Nicholas Ray; *Screenplay,* Horace McCoy and David Dortort; *Story,* Claude Stanush; *Photography,* Lee Garmes; *Music,* Roy Webb; *Music Director,* C. Bakaleinikoff; *Art Directors,* Albert S. D'Agostino and Alfred Herman; *Editor,* Ralph Dawson. Running time: 112 minutes.

Mitchum's finest work during his ten years of indenture to RKO is seen in *The Lusty Men,* the Nicholas Ray film about modern-day rodeo life—a pioneer in the genre that began an early fifties cycle of imitations (*Rodeo, Arena,* etc.) and strangely apart from the run-of-the-mill RKO product. For the services of Mitchum's leading lady, Susan Hayward, Howard Hughes uncharacteristically went off the lot and struck a deal with Darryl F. Zanuck. In exchange, Hughes loaned Mitchum to Zanuck to costar with her in the later *White Witch Doctor.* Filming on *The Lusty Men* was done in the late summer of 1951—the movie then was entitled *Cowpoke,* and subsequently renamed *This Man Is Mine*—and, following RKO tradition, shelved for a year.

The multilevel story finds ex-champ Jeff McCloud (Mitchum) returning to Oklahoma penniless after eighteen years on the rodeo circuit. There he meets Wes Merritt (Arthur Kennedy), a rodeo novice, and his wife, Louise (Susan Hayward), fresh from behind the counter of a tamale joint. The Merritts are trying to put

With Arthur Kennedy in *The Lusty Men.*

together enough money to buy a small ranch of their own. Wes helps Jeff obtain work as a cowhand, and then asks the champ to teach him the arts of the rodeo game. Louise, though, has serious misgiving as Jeff agrees to coach Wes and manage his rodeo career, sharing an equal partnership.

Soon Wes is winning a steady series of competitions, and, punch-drunk with success, he bull-

With Arthur Kennedy and Marshall Reed in *The Lusty Men.*

headedly refuses Louise's pleas to quit and begins squandering his earnings. When Louise goes to Jeff for help with Wes, Jeff suggests instead that she dump her husband for him. He accepts her refusal and tells her he will try to steer his star pupil back to reality. In the showdown, though, Wes calls Jeff a cowardly has-been, and Jeff becomes determined to show he is still a star in the arena. In ensuing contests, Jeff proves he's still the champ, but is fatally injured when his foot catches in a stirrup and he is dragged beneath the hoofs of a wild bronc. Jeff's tragic death sobers Wes and he leaves the rodeo circuit to settle down finally with Louise on their own ranch.

In *The Nation,* critic Manny Farber wrote: "During Howard Hughes' reign at RKO, a number of good movie ideas and artists were stopped in their tracks by the boss' slutty taste and inveterate kibitzing on every production. *The Lusty Men,* one of Hughes' last jobs, however, has a refreshing story idea, with a more humanized version of the Hughes formula. . . . Mitchum is the most convincing cowboy I've seen in horse opry, meeting every situation with the lonely, distant calm of a master cliche-dodger."

Bosley Crowther found the film "vivid and pungent" and felt that "Director Nicholas Ray has really captured the muscle and thump of rodeos." Critic Crowther observed: "Mr. Mitchum is most authentic as a hard-bitten rodeo 'tramp' who has gone on the shelf because of injuries and devotes himself to handling a new man." Other reviewers similarly were impressed with the actor's performance. *Newsweek* commented: "Robert Mitchum is excellent as a jaded former world champion." Arthur Knight, in *Saturday Review,* agreed: "Robert Mitchum, as the rodeo has-been, is outstanding in a generally superior cast."

The British *Monthly Film Bulletin* was among the few nay-sayers, finding that "Robert Mitchum, who appears to be type cast, is unable to lend to his part the strength and depth which it demands."

Of the film itself, critic Otis L. Guernsey viewed *The Lusty Men* as "a happy example of conventional screen fare, with the camera bringing details of the rodeo game close up in a tale of greed and passion . . . it is almost as much fun as the rodeo itself, a solid staple of movie entertainment." *The Lusty Men,* coincidentally, premiered at the Criterion Theatre in New York the day after Mitchum's *One Minute To Zero* closed. Both played together on a double bill for a day of previews at the Broadway house.

47
Angel Face
RKO Radio, 1952

THE CAST:

Frank Jessup, ROBERT MITCHUM; *Diane Tremayne*, JEAN SIMMONS; *Mary Wilton*, Mona Freeman; *Dr. Charles Tremayne*, Herbert Marshall; *Fred Barrett*, Leon Ames; *Catherine Tremayne*, Barbara O'Neill; *Bill Crompton*, Kenneth Tobey; *Arthur Vance*, Raymond Greenleaf; *Judge*, Griff Barnett; *Miller*, Robert Gist; *District Attorney Judson*, Jim Backus; *Harry (Bartender)*, Morgan Brown; *Juror*, Morgan Farley; *Doctor*, Herbert Lytton; *Satsuma*, Frank Kumagai; *Waitress*, Lucille Barkley; *Barrett's Secretary*, Bess Flowers; *Prison Chaplain*, Grandon Rhodes.

Producer, Howard Hughes; *Director*, Otto Preminger; *Screenplay*, Frank Nugent and Oscar Millard; *Story*, Chester Erskine; *Photography*, Harry Stradling; *Music*, Dimitri Tiomkin; *Music Director*, C. Bakaleinikoff; *Art Directors*, Albert S. D'Agostino and Carroll Clark; *Editor*, Frederic Knudston. Running time: 90 minutes.

With Jean Simmons in *Angel Face.*

With Jean Simmons in *Angel Face.*

Robert Mitchum's authoritative presence in *Angel Face,* one more assignment toward wrapping up his contract, made him a reluctant participant in Howard Hughes's ill-fated crash program in the Americanization of Jean Simmons. Hughes rightly concluded he needed the Mitchum name for marquee lure, and Mitchum did his job professionally. Even unlikelier, though, than the "sizzling love combination burning up the screen" was the assignment of Otto Preminger to direct. "He [Hughes] sent me a script called *Murder Story,* and it was awful," Preminger has admitted. And to hear Preminger tell it, Hughes's main reason for making this unpleasant little exercise in murder was because of a dispute Hughes was having with Miss Simmons. "If you don't like the story," Preminger has said Hughes told him, "get some other writers. Do anything you want." Hughes simply presented Preminger with a cast and crew.

RKO's Christmas release (!)—it officially went into distribution on December 11, 1952, although most exhibitors put off showing it as long as possible and it did not open in Manhattan until after the following Easter—*Angel Face* (originally

The Bystander) begins when ambulance driver Frank Jessup (Mitchum) responds to an emergency call from socialite Diane Tremayne (Jean Simmons), whose stepmother (Barbara O'Neil) has been overcome by gas from a jet mysteriously left open. Attracted by Frank, Diana follows him back to the hospital, gets him to break a date with his fiance, Mary Bennett (Mona Freeman), and has him take her dancing. Frank soon learns from Diane that she loves her novelist

With Morgan Brown and Jean Simmons in *Angel Face*.

father (Herbert Marshall) but loathes the woman he married. And Diane discovers that Frank hopes someday to open his own auto repair shop. She promises him that she will try to get her stepmother to finance his garage, and then persuades him to become the family chauffeur, convincing him that it will help influence her stepmother into putting up the needed money.

Frank is alternately drawn to and repelled by Diane, and the two carry on a secret romance. Gradually, though, he becomes fed up with the whole deal, especially when Diane comes to him with a story about an attempt on her life and begs him in vain to take her away. The following day, Diane's stepmother and father are killed when their car rockets backwards and plunges over a cliff. Diane, who had tampered with the car, is distraught over the unintentional death of her father, and she and Frank both are arrested, but lawyer Fred Barrett (Leon Ames) convinces Frank that he must marry Diane as the only way to beat the murder charge. He then manages to get them both off after a long trial.

Convinced of Diane's guilt, Frank decides to leave for Mexico to divorce her. Upset, she offers to drive him to the bus depot. They get into her Jaguar, and Diane quickly throws the car into reverse, sending the two of them over the same cliff where her parents had died.

A smattering of favorable reviews turned up. *Newsweek* called it "a good, unwholesome picture, and, as directed by Otto Preminger, moves at an alarming pace [with] a thoroughly consistent and shocking ending. It is a good thriller." And *Variety* found it "a fair suspense melodrama. . . . Mitchum and Jean Simmons make a good team." Less enthusiastic was Manny Farber, critic for *The Nation*, who wrote: "Unlike many of Howard Hughes' hard-working murder films, this one is too often verbal instead of visual, with a lot of time spent in a dimly-lit boudoir where Robert Mitchum and Jean Simmons mutter forlornly and wear dressing gowns." Assessing the film for *The New York Times*, Howard Thompson called it "an exasperating blend of genuine talent, occasional perceptiveness and turgid psychological claptrap that enhances neither RKO, which should know better, nor the participants. . . . Mr. Mitchum's laconic utterances may or may not be perfectly in keeping with the chain of events . . . and why the film itself commits hari-kiri only the Sphinx knows."

48
White Witch Doctor
20th Century-Fox, 1953

With Susan Hayward and Walter Slezak in *White Witch Doctor*.

THE CAST:

Ellen Burton, SUSAN HAYWARD; *Lonni Douglas*, ROBERT MITCHUM; *Huysman*, Walter Slezak; *Jacques*, Mashood Ajala; *Utembo*, Joseph E. Narcisse; *Kapuka*, Elzie Emanuel; *Jarrett*, Timothy Carey; *Bakuba King*, Everett Brown; *Bakuba Boy*, Otis Greene; *Witch Doctor*, Paul Thompson; *Witch Doctor*, Naaman Brown; *Aganza*, Myrtle Anderson; *Chief's Wife*, Dorothy Harris; *DeGama*, Michael Ansara; *Paal*, Michael Granger; *Chief*, Floyd Shackelford; and Charles Gemora, Leo C. Aldridge-Miles; Louis Polliman Brown, Henry Hastings, Anyaogu, Gabriel Ukaegbu, Elechukwu N. Njakar, Nnaemeka Akosa, John Iboko, Chukemeka Okeke.

Producer, Otto Lang; *Director*, Henry Hathaway; *Screenplay*, Ivan Goff and Ben Roberts; *Based on the Novel by* Louise A. Stinedorf; *Photography*, Leon Shamroy; *Music*, Bernard Herrmann; *Art Directors*, Lyle Wheeler and Mark-Lee Kirk; *Editor*, James B. Clark. Technicolor. Running time: 95 minutes.

Henry Hathaway's *White Witch Doctor*, promoted by 20th Century-Fox as its successor to *The Snows of Kilimanjaro*, was one of Mitchum's rare loan-out assignments during his ten years with RKO. Teamed once again with Susan Hayward, he was cast as a cynical trapper/hunter in "a sort of jungle soap opera with action," as *Variety* described the film. It was based on Louise Stinedorf's schmaltzy best-seller and utilized enough African location shots behind the backlot-based stars to give a reasonable impression of actually having been filmed amid the flora and fauna of the Congo, and brought a bundle into the coffers at 20th as that studio was gearing up for its introduction of CinemaScope. *White Witch Doctor* was, in fact, the studio's last major small-screen production.

The scene is the Congo of 1907. Nurse Ellen Burton (Susan Hayward) is on her way to an interior village adjoining a region inhabited by the dreaded Bakuba tribe. Huysman (Walter

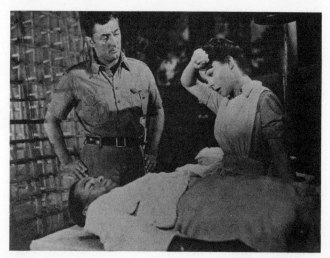

With Susan Hayward in *White Witch Doctor*.

Slezak), a Dutch trader hoping to locate a gold treasure in Bakuba territory, arranges for his partner, Lonni Douglas (Mitchum), to guide Ellen to her destination. The trek brings Ellen and Lonni to a mutual understanding and admiration. At the jungle hospital, Ellen discovers that a number of villagers are in desperate need of medical attention, and within a few days, she is summoned to the Bakuba village to treat a boy who had been mauled by a lion. Lonni agrees to accompany her.

At the village, Ellen administers to the dying boy while Huysman prepares to invade the Bakuba land with an armed gang. Lonni persuades the tribal chief to permit him to deal with Huysman while Ellen stays behind as hostage, and in a gun fight, Lonni kills Huysman and routs his henchmen. Meanwhile, Ellen has saved the wounded boy's life, and she and Lonni decide to remain together in the Congo to administer to the natives.

Impressed by Mitchum, director Hathaway was said to have told his boss, Darryl F. Zanuck: "This sonofabitch is the most phenomenal actor I've ever seen. He glanced through the script and did six pages of dialogue—four in solid African dialect—letter perfect, with every nuance." Critical acclaim, unfortunately, did not come as easy. John McCarten, critic for *The New Yorker*, observed: "In the role of the hunter, Robert Mitchum is as dispassionate as a hippo." In *The New York Times*, A. H. Weiler wrote: "Mitchum is a strong and not precisely silent type, a hero who has crossed the moviegoers' trail before." Of the film, Weiler said: "[It] is an amazingly unsurprising romantic adventure moving methodically along well-beaten film paths." And in the *New York Herald Tribune*, Joe Pihodna commented: "The dances, authentic or not, are far more interesting than the plot [and] brave as Mitchum is in facing the dangers of the jungle, writers Ivan Goff and Ben Roberts are still braver." *Newsweek*, meanwhile, said simply: "Mitchum sidles through the clearings with wholly masculine aplomb." That is probably the best notice he received for this film.

49
Second Chance

RKO Radio, 1953

With Linda Darnell in *Second Chance*.

THE CAST:

Russ Lambert, ROBERT MITCHUM; *Clare Shepard*, LINDA DARNELL; *Cappy Gordon*, JACK PALANCE; *Cable Car Conductor*, Sandro Giglio; *Vasco*, Rodolfo Hoyos, Jr.; *Mr. Woburn*, Reginald Sheffield; *Mrs. Woburn*, Margaret Brewster; *Charley Malloy*, Roy Roberts; *Hernandez*, Salvador Baquez; *Fernando*, Maurice Jara: *Maria*, Jody Walsh; *Felipe*, Dan Seymour; *Hotel Manager*, Fortunio Bonanova; *Edward Dawson*, Milburn Stone; *Rivera*, Abel Fernandez; *Antonio*, Michael Tolan; *Pablo*, Richard Vera; *Blonde in Bar*, Virginia Linden; *Waiter*, Manuel Paris; *Bellhop*, Eddie Gomez; *Don Pasqual*, Martin Garralaga; *Rug Dealer*, Jose Dominguez; *Hotel Clerk*, Luis Alvares; *Priest*, Oresta Seragnoli; and Tony Martinez, Tina Menard, Orlando Beltran, Judy Landon, Marc Wilder, Pete Rand, Max Wagner, Ricardo Alba, Dan Bernaducci, Bob Castro, John Cliff, Henry Escalante, Joe Herrara, Eddie Kerrant, Eddie LeBaron, David Morales, George Navarro, Shirley Patterson, Tony Roux.

A Howard Hughes Presentation. *Executive Producer*, Edmund Grainger; *Producer*, Sam Wiesenthal; *Director*, Rudolph Maté; *Screenplay*, Oscar Millard and Sydney Boehm; *Story*, D. M. Marshman, Jr.; *Photography*, William E. Snyder; *Music*, Roy Webb; *Music Director*, C. Bakaleinikoff; *Art Directors*, Albert S. D'Agostino and Carroll Clark; *Editor*, Robert Ford. Filmed in 3-D and Technicolor. Running time: 82 minutes.

With Linda Darnell in *Second Chance*.

Howard Hughes ordered up another two-fisted action film for Mitchum, added Linda Darnell as his leading lady and Jack Palance to skulk along behind as the menace, and dolled up the proceedings—strictly formula, of course—with Color by Technicolor and 3-D. The two-tough-guys-fighting-for-one-luscious-babe standard RKO plot occupied most of the running time until the sensational climax—a muscular fight between Mitchum and Palance atop a funicular car strung between two Andes peaks (despite the fact that the action supposedly took place in Mexico—a little item never explained). Rugged Bob and tough Jack have at it on the porch of the dangling car, with cables snapping around them and all the three-dimensional gimmicks director Rudolph Maté can reasonably add to involve his audience.

"Crashing thrills! Crushing kisses!" was the ad-line that RKO used the sell the film. "So real . . . it puts *you* so close to the lovers, you feel everything they feel!" So goes *Second Chance,* a south-of-the-border melodrama in which Russ Lambert (Mitchum), an American prizefighter, is barnstorming to try to forget that he once had accidentally killed a ring opponent. He meets Clare Shepard (Linda Darnell), a gangster's moll who is being stalked by professional killer Cappy Gordon (Jack Palance), sent to silence her before a Senate crime committee can find her to testify about her ex-boyfriend. Russ remains unaware of Clare's dilemma until he takes her on an outing and they end up, as well as Cappy, on a broken cable car that threatens to plunge to earth momentarily as it sways between two mountain peaks. Russ, swinging from a dangling rope, manages to get a foothold on a mountain ledge and goes for help. He returns on an auxiliary cable with two basket-like carts that can hold all but one of the passengers. In the showdown that follows, Cappy falls to his death and Russ scrambles into the rescue cart with Clare just as the

With Jack Palance in *Second Chance*.

disabled car falls thousands of feet into the gorge.

Robert Mitchum told Hedda Hopper, on location with *Second Chance*, "I make no suggestions. Of course, if everybody's bumping into each other, I might make a slight one. But I said to RKO, 'This is your baby. I'm gonna read the lines like they're written.' That's my job. . . . When I'm interested, I know my lines and everyone else's. When I'm not, I go on the set and say, 'Tell me what to say.' No fret, no pain, no strain. . . . I've just got one year left with RKO." *Second Chance*, it turned out, was Mitchum's last for the studio. (*She Couldn't Say No*, released the following year, had been filmed earlier and sat on the shelf along with other RKO features.)

Time Magazine's reviewer said; "The third dimension . . . is the least thing wrong with *Second Chance*. According to some touching publicity releases, Bob and Linda are trying to communicate 'a love story that is a pattern for faith.' It may be a spiritual light that comes into Mitchum's eyes when he gets a glom of Linda, or then again it may only be the glare of some passing headlights."

Reviewing for the *New York Herald Tribune*, Paul V. Beckley called the film "a Technicolor thriller in 3 dimensions, with people such as Robert Mitchum and Linda Darnell for nice closeups. . . . It's nice to be able to say it is the best I've seen in this new medium." *Newsweek,* also writing favorably, felt that the film "displays a very respectable example of thrilling writing. And if there is a good deal of the preposterous in the outcome, director Rudolph Maté has used his 3-D skillfully to produce a general audience sweat."

Of the star, Britain's *Monthly Film Bulletin* wrote succinctly; "Mitchum gives a characteristically nonchalant performance."

50
She Couldn't Say No

RKO Radio, 1954

THE CAST:

Corby Lane, JEAN SIMMONS; *Doc*, ROBERT MITCHUM; *Otley*, Arthur Hunnicutt; *Ad Meeker*, Edgar Buchanan; *Joe*, Wallace Ford; *Judge Holbert*, Raymond Hatton; *Mrs. McMurtry*, Hope Landin; *Digger*, Jimmy Hunt; *Sheriff*, Ralph Dumke; *Ed Gruman*, Gus Schilling; *Sally*, Eleanor Todd; *Elmer Wooley*, Pinky Tomlin; *Amos*, Burt Mustin; *Nora*, Edith Leslie; *Mrs. Holbert*, Martha Wentworth; *Barbara*, Gloria Winters; *Clerk*, Barry Brooks; *Minister*, Wallis Clark; *Mrs. Gruman*, Florence Lake; *Mr. Bentley*, Jonathan Hale; *TV Announcer*, Keith Harrington; *Plumber*, James Craven; and Tol Avery, Mary Bayliss, Joy Hallward, Morgan Brown, Clyde Courtwright, Coleman Francis, Mike Lally, Leo Sulky, Clarence Muse, Maxie Thrower, Dabbs Greer, Dan White, Bob Hopkins, Charles Watts, Ruth Packard, Teddy Mangean, Sammy Shack, Carl Sklover, Charles Cane, Tony Merrill, Marjorie Holliday, Marilyn Gladstone.

A Howard Hughes Production. *Producer*, Robert Sparks; *Director*, Lloyd Bacon; *Screenplay*, D. D. Beauchamp, William Bowers, and Richard Flourney; *Based on the Story* "Enough for Happiness" *by* D. D. Beauchamp; *Photography*, Harry J. Wild; *Music*, Roy Webb; *Music Director*, C. Bakaleinikoff; *Art Directors*, Albert S. D'Agostino and Carroll Clark; *Editor*, George Amy. Running time: 89 minutes.

Mitchum's second teaming with Jean Simmons was in Howard Hughes's futile attempt to resurrect the fondly recalled screwball comedies of the thirties and forties. To direct, Hughes hired veteran Lloyd Bacon (it was his next-to-last film), gave him the studio's two best contract stars plus a clever story overworked by too many authors—*Time* subsequently noted that it took three writers to concoct this tale while only one was needed to do *War and Peace*—and then agonized over the finished product for sixteen months (it was filmed in November 1952). Hughes even had difficulty zeroing in on a final title, calling the production at various times *Beautiful But Dangerous, Enough for Happiness,* and *She Had To Say Yes.* He finally settled on *She Couldn't Say No.* It marked the end

of the Jean Simmons epoch at RKO, and, in order of release, it also was Mitchum's last on the lot.

The predictable tale describes the return of a poor little rich girl, Corby Lane (Jean Simmons), to her hometown of Progress, Arkansas, where she plans to repay the town's long ago kindnesses to her late father. Her appearance is soon followed by a mysterious shower of cash gifts that rapidly threatens the town's economy, which had been surviving nicely on the barter system. The community's lone doctor (Mitchum) soon discovers the source of the town's sudden cash windfall, but, attracted to Corby, he decides to guard her secret.

The anonymous gifts begin to show their effects: town drunk Otley (Arthur Hunnicutt) nearly dies from too much good Scotch; Joe (Wallace Ford), the local vet, decides to move to sunny California; Judge Holbert (Raymond Walburn) seeks a more elegant life elsewhere; general store proprietor Ad Meeker (Edgar Buchanan) locks up his business; postman Elmer Wooley (Pinky Tomlin) stops making his rounds; the town simply ceases to function. News of Progress' progress receives national coverage, and hordes of money-grabbers begin invading the town. Alarmed, Corby reveals her identity and prepares to leave. Doc calms the crisis and convinces her to stay as his bride.

Newsweek felt that *She Couldn't Say No* "wastes the talents to two of Hollywood's finest properties, Jean Simmons and Robert Mitchum, in a disastrously flat comedy. . . . Students of the art of making next-to-nothing out of virtually nothing may find director Lloyd Bacon's picture of interest," while Howard Thompson bemoaned in *The New York Times* that the film "teams that gifted British miss, Jean Simmons, and the estimable Robert Mitchum in possibly their thinnest assignments to date." And *Time* wrote that it was "a hymn to a sexy title. It is sung in praise of small-town life but there are rather too many verses and the performers do not seem to know the tune." *Variety,* however, was kind to the stars, observing that "Mitchum and Miss Simmons deliver likeably."

RKO's advertising approach to *She Couldn't Say No* closely resembled the one used for *Every Girl Should Be Married,* their Cary Grant/Betsy Drake comedy several years earlier. This time out, a sexy photo of a surprisingly voluptuous Jean Simmons checking the heartbeat of non-plussed doctor Robert Mitchum was tagged by the intriguing copy line: "Just wait'll you see 'Doc' Mitchum operate . . . what a bedside manner!"

With Jean Simmons and Jimmy Hunt in *She Couldn't Say No.*

With Jean Simmons in *She Couldn't Say No.*

With Jean Simmons in *She Couldn't Say No.*

51 River of No Return

20th Century-Fox, 1954

With Marilyn Monroe in *River of No Return*.

THE CAST:

Matt Calder, ROBERT MITCHUM; *Kay Weston*, MARILYN MONROE; *Harry Weston*, RORY CALHOUN; *Mark Calder*, Tommy Rettig; *Dave Colby*, Murvyn Vye; *Sam Benson*, Douglas Spencer; *Gambler*, Ed Hinton; *Ben*, Don Beddoe; *Surrey Driver*, Claire Andre; *Croupier*, Jack Mather; *Barber*, Edmund Cobb; *Merchant*, Will Wright; *Dancer*, Jarma Lewis; *Drunk Cowboy*, Hal Baylor; *Minister*, Arthur Shields; *Spectator at Black Nugget*, John Doucette; *Blonde Dancer*, Barbara Nichols; *Prospector*, Paul Newlan; *Bartender*, Ralph Sanford; and Mitchell Lawrence, John Veich, Larry Chance, Fay Morley, Harry Seymour, Jerome Schaeffer, Ann McCrea, Geneva Gray, John Cliff, Mitchell Kowal.

Producer, Stanley Rubin; *Director*, Otto Preminger; *Screenplay*, Frank Fenton; *Story*, Louis Lanz; *Photography*, Joseph LaShelle; *Music*, Cyril Mockridge; *Music Director*, Lionel Newman; *Songs*, Lionel Newman and Ken Darby; *Choreography*, Jack Cole; *Art Directors*, Lyle Wheeler and Addison Hehr; *Special Effects*, Ray Kellogg; *Editor*, Louis Loeffler. CinemaScope and Technicolor. Running time: 91 minutes.

Mitchum's first role as a free-lance actor teamed him with Marilyn Monroe and again with Otto Preminger, and befitting his stardom, he even managed a major concession from Darryl F. Zanuck: top-billing over 20th Century-Fox's biggest attraction! Despite the obvious pitfalls in accepting a role opposite Monroe, to whom most of the scenes were to be given on orders from the front office, Mitchum carefully carved out a characterization in his now-familiar strong, quiet outdoorsman image. He simply refused to be intimidated by the expansiveness of either Marilyn Monroe or the Canadian Rockies. Zanuck's obvious idea for *River of No Return* was to give his studio's number-one commodity a chance to be as sexy in shirt and jeans as she previously had established herself in clinging dresses and spangled tights. Mitchum only had to don cowboy duds

With Tommy Rettig in *River of No Return*.

134

With Marilyn Monroe and Tommy Rettig in *River of No Return.*

again to be his ruggedly familiar, Gibraltar-like self.

The story is set in the northwest of 1875 with recently-paroled Matt Calder (Mitchum) turning up in a tent city to pick up his ten-year-old son Mark (Tommy Rettig). Matt and the boy head for open country after Matt thanks saloon singer Kay Weston (Monroe) for looking after the lad. The Calders return to Matt's farm on the edge of the River of No Return, things progress well, and Mark learns to idolize his dad. Spotting an out-of-control raft on the surging river one morning, Matt rescues Kay and her gambler husband, Harry (Rory Calhoun), on their way to register a gold claim Harry had won at poker. When Matt tries to warn them of the dangers of the river, the impatient Harry knocks him out, steals his gun and horse, and goes off alone while Kay, angered, stays behind to look after the injured Matt.

Soon afterwards, an Indian attack forces Matt to hustle Kay and Mark aboard a raft and try to make their escape by river despite its dangers. Matt is determined to take revenge on Harry and between sieges with the savages and negotiating the rapids, he has run-ins with Kay, who, in a burst of anger at one campsite, tells Matt she knows of his past. Mark overhears and refuses to believe his father's explanation of a long-ago killing. When they finally reach Council City, Kay finds Harry and begs him to face Matt. Instead, he pulls a gun. Kay tries to wrestle it away as young Mark, examining a rifle in the nearby general store, sees what is happening and shoots Harry. Kay assures the dazed youngster that his action had been justified. Matt berates Kay for interfering, and she goes off huffily. Matt then arranges for a wagon to get back to the farm, storms into the saloon and without a word, tosses Kay over his shoulder, and embarks on a new life with Mark and her.

"Seldom have I seen an actor maintain an air of

aloofness in the face of proceedings like shooting rapids on a raft, fighting a mountain lion, and dodging the arrows of outraged redmen," critic John McCarten wrote of Mitchum in *The New Yorker*. And in the *New York Herald Tribune*, Otis L. Guernsey said: "Accustomed as he is to leathery roles, Mitchum is taxed to the limit in this script. In one sequence, he wrestles with (1) Marilyn Monroe, (2) a mountain lion, and (3) a bully with a knife, in that order and in rapid succession. He is undismayed by Indian arrows, a swim in the rapids, and a line of dialogue borrowed from Joe Louis ["He can run, but he can't hide"], and he winds through to the end without seriously damaging his composure."

Of *River of No Return*, Otto Preminger has said:

"I remember little of it. I liked the script, and I was interested in using the new lenses called CinemaScope." Of Mitchum: "I remember Bob as a man of professional integrity, and I would like to work with him again whenever it's possible. Beyond that, while I see him too rarely, when I do it's as if we had parted only yesterday. Bob has a warmth, a feeling apart from his intelligence that makes him a friend for life even if you've only had a fleeting experience of work or personal contact with him." This praise obviously was proferred before the well-publicized tiff causing Mitchum to leave the set of Preminger's *Rosebud* in 1975, the film that was to have reunited the actor and the director.

52 Track of the Cat

Warner Bros., 1954

With Tab Hunter and Carl "Alfalfa" Switzer in *Track of the Cat*.

THE CAST:

Curt Bridges, ROBERT MITCHUM; *Grace Bridges*, TERESA WRIGHT; *Gwen Williams*, DIANA LYNN; *Harold Bridges*, TAB HUNTER; *Ma Bridges*, Beulah Bondi; *Pa Bridges*, Philip Tonge; *Arthur Bridges*, William Hopper; *Joe Sam*, Carl "Alfalfa" Switzer.

A Wayne/Fellows Production. *Director*, William A. Wellman; *Assistant Director*, Andrew V. McLaglen; *Screenplay*, A. I. Bezzerides; *Based on the Novel by* Walter Van Tilburg Clark; *Photography*, William H. Clothier; *Music*, Roy Webb; *Art Director*, Al Ybarra; *Editor*, Fred MacDowell. CinemaScope and WarnerColor. Running time: 102 minutes.

William Wellman's arty *Track of the Cat* offered Mitchum, who had worked with Wellman in *The Story of G.I. Joe*, his first starring villain role. Not only was it Mitchum's finest performance to that time—"a back-country Cain" as *Time* referred to his character—but it also showed how he had

matured as an actor of considerable depth and ability. The allegorical tale, stunningly filmed in black and white by William Clothier's color cameras, was the realization of director Wellman's dream to photograph a bold theme in the starkest terms, interrupted only occasionally by a spot of vivid color—Mitchum's red mackinaw, Diana Lynn's yellow scarf.

Variously termed innovative and self-indulgent, *Track of the Cat* since has been categorized as a cinematic curio and an intriguing failure. It is a grim, philosophical melodrama about a group of bitter, twisted people snowbound on their northern California ranch, living

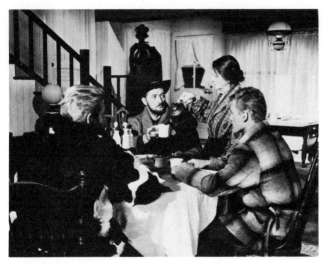

With William Hopper, Beulah Bondi, and Tab Hunter in *Track of the Cat.*

With Diana Lynn and Teresa Wright in *Track of the Cat.*

in dread of a killer panther stalking the area. Beulah Bondi is the self-righteous, unloving matriarch of the family; Philip Tonge, her oratorical, alcoholic husband. William Hopper plays Arthur, the quiet, gifted eldest son; Robert Mitchum is Curt, his arrogant, strong-willed brother; Teresa Wright as their sister, Grace, a withered, disillusioned old maid; and Tab Hunter, their young, naive brother, Harold. Diana Lynn is Gwen, the girl from the neighboring ranch who is in love with Harold.

The first winter snow brings terror to the remote Bridges spread, for with it comes a huge mountain lion that begins killing off the vulnerable cattle. Curt and Arthur venture into the hills to track down the cat, but when Curt returns for rations, the animal attacks and kills his brother. Quarreling and snarling, the family prepares to bury the oldest son, and Grace grieves inconsolably when she learns that it was not the hated Curt who was the victim. Young Harold sees to Arthur's burial and then goes in search of Curt, who has vowed to stalk the cat as a lifetime crusade.

Days later, Harold finds Curt's horse and discovers that his embittered brother had lost his food and, in a moment of panic, had run blindly toward home and had fallen over a cliff to his death. Harold, feeling that the destruction of the cat now has become his destiny, tracks down the beast and kills it. This accomplishment brings him to manhood.

"William Wellman's *Track of the Cat* is touched with the icicle finger of nightmare," Otis L. Guernsey wrote in the *New York Herald Tribune*.

"The script of A. I. Bezzerides is a gargoyle of pioneer virtue. . . . It cuts back and forth between Mitchum's adventure in the outdoors and the whinings and bitterness indoors, worrying its subject like an animal prolonging the kill." Bosley Crowther called the film "a sort of Eugene O'Neillized Western drama," and felt that "the illusion of an interrelation is not helped by Robert Mitchum in the role of the hard-bitten, mother-driven brother, since Mr. Mitchum is one of those boys whose screen personality is stubborn and resistance to the subtleties of such a role."

Director Wellman later discussed the film: "It was a flower, a portrait, a vision, a dream come true—it was a flop artistically, financially, and Wellmanly. Neither the critics nor the audiences paid any attention to the unusual color, or rather the lack of color, the non-Easter card type of color we had striven for and succeeded in getting. . . . The black panther was the symbol of the picture. It was the black panther that represented all that was bad in Mitchum and that finally kills him [but] the audience's imagination failed to imagine."

Following *Track of the Cat*, Wellman and Mitchum prepared another project, *Blood Alley*, for John Wayne's Batjac Productions. Filming began during the first week of January 1955. Less than a week later, Mitchum again hit the headlines when Wellman fired him, accusing the actor of a series of pranks—like shoving the company's transportation manager, Warner Bros.' executive George Coleman, into San Francisco Bay. Mitchum was replaced by John Wayne following unsuccessful attempts to get either Gregory Peck or Humphrey Bogart.

53
Not as a Stranger

Stanley Kramer/United Artists, 1955

With Frank Sinatra in *Not As a Stranger*.

THE CAST:

Kristina Hedvigson, OLIVIA de HAVILLAND; *Lucas Marsh,* ROBERT MITCHUM; *Alfred Boone,* FRANK SINATRA; *Harriet Lang,* GLORIA CRAHAME; *Dr. Adams,* BRODERICK CRAWFORD; *Dr. Runkleman,* CHARLES BICKFORD; *Dr. Snider,* Myron McCormick; *Joe Marsh,* Lon Chaney; *Ben Cosgrove,* Jesse White; *Oley,* Harry Morgan; *Brundage,* Lee Marvin; *Bruni,* Virginia Christine; *Dr. Dietrich,* Whit Bissell,; *Dr. Lettering,* Jack Raine; *Miss O'Dell,* Mae Clarke.

Producer/Director, Stanley Kramer; *Assistant Director,* Carter DeHaven, Jr.; *Screenplay,* Edna and Edward Anhalt; *Based on the Novel by* Morton Thompson; *Photography,* Franz Planer; *Music Director,* George Antheil; *Orchestrations,* Ernest Gold; *Title song,* James Van Heusen and Buddy Kaye; *Art Director,* Howard Richmond; *Gowns,* Don Loper; *Editor,* Frederick Knudtson. Running time: 135 minutes.

With Frank Sinatra and Olivia de Havilland in *Not As a Stranger*.

For his directorial debut, producer Stanley Kramer assembled an all-star cast, among them Robert Mitchum in his biggest film to date. As Lucas Marsh, the ambitious, callous medical student who marries a girl he doesn't love to continue his studies on her meager savings, Mitchum carefully underacted almost to the point of chilly detachment. Kramer managed to mix a fine sense of hospital realism with the ponderous melodramatics of the sudsy script that Edward and Edna Anhalt had fleshed from Morton Thompson's epic-sized best seller, and turned it into one of 1955's top film hits.

Eliminating the book's early chapters telling of Lucas Marsh's boyhood, the film begins with his medical school days, where Lucas slaves long hours in his single-minded dedication to become a great doctor. When he is about to be discharged for lack of tuition funds, Lucas tries to borrow from his best friend, Alfred Boone (Frank Sinatra) and from his professor, Dr. Aarons (Broderick Crawford); then, learning that one of the hospital's nurses, Kristina Hedvigson (Olivia de Havilland), has a modest bankroll, he woos and shortly thereafter marries her, continuing his studies on her money. Unable to bring himself to accept the fact that a doctor is an ordinary man, Lucas slowly allows his idealism to make him hypercritical.

After graduation, Lucas becomes assistant to Dr. Runkleman (Charles Bickford), a gruff, lovable, small-town practitioner, and has a half-serious love affair with wealthy Harriet Lang (Gloria Grahame), one of his patients. Lucas soon discovers that Runkleman has a serious heart condition, but refuses to see any specialists. At the same time, Lucas clashes with Dr. Snider (Myron McCormick), head of the local hospital, over the latter's treatment of a charity case that proves to be typhoid. Kris returns to nursing in the typhoid

With Olivia de Havilland in *Not As a Stranger*.

emergency. Lucas asks her to continue her duties after the crisis subsides, but Kris turns wearily away. Only that morning, she had learned from their friend, Al Boone, now a successful city doctor, that she was pregnant. Despite this, she asks Lucas for a separation, but he is told of her condition from Al at about the time that Runkleman suffers a heart attack. Lucas performs emergency surgery but makes a serious miscalculation and Runkleman dies. Heartsick, Lucas drags himself back to Kris, knowing at last he is neither infallible nor perfect, and needs her love.

"[Kramer's] direction of the good cast has little depth and exposes the thinness of the script," thought Philip T. Hartung, critic for *Commonweal*. "Robert Mitchum plays the lead role in a sort of stunned lethargy that hardly suggests the brainy student of medicine." John McCarten wrote in *The New Yorker:* "Robert Mitchum . . . is extraordinarily adept at concealing his emotions. I suppose that the hooding of normal responses to any given situation is an occupational necessity for doctors, undertakers and gamblers, but I can see no real point in having the actor hide from his audience what is eating him, as Mr. Mitchum does here most of the time."

In the yes-no opinion of William K. Zinsser of the *New York Herald Tribune*: "Unfortunately [Kramer] made two mistakes. He cast Robert Mitchum in the crucial central role, and he decided to direct the picture himself. . . . Much of *Not As a Stranger* is Mitchum's fault. He hardly changes expression or conveys any emotion from beginning to end. It is a monotonous performance in a role that could have been intriguing." Similarly, Bosley Crowther found that "the fact that Mr. Kramer has not managed to force a clear understanding of his man is quite as much a shortcoming of the picture as is the flat performance of Robert Mitchum . . . the stiff-backed individual that [he] plays. He is the screen's most elusive and imponderable medical man."

Mitchum himself has remembered the picture as "all right," and Kramer recalls it as "ten weeks of hell." Buffs recall its many gaucheries, like the classic scene in which Mitchum releases a panting stallion from its stall, and as it charges a nearby mare, he charges nearby Gloria Grahame.

54
The Night of the Hunter

United Artists, 1955

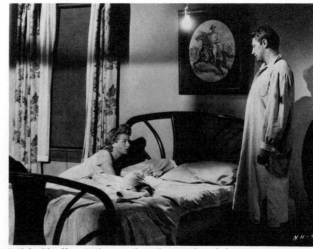

With Shelley Winters in *The Night of the Hunter*.

THE CAST:

Preacher Harry Powell, ROBERT MITCHUM; *Willa Harper*, SHELLEY WINTERS; *Rachel Cooper*, Lillian Gish; *Birdie*, James Gleason; *Icey Spoon*, Evelyn Varden; *Ben Harper*, Peter Graves; *Walt Spoon*, Don Beddoe; *John*, Billy Chapin; *Pearl*, Sally Jane Bruce; *Ruby*, Gloria Castillo; *Clary*, Mary Ellen Clemons; *Mary*, Cheryl Callaway.

Producer, Paul Gregory; *Director*, Charles Laughton; *Screenplay*, James Agee; *Based on the Novel by* Davis Grubb; *Photography*, Stanley Cortez; *Music Director*, Walter Schumann; *Assistant Director*, Milton Cartor; *Art Director*, Hilyard Brown; *Editor*, Robert Golden. Running time: 93 minutes.

Following his appearance in the most successful (financially) picture he had made to that time, Mitchum starred in the least successful one, a gripping if somewhat electric horror tale. It was the only film ever directed by Charles Laughton, who, Mitchum remembered, "called me up and said, 'You play a diabolical crud.' 'Present!' I replied. Charles said, 'I'm not supposed to know about such things. I am a professional non-crud.' 'Charles,' I said, 'I will take care of that department.' Then I read the book." Producer Paul Gregory, with whom Laughton then was engaged in several theatrical ventures (*Don Juan in Hell* and *John Brown's Body*), had come up with the independent financing to bring Davis Grubb's best-selling novel to the screen with a scenario by James Agee, and got from Laughton a minor film classic, a nightmarish exercise in pity and terror, bordering somewhat on the arty.

During the Depression in a small West Virginia community, unemployed Ben Harper (Peter Graves), holds up a bank and kills two men. Before being apprehended, he manages to hide the money from the stickup, swearing his two children, John (Billy Chapin) and Pearl (Sally

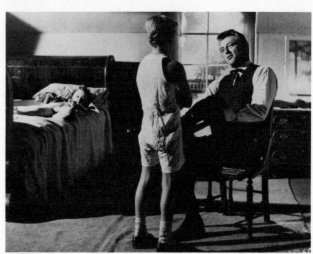

With Sally Jane Bruce and Billy Chapin in *The Night of the Hunter*.

In *The Night of the Hunter*.

140

In *The Night of the Hunter.*

Jane Bruce), to secrecy. Harper's cellmate during his last days before his hanging is an itinerant, self-styled preacher, Harry Powell (Mitchum). After the execution, Powell seeks out Harper's widow, Willa (Shelley Winters), who, starved for affection, accepts his eventual marriage proposal. Soon convinced that Willa cannot lead him to the stolen loot that Harper had hidden, Powell begins badgering the children into revealing its location. He finally murders Willa and attempts to terrorize John and Pearl, but they manage to escape in a small boat and drift down the Ohio River, with Powell in pursuit on horseback.

The children stumble upon the home of Rachel Cooper (Lillian Gish), who takes them in and cares for them until Powell eventually catches up with them. He tries to force Rachel into surrendering the children, but she is not one to be terrorized, and she holds him at bay until the police arrive. Powell is executed for his crimes, and the children find a loving home with Rachel.

Hollis Alpert remarked in *Saturday Review:* "Robert Mitchum, as the preacher, has by far his best role to date. His harsh voice, his homely drawl are perfect. The monstrousness of the man he plays is kept in bounds—he's scary, but not too scary, which is as it should be." In *The New York Times,* Bosley Crowther noted: "Robert Mitchum plays the murderous minister with an icy unctuousness that gives you the chills. There is more than malevolence in his character. There is a strong trace of Freudian aberration, fanaticism and iniquity."

William K. Zinsser wrote in the *New York Herald Tribune:* "Mitchum, whose acting has perhaps never been praised before, gives a superb performance that will surprise almost everybody. . . . On any plane, *The Night of the Hunter* is fine entertainment, and one of the best movies of the year."

From director Laughton: "Mitchum is one of the best actors in the world. He won't thank you for destroying the tough image he's built up as a defense. In fact, he's a tender man and a very great gentleman."

Several sequences in *The Night of the Hunter* are frequently recalled as brilliant cinema. In the most striking, Mitchum is seen riding across the horizon in the moonlight, outlined on his horse against the night sky, slowly approaching the barn where John and Pearl are hiding. Another is the memorable scene in which Mitchum delivers a chilling sermon on good and evil, using his hands that have L-O-V-E and H-A-T-E tattooed on the fingers. Or the wedding night sequence in which the sex-starved widow awaits her new husband but is greeted only with a harangue about the evils of sex and "sinful" women. And there is the showdown between Lillian Gish and Mitchum, as they join in an ironic religious duet while she sits indoors with a shotgun in the dead of night, protecting the children, and he bides his time just beyond her front gate.

55
Man with the Gun

United Artists, 1955

THE CAST:

Clint Tollinger, ROBERT MITCHUM; *Nelly Bain*, JAN STERLING; *Stella Atkins*, Karen Sharpe; *Marshal Sims*, Henry Hull; *Saul Atkins*, Emile Meyer; *Jeff Castle*, John Lupton; *Ann Wakefield*, Barbara Lawrence; *Dade Holman*, Joe Barry; *Rex Stang*, Ted deCorsia; *Ed Pinchot*, Leo Gordon; *Drummer*, James Westerfield; *Doc Hughes*, Florenz Ames; *Virg Trotter*, Robert Osterloh; *Cal*, Jay Adler; and Amzie Strickland, Stafford Repp, Thom Conroy, Maudie Prickett, Mara McAfee, Angie Dickinson, Norma Calderon.

Producer, Samuel Goldwyn, Jr.; *Director*, Richard Wilson; *Screenplay*, N. B. Stone, Jr., and Richard Wilson; *Photography*, Lee Garmes; *Music*, Alex North; *Music Director*, Emil Newman; *Art Director*, Hilyard Brown; *Editor*, Gene Milford. Running time: 78 minutes.

Following his forays into other realms, Mitchum reestablished his more familiar image as a two-fisted towntamer on horseback in *Man with the Gun*, the maiden production of Samuel Goldwyn, Jr., following in the footsteps of his legendary father. Director Richard Wilson, also making his

With Jan Sterling in *Man with the Gun.*

With Jan Sterling in *Man with the Gun*.

With Barbara Lawrence in *Man with the Gun.*

debut, creatively established this action drama several cuts above the average western of its type, infusing it with adult dialogue and characterizations, a touch of suspense, stunning photography, and a gem of a musical score by Alex North.

Mitchum, billed alone above the title for the first time, stars as Clint Tollinger, a gunslinger who arrives in Sheridan City in search of his estranged wife, Nelly Bain (Jan Sterling). Now the town madame, Nelly refuses to see him though she still loves him. Learning that the town is being run by Dade Holman (Joe Barry), a wealthy rancher whose gunmen enforce his rule, Clint has himself deputized by Sims (Henry Hull), the do-nothing marshal, insisting only that he work alone in "taming" Holman and his men. His first act as deputy is to post signs around town barring the wearing of guns. Infuriated, Holman and his men come into town in a body, and are disarmed by Clint who cleans up Sheridan City by shooting several of Holman's men. Clint finishes

his job by burning down the Palace Saloon and killing its owner, Rex Stang (Ted De Corsia), in self defense. The burning, though, turns the town against him.

Taking advantage of the citizens' rumblings, Holman uses Ann Wakefield (Barbara Lawrence), one of Nelly's girls, as a decoy to set up Clint for an ambush. Clint is wounded before he can gun Holman down, and this leads to a reconciliation with Nelly. Clint then offers himself for the job of town sheriff.

"As the man with the gun," wrote A. H. Weiler in *The New York Times,* "Mr. Mitchum convincingly enacts the role of a dedicated citizen who has seen his unarmed father mowed down and therefore loves his bloody profession." In *Commonweal,* critic Philip T. Hartung said of Mitchum: " . . . certainly one of the best performances he has ever given," while John McCarton, in *The New Yorker,* felt that "[the film] offers Robert Mitchum as a fierce fellow with a six-shooter who puts down a gang of bad types in an 1870-vintage cowtown and then gets to be a difficult chap to have around himself . . . the picture, I can assure you, is no *High Noon.*"

The *New York Herald Tribune* critic, Joe Pihodna, thought: "Mitchum is a real tough guy in this expedition. He catches his badmen off guard and shoots them down without moving a muscle in his face. This sort of melodrama ends up in ridiculous situations. It is easy to knock off the bad guys when the script is stacked for you [and] hardly anyone counts in the story except Mitchum."

Time wrote of the film (originally called *The Deadly Peacemaker*) that it "has all the splendid cardboard heroics of the classic Western with flint-eyed, flint-faced Robert Mitchum," while *Newsweek* commented: "Artistically, it is no more than a fast-moving step ahead of routine Westerns as its poker-faced star, Robert Mitchum, rids Sheridan City of a scheming rancher."

The critic for *Variety* was more enthusiastic, calling the movie "excellent Western suspense melodrama . . . a humdinger of an outdoor actioner, sure to win favor with the shoot-'em-up fans, but offering sufficient otherwise to strike the fancy of many who do not usually take to bang-bang sagebrush feature film entertainment."

56
Foreign
Intrigue

United Artists, 1956

In *Foreign Intrigue.*

THE CAST:

Dave Bishop, ROBERT MITCHUM; *Dominique,* Genevieve Page; *Britta Lindquist,* Ingrid Tulean (Thulin); *Joltan Spring,* Frederick O'Brady; *Pierre Sandoz,* Eugene Deckers; *Mrs. Lindquist,* Inga Tidblad; *Tony Forrest,* John Padovano; *Carl Mannheim,* Frederick Schrecker; *Jones,* Lauritz Falk; *Brown,* Peter Copley; *Smith,* Ralph Brown; *Dr. Thibault,* George Hubert; *Baum,* Mil Sperber; *Victor Danemore,* Jean Galland; *Bistro Owner,* Jim Gerald; *Starky,* John Starck; *Dodo,* Gilbert Robin; *Charwoman,* Valentine Camax; *Charles,* Robert Le Beal; *Information Desk Clerk,* Albert Simmons.

A Sheldon Reynolds Production. *Producer/Director,* Sheldon Reynolds; *Associate Producer,* Nicole Millenaire; *Assistant Producer,* John Padovano; *Screenplay,* Sheldon Reynolds; *Story,* Sheldon Reynolds, Harry Jack Bloom, and Gene Levitt; *Photography,* Bertil Palmgren; *Music,* Paul Durand; *"Foreign Intrigue" Concerto,* Charles Norman; *Art Director,* Maurice Petri; *Editor,* Lennart Wallen. Eastman Color. Running time: 106 minutes.

It was Mitchum's box-office clout, undoubtedly, that convinced producer/director Sheldon Reynolds to offer him a partnership, a hefty percentage of the gross, and his name twice the size of the title to carry the feature-length version of Reynolds's extremely successful *Foreign Intrigue* television series. The theatrical *Foreign Intrigue* remains the archetypal trenchcoated secret agent film of its era and did much to spark a trenchcoat rage throughout Europe and into the United States in the mid-1950s. As the only American actor in the large cast, Mitchum traipsed all over Europe in this overlong, highly convoluted spy tale. As a suspense yarn of international skullduggery, *Foreign Intrigue* offered Mitchum the opportunity to once again understate his undenied star quality (the pressbook for the film inflated Mitchum's screen credits to an incredible 108!) as he worked his way through story twists that would have been more than enough for three separate movies. His two

With Genevieve Page in *Foreign Intrigue.*

With Ingrid Tulean and Genevieve Page in *Foreign Intrigue*.

With Frederick O'Brady in *Foreign Intrigue*.

leading ladies in this one were foreign: French actress Genevieve Page, best known in the U. S. for her later performance as Countess Marie in *Song Without End*, and Swedish star Ingrid Tulean, who, with her name later spelled Thulin, became one of Ingmar Bergman's leading actresses.

Mitchum, in *Foreign Intrigue*, is Dave Bishop, a press agent who decides to delve into the background of his late employer, Victor Danemore (Jean Galland), an international tycoon who has died mysteriously. Bishop's quest leads him to Vienna where he discovers that Danemore also had been a blackmailer. Before he can lay his hands on documented proof, however, his contact is murdered, and evidence points to the tycoon's widow, Dominique (Genevieve Page). Learning that Zoltan Spring (Frederick O'Brady), a professional spy also has been hired to look into Danemore's activities, Bishop agrees to a shaky alliance while each man continues his own investigation.

Bishop's trail leads him next to Stockholm, where he meets and falls in love with Brita Lindquist (Ingrid Tulean), whose father, a traitor during the war, had been blackmailed and driven to suicide by Danemore. Back in Vienna, Bishop is introduced to four men who tell him the story behind his late boss. They are intelligence agents from England, Sweden, Switzerland, and the United States. Danemore had discovered that during the war Hitler had made pacts with certain individuals in each country he invaded, but four countries on the Nazi list were never taken and the four traitors who had made pacts remained unrevealed except to Danemore, who was blackmailing them. The key to the puzzle is Zoltan Spring's employer, the English traitor. Bishop is asked to continue working with Spring to learn the man's identity.

As Bishop waits for Spring on a deserted Viennese sidestreet, Brita suddenly turns up to warn him about Dominique. Bishop pulls Brita out of the light and is confronted by Dominique holding a gun. She proposes that he join her in blackmailing the traitors, but he refuses and she is disarmed before Spring's arrival. Bishop then walks off into the night with Spring, on his way to apprehending the traitors.

Critical opinion of *Foreign Intrigue* was far from kind. One of the nicest things said was the comment by the *Variety* critic that "Mitchum gives a good account of himself in the lead role." *Time* wrote that "sleepy-eyed Robert Mitchum . . . yawningly tangles with a Babel of exotic agents, negligently disposes of spies, counterspies, a treacherous brunette and a seductive blonde."

Most hostile was Bosley Crowther who commented: "It is shot through with hackneyed situations . . . and the acting is downright bad. . . . Mr. Mitchum, whose mental processes have never appeared overly alert, is favored, at least in this instance, by not being overly taxed." Critic Crowther's New York confrere, William K. Zinsser, called Mitchum "as stony and impassive as ever." and John McCarten wrote in *The New Yorker:* "Mr. Mitchum seems even more bored than usual."

For the actor, though, it was a free trip to Europe for the Mitchums, and another bundle of money in the bank.

57
Bandido!

United Artists, 1956

THE CAST:

Richard Wilson, ROBERT MITCHUM; *Lisa Kennedy*, URSULA THIESS; *Jose Escobar*, GILBERT ROLAND; *Kennedy*, ZACHARY SCOTT; *Gonzalez*, Jose I. Torvay; *Gunther*, Henry Brandon; *McGhee*, Douglas Fowley; *Sebastian*, Rodolfo Acosta; *General Lorenzo*, Victor Junco; *General Brucero*, Alfonso Sanchez Tello; *Adolfo*, Arturo Manrique; *Santos*, Margarito Luna; *Driver*, Jose A. Espinosa; *Priest*, Miguel Inclan; *Man in Wagon*, Manuel Sanchez Navarro; *Scout*, Albert Pedret; *Indian Boy*, Antonio Sandoval.

A Robert L. Jacks/Bandido Production. *Producer*, Robert L. Jacks; *Director*, Richard Fleischer; *Screenplay*, Earl Felton; *Photography*, Ernest Laszlo; *Music Director*, Max Steiner; *Art Director*, John Martin Smith; *Editor*, Robert Golden, CinemaScope and DeLuxe Color. Running time: 92 minutes.

With Rodolfo Acosta and Gilbert Roland in *Bandido.*

"No one ever rocked the screen like this gun-running, woman-hungry adventurer, who grenaded his way across the roaring inferno called Mexico to the cry—BANDIDO!" That was United Artists' come-on for Mitchum's muscular potboiler that provided him with a free trip below the border; he in turn lent it his machismo image with tongue planted firmly in cheek. A fanciful tale written especially for him, *Bandido!* was an energetic dime-thriller yarn spiced with sex, lots of hard riding, and even more noise, and has Mitchum wrestling with Ursula Thiess, holding off a platoon of soldiers while sitting atop an ammunition dump, and demolishing half an army with grenades casually tossed over his shoulder while he's sipping drinks on a balcony.

Soldier of fortune Richard Wilson (Mitchum) saunters into a sleepy Mexican town of 1916 where a pitched battle between the bandidos and the Regulares is at a Mexican standoff. Lobbing a few well-placed grenades at the more vulnerable Regulares, Wilson immediately endears himself to Jose Escobar (Gilbert Roland), the bandit leader, who offers him a handsome fee to help the bandidos intercept a cache of arms destined for the Regulares. The guns are in the hands of an American named Kennedy (Zachary Scott), who is traveling with his wife, Lisa (Ursula Thiess), and Gunther (Henry Brandon), a go-between for the government. Rapidly developing an interest in Kennedy's wife as well as his arms, Wilson leads a rebel attack and captures Kennedy, Lisa, and Gunther. After Kennedy lies about the hiding place of the arms and Lisa leads them on a wild goose chase, Escobar's men prepare to have her shot, but Wilson comes to her rescue.

Captured by the Regulares, Wilson escapes during a sudden rebel attack but is again imprisoned by Escobar for engineering Lisa's escape. Locked in a cell with Kennedy, Wilson offers to help him get away in return for the weapons. Desperate, Kennedy agrees, but in the race to freedom, made possible by one of Wilson's ever-handy grenades, he is severely wounded and later killed by Escobar. Wilson then goes off with Escobar to retrieve the arms, with the Regulares in pursuit. Aboard one of the barges where, Kennedy had told Wilson, the weapons had been secreted, the two set up a machine gun and hold off the government troops until the rebels arrive. The battle is going badly until Wilson blows up the other barge and routs the Regulares. The victorious rebels unload the remaining guns and Wilson rides off for a rendezvous with Lisa.

Newsweek, one of the few publications to print a

With Zachary Scott in *Bandido.*

With Ursula Thiess in *Bandido.*

review of the film (it never received a first-run Manhattan play-date), noted that "*Bandido!* has a south-of-the-border soldier of fortune, Robert Mitchum . . . and the baroque magnificence of Mexico in color, plus the almost constant noise of gunfire. What it lacks is humor and Douglas Fairbanks." And *Variety* wrote that "Robert Mitchum is a likeable, not always understandable sort of hero-heavy . . . who likes war because it gives him a chance to make some money gunrunning, besides finding amusement in his profession."

Shirley Cobham, in Britain's *Films and Filming*, commented: "I am always surprised when Robert Mitchum kisses women in his films—it is too frivolous an occupation for him. I am even more surprised that here he kisses Ursula Thiess, who lisps disinterestedly from scene to scene."

58
Heaven Knows, Mr. Allison

20th Century-Fox, 1957

THE CAST:

Sister Angela, DEBORAH KERR

Corporal Allison, ROBERT MITCHUM

Producer, Buddy Adler and Eugene Frenke; *Director,* John Huston; *Screenplay,* John Lee Mahin and John Huston; *Based on the Novel by* Charles Shaw; *Photography,* Oswald Morris; *Music,* Georges Auric; *Music Director,* Lambert Williamson; *Art Director,* Stephen Grimes; *Editor,* Russell Lloyd. CinemaScope and Deluxe Color. Running time: 107 minutes.

Robert Mitchum, in *Heaven Knows, Mr. Allison,* co-starred for the first time with the lady who subsequently became his biggest booster, Deborah Kerr. The film began Mitchum's—and director John Huston's—three-picture deal with 20th Century-Fox, and took him to Tobago, from where he had just returned after completing *Fire Down Below* (released later). There, in September of 1956, the trio went to work on a two-character movie, unnecessarily filmed in CinemaScope, about an American Marine corporal and an Irish nun who are trapped together on a South Pacific island during World War II. The original novel

With Deborah Kerr in *Heaven Knows, Mr. Allison.*

With Deborah Kerr in *Heaven Knows, Mr. Allison*.

With Deborah Kerr in *Heaven Knows, Mr. Allison*.

had been purchased in 1952 as a vehicle for director William Wyler, who submitted various story treatments over the years but had trouble getting them past church authorities. When Wyler moved finally to other projects, *Heaven Knows, Mr. Allison* was put on the shelf. It was reactivated for Huston, who worked on the screenplay with John Lee Mahin. "In our version," Huston has pointed out, "the girl had not taken her final vows. Even so, we kept away from any implication of sex . . . there was nothing censorable anywhere in it."

Though the tasteful Huston/Mahin screenplay is totally devoid of sensationalism, the film allowed, strangely, for virtually no character development despite the perceptive Mitchum and Kerr performances. They are introduced to their situation and then trapped in it until some Japanese troops land near the film's conclusion and permit a bit of plot movement. Up to this point, Sister Angela remains unswervingly steadfast and Corporal Allison maintains a detached respect for her, wavering briefly during a drunk scene. Director Huston manages a bit of humor and suspense by way of a turtle hunt and a desperate secret raid by the Marine and the nun on the enemy's food stores. Eventually, though, they are rescued and go their separate ways.

Considered nothing more than merely pleasant, the film is regarded as one of John Huston's lesser efforts. Arthur Knight, though, raved over Mitchum's performance in *Saturday Review:* "What makes this off-beat romantic drama so appealing and affecting are the performances of its two stars. ... The revelation is Robert Mitchum. Not since his portrayal of the doomed and desperate company commander in *The Story of G.I. Joe* has he shown such capacity for tenderness, for understatement, and the creation of a three-dimensional, believable, likeable human being." Similarly enthusiastic about Mitchum was critic William K. Zinsser in the *New York Herald Tribune:* "What is surprising is that he is so tender. When he blurts out a personal question or does an act of kindness that embar-

rasses him, he is like an awkward schoolboy, and suddenly a sensitive quality shines through his crude exterior that we—and he—didn't know he had. His character grows in depth; he is not just another Marine on a desert island."

The opinion of the *Time* reviewer was that "actor Robert Mitchum, even though he does nothing but slob around the screen, has succeeded for once in carrying off his slobbing with significance." And Richard Coe admitted in the *Washington Post:* "Mitchum never has been a favorite of mine, but this picture puts him near the top of my own favorite actor list. Here is a grand performance, a shrewd mixture of vigor and tenderness." Britain's *Monthly Film Bulletin* concluded that "CinemaScope and censorship effectively destroyed its chances for distinction. The film is nonetheless good entertainment, technically competent, and perceptive in the characterizations of Mitchum and Deborah Kerr."

John Huston's words on Mitchum: "Bob is a wonderful guy . . . amusing, intellectual . . . very much in the Bogart mold."

59
Fire Down Below

Warwick/Columbia Pictures, 1957

THE CAST:

Irena, RITA HAYWORTH; *Felix,* ROBERT MITCHUM; *Tony,* JACK LEMMON; *Harbor Master,* Herbert Lom; *Lt. Sellers,* Bonar Colleano; *Dr. Sam,* Bernard Lee; *Miguel,* Anthony Newley; *Jimmy Jean,* Edric Conner; *Captain of the Ulysses,* Peter Illing; *Mrs. Canady,* Joan Miller; *Hotel Owner,* Eric Pohlmann; *The American,* Lionel Murton; *Bartender,* Murray Nash; *Waitress,* Maya Koumani; *Young Man,* Phillip Baird; *Drunk,* Keith Banks; *Sailors,* Vivian Matalon, Gordon Tanner, and Maurice Kaufmann; *Dancers,* Dean Mostyn, Greta Remin, Lorna Wood, Barbara Lane, Shirley Rus, Gina Chare, Anatole Smirnoff, Terry Shelton, Robert Nelson.

With Jack Lemmon in *Fire Down Below.*

With Rita Hayworth and Jack Lemmon in *Fire Down Below.*

Producers, Irving Allen and Albert R. Broccoli; *Associate Producer,* Ronald Kinnoch; *Director,* Robert Parrish; *Screenplay,* Irwin Shaw; *Based on the Novel by* Max Catto; *Photography,* Desmond Dickinson and Cyril Knowles; *Music,* Arthur Benjamin; *Music Director,* Muir Mathieson; *Title Song,* Jack Lemmon; *Sung By* Jeri Sothern; *Steel Band Music,* Katzenjammers of Trinidad; *Choreography,* Tutte Lemkow; *Editor,* Jack Slade. CinemaScope and Technicolor. Running time: 116 minutes.

"It's doubtful that the makers of *Fire Down Below* set out to create a new art form," *Newsweek* assessed, "but that is what they wound up with—something which might be called the one-picture double bill. In the present instance, one watches a steaming tropical love triangle for about an hour, and then without warning, the picture abruptly becomes a suspense thriller which quickly drives the other movie completely out of mind." Made by Columbia, in co-production with British-based Warwick Films, primarily to bolster the waning

glamour girl career of its erstwhile number one star, Rita Hayworth, *Fire Down Below* flanked her with rugged Robert Mitchum and, in an early dramatic role, house light comedian Jack Lemmon.

The three stars were shuttled between the Elstree Studios in London and the Caribbean island of Tobago (*before* Mitchum subsequently made *Heaven Knows, Mr. Allison,* also in Tobago). "Spontaneous combustion!" the ads for the film shouted. "Hayworth sizzles ... Mitchum explodes ... Lemmon burns!" Mitchum and Lemmon are Felix and Tony (the original odd couple), a pair of vagabond, minor-league smugglers, knocking about the West Indies in their small boat. The two are approached by Irena (Hayworth), a stateless lady who is anxious for transport to the vague island of Santa Nada where passports are less important. En route, the less-than-worldly Tony falls for her while the bored Felix tries to save his partner from the wiles of their sultry passenger. ("I'm no good for you.

With Jack Lemmon, Rita Hayworth, Lionel Murton, and Anthony Newley in *Fire Down Below*.

No good for anyone. Armies have marched over me," she confesses to Tony in one of the story's more notable bits of dialogue).

Harsh words between the men causes a rift in their partnership, and Felix subsequently betrays Tony's smuggling activities to the Coast Guard. Tony eludes the law, ships aboard a tramp steamer, and heads for Felix's hideaway planning to kill him. In a dense fog, the steamer collides with another freighter, and Tony, pinned in the wreckage, is abandoned. With the cargo set to explode in hours, Felix manages to rescue his antagonistic ex-partner. Ashore, Tony at last realizes that Irena really belongs to Felix and gracefully bows out of the scene.

Critic William K. Zinsser began his review complaining that the first half of the film, dealing with the romantic triangle, was "pretty bad; the writing is purple, the plot obvious, the acting indifferent. Then suddenly *Fire Down Below* comes to life as if a whole new team had taken over, and the second half is quite good." Zinsser went on to point out that "Mitchum is competent as the laconic tough guy"—a line that seems to have appeared in dozens of previous critiques for the actor's countless performances.

Time noted that "Sleepy-eyed Bob Mitchum never will wake up, but here his somnolence is quite effective. . . . *Fire Down Below* is a triangle story with unusual tensile strength." In *Commonweal,* reviewer Philip T. Hartung was convinced that "at times *Fire Down Below* is an unusual and interesting study in realism and cynicism . . . but the picture as a whole is peculiarly put together."

On the other hand, Bosley Crowther sighed: "No need to call the fire department to handle *Fire Down Below*. . . . It has its own built-in cold water which is turned on about halfway through the damps down the modest conflagration Rita Hayworth has going up to then. . . . How they persuaded Miss Hayworth and Mr. Mitchum to step aside and turn the picture over to Mr. Lemmon is a secondary concern. Why Mr. Shaw failed to notice he had doused the story is what we'd like to know."

Mitchum and Hayworth were, for all practical purposes, written out of the film for Lemmon's tour-de-force in the burning ship, easing back in for the wrap-up in which Jack surrenders Rita to Bob and allowing for a few more lines of unforgettable dialogue, such as the mid-picture exchange in which Mitchum kisses Hayworth, gets a cold response, and confesses, "I'm proud," and then thrusting her away, "I don't make love to the dead."

60
The Enemy Below

20th Century-Fox, 1957

In *The Enemy Below*.

THE CAST:

Captain Murrell, ROBERT MITCHUM; *Von Stolberg,* CURT JURGENS; *Lt. Ware,* Al (David) Hedison; *Schwaffer,* Theodore Bikel; *Doctor,* Russell Collins; *Von Holem,* Kurt Kreuger; *C.P.O. Crain,* Frank Albertson; *Quartermaster,* Biff Elliot; *Mackerson,* Alan Dexter; *Ensign Merry,* Doug McClure; *Corky,* Jeff Daley; *Ellis,* David Blair; *Robbins,* Joe di Reda; *Lt. Bonelli,* Ralph Manza; *Messenger,* Ted Perritt; *Quiroga,* Jimmy Bayes; *Kunz,* Arthur La Ral; *Braun,* Frank Obershall; *Chief Engineer,* Robert Boon; *Mueller,* Werner Reichow; *Andrews (Radio Operator),* Peter Dane; *American Sailor,* Ronnie Rondell; *Striker,* Lee J. Winters; *Lewis,* David Post; *Fireman,* Ralph Reed; *Cook,* Maurice Donner; *German Sailor,* Jack Kramer; *Torpedo Officer,* Robert Whiteside; and Dan Tann, Dale Cummings, Sasha Harden, Michael McHale, Joe Brooks, Thomas Beyl, Richard Elmore, Vincent Deadrick, Dan Nelson, Roger Cornwell.

Producer/Director, Dick Powell; *Screenplay,* Wendell Mayes; *Based on the Novel by* Cmdr. D. A. Rayner; *Photography,* Harold Rosson; *Music,* Leigh Harline; *Music Director,* Lionel Newman; *Art Directors,* Lyle R. Wheeler and Albert Hogsett; *Special Effects,* L. B. Abbott: *Editor,* Stuart Gilmore. Cinema-Scope and DeLuxe Color. Running time: 98 minutes.

With Alan Dexter and player in *The Enemy Below*.

The first of two war movies Robert Mitchum made for Dick Powell (whose directing career was more illustrious than his acting had been), *The Enemy Below* is one of the screen's more under-rated military films—a stunning confrontation movie between two dedicated officers who come to relish the "chess game" in which they have engaged themselves. Mitchum's leadership image is the backbone of his role in *The Enemy Below*, and he turns in a top-notch performance as the captain of the U.S. destroyer *Haines*, involved in a cunning sea duel with German submarine commander Curt Jurgens (in his American film debut). The two are given crisp, intelligent dialogue in Wendell Mayes's literate adaptation that interweaves three conflicts: the destroyer versus the submarine; the destroyer's captain versus the submarine's commander; the de-

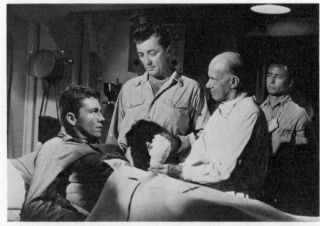

With David Blair, Russell Collins and player in *The Enemy Below*.

stroyer and the submarine versus the sea.

Mitchum is the fatigued, ailing, admired American naval officer who takes pride in his job while remaining coldly professional. "I don't want to know the man I'm trying to destroy," he tells his executive officer (Al Hedison) at one point. His adversary, Jurgens, is a war-weary *Unterboatenkommandant* who, while thoroughly disillusioned with Hitler's philosophies, recovers his martial zest in this duel with a worthy opponent. The two men track and stalk each other across the North Atlantic until the destroyer is torpedoed and the submarine rammed when it closes in. The survivors of both are recovered by a third vessel, and the two opponents, meeting briefly, manage to express to one another, wordlessly, a keen admiration.

Paul V. Beckley, critic for the *New York Herald Tribune*, called the film "strong, almost ruthlessly realistic" and felt that "both Mitchum and Jurgens have turned in excellent portrayals." Stanley Kauffmann wrote in the *New Republic:* "Sheer excitement is distilled by means of the acute camera work, the literate dialogue . . . and the solid performances of Curt Jurgens and, if you please, Robert Mitchum [who] probably owes a debt here to his director, Dick Powell."

The National Board of Review of Motion Pictures named the film among the year's Ten Best, and in its magazine, *Films In Review,* wrote: "Robert Mitchum is surprisingly effective as the destroyer's commander. In fact, Mitchum has become an able actor and should no longer be dismissed as merely a dimpled chin." And *Time* spoke of *The Enemy Below* as "the best game of poker a man could ever hope to kibitz. . . . Dick Powell, whose direction is far more exciting than his crooning ever was, plays it to a fare-thee-well."

In the dissenting column were Robert Hatch, critic for *The Nation,* who saw the movie as "an old and hackneyed piece of emotional nonsense," and Richard W. Nason, third-string reviewer for *The New York Times,* who called it "a standard naval melodrama with only a faint overlay of the psychological duel between the two commanders remaining. The keen intelligence that appreciates such a battle as an abstract mathematical wonder is further obscured by some hoaky plot elements," and thought that the destroyer's skipper was "played in a cold, casual way by Robert Mitchum."

20th Century-Fox's selling angle for the film was curious, trying apparently to cover the fact that it was strictly a man's movie with an all-male cast: "Robert Mitchum—more beloved than in *Heaven Knows Mr. Allison* . . . Curt Jurgens—romantic Continental star in his American debut . . . as the amazing men who lived the sea's most amazing adventure!" The ads, though, failed in their purpose, and the film failed at the box-office.

61
Thunder Road

United Artists, 1958

THE CAST:

Lucas Doolin, ROBERT MITCHUM; *Troy Barrett,* Gene Barry; *Carl Kogan,* Jacques Aubuchon; *Francie Wymore,* Keely Smith; *Vernon Doolin,* Trevor Bardette; *Roxanna Ledbetter,* Sandra Knight; *Robin Doolin,* James Mitchum; *Mary Barrett,* Betsy Holt; *Sarah Doolin,* Frances Koon; *Singer/guitarist,* Randy Sparks; *Jed Moultrie,* Mitch Ryan; *Stacey Gouge,* Peter Breck; *Lucky,* Peter Hornsby; *Niles Penland,* Jerry Hardin; *Preacher,* Robert Porterfield.

With James Mitchum in *Thunder Road.*

A D.R.M. Production. *Director,* Arthur Ripley; *Screenplay,* James Atlee Phillips and Walter Wise; *Story,* Robert Mitchum; *Photography,* Alan Stensvold and David Ettenson; *Music,* Jack Marshall; *Song* "Whippoorwill," Don Raye and Robert Mitchum; *Sung by* Keely Smith; *Special Effects,* Jack Lannan and Lester Swartz; *Editor,* Harry Marker. Running time: 92 minutes.

With James Mitchum in *Thunder Road.*

"Robert Mitchum blasts the screen!" "Mitchum roars down the hottest highway on earth!" These tag-lines sold what is regarded as Mitchum's most personal film: his first for his own production company, from his own original story, acting with his look-alike son, James, then sixteen. Mitchum also wrote its main song; he did not sing it in the film but later had a hit recording of it. *Thunder Road* occupies a special nitch among Mitchum buffs and remains the model against which all subsequent "moonshiner vs. revenooer" movies are compared. Its long-standing reputation as an underground classic as well as an interesting slice of contemporary Americana belie the scant— even scornful—notice it received during its initial run in urban movie markets. It never played first run in New York City, for instance, but was hugely successful among what *Variety* lovingly terms "the yahoo trade." In his lengthy treatise on *Thunder Road,* film historian Richard Thompson calls it "a work whose charm is open only to those who have first-hand knowledge of the world it depicts."

Mitchum plays Lucas Doolin, a Korean War veteran who takes over the family's bootleg hootch business. Known locally as "the best backroad lightnin' around," Luke soon finds himself trying to discourage his kid brother, Robin (James Mitchum), from getting into the trade while battling syndicate gangster Carl Kogan (Jacques Aubuchon), who wants a large piece of the Doolin business, and outsmarting the Feds, headed by agent Troy Barrett (Gene Barry). Kogan sends his men around to intimidate the Doolins, and when they refuse to sell their entire output to him, he has one of their trucks ambushed and its driver killed. Luke retaliates by roughing up Kogan, and open warfare begins. Finally captured by Kogan, Luke escapes with Robin's help. Barrett arrests Kogan and then takes off after Luke. During a high-speed chase through the back country, Luke crashes into a high-tension transformer and is electrocuted at the wheel.

Robert Mitchum, historian Thompson has noted, "put longtime enigma Arthur Ripley in the director's chair. The brilliance of this strategy rests on two phenomena: (a) Ripley's Stone Age flat shooting style; (b) the complete dissipation of Ripley's minor personal style into ecstatic incoherence whenever a profound theme sneaks into his films. *Thunder Road*'s themes push Ripley over the line, leaving Mitchum's conception virtually unaltered."

"This is a highly efficient thriller," wrote Britain's *Monthly Film Bulletin.* "Appropriately picturesque playing from Robert Mitchum, who gives his monosyllabic performance, is somewhat let down by the acting of his son, who merely parodies his father's mannerisms." *Variety* found the film "mainly interesting because of a series of auto chases and spectacular accidents," and thought that "Mitchum's performance is rather colorless due to lack of strong situations to give him opportunity for much more than a walk-on."

Films in Review appreciated that "the little Americana in this 'B' has the force of welcome novelty. . . . The moonshiners are presented with some awareness of their American background." The magazine's critic also felt that "Mitchum played the lead with a skill that again proved he is more than a dimpled chin."

Thunder Road, initially to have been called *Jack*

With Keely Smith in *Thunder Road*.

O'Diamonds and then *The Whippoorwill* (which became the title of the movie's theme song), was directed rather leisurely by Arthur Ripley, whose few screen credits indicate a somewhat erratic career, and featured a score by Jack Marshall that set traditional-sounding mountain music into an incongruous Russian balalaika milieu. In 1975, son James starred in a similarly themed film, *Moonrunners,* which offered an appreciative bow to its predecessor by using as its ad-line: " 'Thunder Road' was only a practice run. This is the real thing! Like father . . . like son, BIG JIM MITCHUM—gear-grinding, tire-screaching, hot-rodding bootleg shine!"

62
The Hunters
20th Century-Fox, 1958

With May Britt in *The Hunters*.

THE CAST:

Major Cleve Saville, ROBERT MITCHUM; *Lt. Ed Bell*, ROBERT WAGNER; *Col. "Dutch" Imil*, RICHARD EGAN; *Kristina Abbott*, MAY BRITT; *Lt. Carl Abbott*, Lee Philips; *Lt. Corona*, John Gabriel; *Col. "Monkey" Moncavage*, Stacy Harris; *Korean Farmer*, Victor Sen Yung; *Korean Child*, Candace Lee; *Casey Jones*, Leon Lontoc; *Sergeant*, John Doucette; *Korean Bartender*, Vinnie De Carlo; *Capt. Owynby*, Larry Thor; *Gifford*, Ralph Manza; *Japanese Clerk*, Nobu McCarthy; *WAF Lieutenant*, Nina Shipman; *Mrs. Mason*, Alena Murray; *Major Dark*, Jay Jostyn; *Jackson*, Robert Reed; *Greek Sergeant*, Jimmy Baya: and John Caler, Bob Olen, Mae Maeshire, Frank Kumagai, Chiyoko Tota Baker, Kam Tong, Rachel Stephens, Mary Song, James Yagi, Whamok Kim, Mabel Lim, Frank Tang.

Producer/Director, Dick Powell; *Screenplay*, Wendell Mayes; *Based on the Novel by* James Salter; *Photography*, Charles G. Clarke; *Music*, Paul Sawtelle; *Art Directors*, Lyle R. Wheeler and Maurice Ransford; *Editor*, Stuart Gilmore. Cinema-Scope and DeLuxe Color. Running time: 108 minutes.

In his second straight war movie for producer/director Dick Powell, Robert Mitchum starred as a World War II ace seeking new laurels as a jet pilot in Korea. Originally, he was to have acted in *Battle Hymn*, the true-life film story of Colonel Dean Hess, the "flying parson" who mingled aerial fighting and caring for orphans in Korea. Hess, though, personally vetoed Mitchum, saying "I couldn't allow an actor who had been jailed for taking drugs to play me on the screen," and the role went to Rock Hudson.

This Mitchum/Powell collaboration advanced the contention that Mitchum in action, leading men into battle, is more convincing than Mitchum playing melodrama, particularly when the romantic angles are less than enthralling as they appear to be in *The Hunters*. While aloft, the film soars with vivid scenes of combat flying and jet contrails streaming across the CinemaScope screen. Aground, though, the soapy romantic triangle plot intruded, with Mitchum wooing the willing wife of a neurotic boozer under his command.

With Richard Egan in *The Hunters*.

The love affair blooms soon after Major Cleve Saville (Mitchum) arrives in Kyoto to assume command of a jet fighter squadron and meets Kris Abbott (May Britt), the cool, blonde wife of a young lieutenant (Lee Philips) in his outfit. Saville manages to keep the command in crack shape, and, because of his feelings for Kris, he goes out on a limb to cure Lt. Abbott's flying fears. On one mission, Abbott is forced down behind enemy lines, and Saville risks his own neck to stage a rescue, going in with his daredevil wing man, Lt. Ed Pell (Robert Wagner). After crash landing, and dealing with a Red patrol, the three pilots make their way back across Communist lines to safety, linking up with a Greek patrol. Back in Japan, Saville reassures Abbott of his abilities as a pilot, and the young officer begs his wife to give their marriage a fresh start. Kris sees Saville one final time to say goodbye.

In *The Hunters.*

"Were it not for its shots of our Air Force jets in action," Hollis Alpert wrote in *Saturday Review,* *"The Hunters* might be dismissed as another routine war epic, for its cozy little plot involves near adultery in Japan while the boys zoom through the deadly wild blue yonder in Korea."

In the *New York Herald Tribune,* Paul V. Beckley thought: "The occasional lethargy of the romantic passages is overcome by the aerial shots. . . . There is considerable emphasis on character, and Mitchum plays the deadly major with a sardonically convincing air." *Newsweek* commented that "the distinction of *The Hunters* . . . lies in some stirring sequences of aerial battle. These scenes, however, last no longer than sky writing, and the movie otherwise struggles in the cramped quarters of an earthbound triangle [led by] Robert Mitchum—a consistent contender for Victor Mature's second-rate position in the acting dodge."

Variety, though, felt that "Mitchum is convincing," although "the story is contrived," and Philip T. Hartung said in *Commonweal:* "Robert Mitchum, more lively than usual, is positively likeable as a World War II ace."

Reviewing *The Hunters* for *The New York Times,* Howard Thompson decided that it was "a respectable, rather neutrally-flavored film that somehow only matters when aloft," and thought it "performed well enough by a pretty good, predominantly male cast, headed by Robert Mitchum, and handsomely produced by Dick Powell." In the romantic sequences, Thompson felt, "Mitchum is completely convincing," but complained "why the realistic Mr. Mitchum, even at Miss Britt's request, would 'protect' a selfish, whimpering and perennially hung-over neurotic stumps us completely."

63
The Angry Hills
Metro-Goldwyn-Mayer, 1959

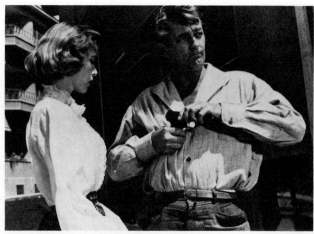

With Gia Scala in *The Angry Hills*.

THE CAST:

Mike Morrison, ROBERT MITCHUM; *Konrad Heisler*, Stanley Baker; *Lisa Keriadkides*, Elisabeth Mueller; *Eleftheria*, Gia Scala; *Dmitrios Tassos*, Theodore Bikel; *Chesney*, Sebastian Cabot; *Leonides*, Peter Illing; *Ray Taylor*, Leslie Phillips; *Dr. Stergiov*, Donald Wolfit; *Colonel Oberg*; Marius Goring; *Maria*, Jackie Lane; *Andreas*, Kieron Moore; *Papa Panos*, George Pastell; *Bluey*, Patrick Jordan; *Kleopatra*, Martita Constantiou; *Papa Phillibos*, Alec Mango; *Tavern Proprietor*, Stanley Van Beers.

A Raymond Stross Production. *Producer*, Raymond Stross; *Associate Producer*, Victor Lyndon; *Director*, Robert Aldrich; *Screenplay*, A. I. Bezzerides; *Based on the Novel by* Leon Uris; *Photography*, Stephen Dade; *Music*, Richard Russell Bennett; *Music Director*, Dock Mathieson; *Art Director*, Ken Adam; *Editor*, Peter Tanner. CinemaScope. Running time: 105 minutes.

With Sebastian Cabot in *The Angry Hills*.

Mitchum lent his boxoffice clout and some of his bankroll to *The Angry Hills*, an international espionage-intrigue potboiler filmed in Greece by Robert Aldrich from one of Leon Uris's kaleidoscopic novels. Released by prestigious MGM, it was, unaccountably, played off around the country as an expensive B movie, and even filled the bottom half of double bills in and around Manhattan. Mitchum has asserted that "originally they wanted Alan Ladd for the part, but when they [the producers] got to his desert home to see him, he had just crawled out of his swimming pool and he was all shrunken up like a dishwasher's hand . . . he was so small they could hardly see him, and they decided he wouldn't do for the big war correspondent." In his typical self-deprecating manner, Mitchum confessed that "Some idiot said, 'Ask Mitchum to play it. The bum will do anything if he's got five minutes free.' Well, I had five minutes, so I did it."

The fanciful tale of an American journalist recruited as an intelligence courier during World War II ended up as a flawed film with a convoluted plot and countless untidy situations at the wrap-up that even the presence of Mitchum and a fine cast of sterling British actors and two Continental sex symbols were unable to resolve. The story's main character is Mike Morrison (Mitchum), a war correspondent in Athens in 1941 who is talked by Greek turncoat Dr. Stergiov (Donald Wolfit) into delivering an important list of names to British Intelligence in London. Wounded by a Nazi collaborator (Theodore Bikel), Mike manages to escape into the hills where he is sheltered and nursed back to health by Eleftheria (Gia Scala), a guerrilla girl. When the Nazis arrive on the scene, Eleftheria takes him to the safety of a nearby convent before she is killed by the Germans. Mike is then smuggled back to Athens by Lisa Keriadkides (Elisabeth Mueller), one of the people on his list.

When Lisa's two children are taken hostage by Nazi chief Konrad Heisler (Stanley Baker), she agrees to turn Mike over to the Germans, but

160

With Leslie Phillips in *The Angry Hills*.

instead, once her children are safe, arranges for his escape. Then she diverts Heisler's attention as Mike makes his way out of Greece with her children.

"Mr. Mitchum," critic Howard Thompson felt in assessing the actor's role, "unfortunately is pretty much of a dope, scribe or no scribe. The most curiously hollow section of the picture—Mr. Mitchum's battered involvement with some brave mountain guerrillas—should have been the strongest. Instead, it slopes off as another episode in a standard chase yarn, with Mr. Mitchum bewilderingly toting a rifle and pawing a fiery Greek girl played by Gia Scala."

Variety reviewed *The Angry Hills* twice—in London and later in Hollywood—and was confused both times. The paper's two critics also had different things to say of Mitchum. One felt that "Stanley Baker and Mitchum give very sound performances," while the other insisted that "Mitchum's character is never defined, nor very pleasing."

The Angry Hills is Mitchum's only film with director Robert Aldrich (although Aldrich had been an assistant to William Wellman on *The Story of G.I. Joe*). The two, it seems, never warmed to one another, and Aldrich has been quoted as saying: "I couldn't get through to him at all. I was totally unable to find any personal or creative or even emotional routes to make Mitchum really function as an actor. I have seen Mitchum be too excellent too often to doubt for one minute that he is an extremely accomplished and gifted artist. And since the performance that I was able to extract from him was neither sensitive nor accomplished nor in any way gifted, my failure to connect with him is a liability that I alone must also assume." Aldrich further claims that MGM butchered the movie, lopping off nearly twenty-five minutes, which might account for various incongruities and questionable motivations of the performers during the final third of the film.

64
The Wonderful Country

United Artists, 1959

THE CAST:

Martin Brady, ROBERT MITCHUM; *Ellen Colton,* JULIE LONDON; *Major Stark Colton,* GARY MERRILL; *Gov. Cipriano Castro,* Pedro Armendariz; *Travis Hight,* Jack Oakie; *Captain Rucker,* Albert Dekker; *Doc Stovall,* Charles McGraw; *Sgt. Tobe Sutton,* Leroy "Satchel" Paige; *Gen. Marcos Castro,* Victor Mendoza; *Pancho,* Mike Kellin; *Ben Turner,* John Banner; *Ludwig "Chico" Turner,* Anthony Caruso; *Peebles (Barber),* Tom Lea.

A D.R.M. Production. *Executive Producer,* Robert Mitchum; *Producer,* Chester Erskine; *Director,* Robert Parrish; *Screenplay;* Robert Ardrey; *Based on the Novel by* Tom Lea; *Photography,* Floyd Crosby and Alex Phillips; *Music,* Alex North; *Art Director,* Harry Horner; *Editor,* Michael Luciano. Technicolor. Running time: 96 minutes.

With Julie London in *The Wonderful Country.*

Robert Mitchum's second film for his own production outfit was a rugged, eye-filling western that never attracted the attention it should have. "*The Wonderful Country* is a wonderful Western," *Variety* wrote. "The color is beautiful, the cast is accurate, the writing is tasteful and realistic, and the characterizations are unusual. . . . [it is] a credit to the taste of producer Chester Erskine and of Robert Mitchum, for whose D.R.M. banner it was filmed."

In his best western role, Mitchum works somewhat uncharacteristically with a Spanish accent and the mannerisms of a Mexican peon (a portrayal one might have expected more from Anthony Quinn). He stars as Martin Brady, an American fugitive and hired gun for the powerful Castro brothers (Pedro Armendariz and Victor Mendoza), the former a petty dictator, the other his army's leader. Sent into Texas on a gun-running mission, Brady breaks his leg when his horse falls, loses his contraband shipment, and is forced to remain in the United States. During his convalescence, he becomes involved with

With Pedro Armendariz in *The Wonderful Country.*

With Leroy "Satchel" Paige in *The Wonderful Country*.

Ellen Colton (Julie London), the unhappy wife of an Army major (Gary Merrill).

Recruited by Captain Rucker (Alber Dekker) of the Texas Rangers to report on Major Colton's activities, Brady soon discovers that the major is doing business with the Castro brothers, hoping to drive out the Apaches so that the railroad can come through the country. After killing a man for insulting Ellen, Brady is forced to cross back into Mexico, where Cipriano Castro and his brother are now vying for control. Holding Brady responsible for the loss of the arms, the Castros keep him a virtual prisoner.

Colton joins forces with the Castros against the Apaches, and at a fiesta, Brady again meets Ellen and Captain Rucker, who offers Brady a chance to join the Texas Rangers. Riding north, Brady runs into Major Colton, whose patrol has been ambushed by Indians. To save the badly wounded major, Brady guides the troops, under Sgt. Tobe Sutton (Leroy "Satchel" Paige), back across the border, where the major dies. In a showdown, Brady kills a pistolero sent by the Castros but loses his beloved horse, Lagrimas. Symbolically laying down his gun by the dead animal, Brady crosses the Rio Grande for the last time to "The Wonderful Country," returning to Ellen and reclaiming his heritage.

Howard Thompson cheered in *The New York Times:* "This is a superior, intelligent film on nearly every count . . . a well-acted, introspective adventure yarn, beautifully paced by Robert Parrish's direction, and magnificently evocative of the locale where it was made [and] Mr. Mitchum is ideally cast as the hard-bitten derelict hero."

Rose Pelswick, critic for the *New York Journal-American,* felt that "Mood and atmosphere are admirably sustained in spite of the rambling script, and Mitchum gives an excellent performance as the harassed pistolero." Reviewer Alton Cook, in the *New York World Telegram and Sun,* said; "*The Wonderful Country* engulfs his dilemma in any number of subplots and leaves its hero on the outskirts frequently [but] Mitchum is just such a compelling personality that he never drifts out of audience attention. . . . He is the actor who makes no apparent effort but always remains the man in closeup."

65
Home from the Hill
Metro-Goldwyn-Mayer, 1960

With Eleanor Parker in *Home from the Hill.*

THE CAST:

Capt. Wade Hunnicutt, ROBERT MITCHUM; *Hannah Hunnicutt*, ELEANOR PARKER; *Rafe Copley*, George Peppard; *Theron Hunnicutt*, George Hamilton; *Libby Halstead*, Luana Patten; *Albert Halstead*, Everett Sloane; *Sarah Halstead*, Anne Seymour; *Opal Bixby*, Constance Ford; *Chauncey*, Ken Renard; *Dr. Reuben Carson*, Ray Teal; *Melba*, Hilda Haynes; *Dick Gibbons*, Charlie Briggs; *Hugh Macauley*, Guinn 'Big Boy' Williams; *Peyton Stiles*, Dan Sheridan; *Ed Dinwoodie*, Orville Sherman; *Bob Skaggs*, Dub Taylor; *Ramsey*, Stuart Randall; *John Ellis*, Tom Gilson; *Foreman*, Joe Ed Russell; *Gas Station Attendant*, Burt Mustin; *Minister*, Rev. Duncan Gray, Jr.

A Sol C. Siegel Production. *Producer*, Edmund Grainger; *Director*, Vincente Minnelli; *Screenplay*, Harriet Frank, Jr., and Irving Ravetch; *Based on the Novel by* William Humphrey; *Photography*, Milton Krasner; *Music*, Bronislau Kaper; *Music Director*, Charles Wolcott; *Art Directors*, George W. Davis and Preston Ames; *Assistant Director*, William McGarry; *Special Effects*, Robert R. Hogue; *Editor*, Harold F. Kress. Cinema-Scope and Metrocolor. Running time: 150 minutes.

With George Hamilton in *Home from the Hill.*

In Vincente Minnelli's vigorous though rambling adaptation of the William Humphrey novel about contemporary Texas, Robert Mitchum gave one of his memorable performances as the lusty Southern rancher, Captain Wade Hunnicutt, a role that, it has been said, was written for Clark Gable. Critics were lavish with their praise for his work. "Certainly Robert Mitchum has not given a performance as good as this in years," Arthur Knight wrote in *Saturday Review*. And "Mitchum delivers his strongest performance in years," cheered *Variety*.

The film's title came from a line by Robert Louis Stevenson: "Here he lies where he longed to be, home is the sailor, home from the sea, and the hunter home from the hill." The hunter here is virile Wade Hunnicutt, whose beautiful wife, Hannah (Eleanor Parker), has continued to live with him only because of their seventeen-year-old son, Theron (George Hamilton). Wade's other

With George Peppard in *Home from the Hill.*

son is the Hunnicutt's hired hand, Rafe Copley (George Peppard), a bastard who has been denied the family name. When Hannah's sheltered upbringing of Theron makes him the butt of local jokesters, Wade forceably assumes his son's education, teaching him marksmanship over Hannah's objections, and placing him under the tutelage of Rafe.

As Theron matures into manhood, he falls in love with a local girl, Libby Halstead (Luana Patten), although her parents (Everett Sloane and Anne Seymour) object to the match fearing that he may be a younger edition of Wade, famed for his wenching. When he discovers the truth about his father and Rafe's real identity, Theron renounces Wade and breaks off with Libby, unaware that she is carrying his child. Rafe, long in love with Libby, steps in and the two are married. At the baby's christening, some of the townsmen joke about the possibility that the child is actually Wade's, and Libby's father storms over to the Hunnicutt spread and guns down the unarmed Wade. Theron tracks the demented Halstead into the woods and shoots him. Then, after a final farewell to Rafe, he leaves to find a new life for himself. Hannah buries Wade under a tombstone marked: Wade Hunnicutt—Husband of Hannah—Beloved Father of Rafe and Theron.

In the film, both George Peppard and George Hamilton are given "introducing" billing, despite the fact that they had made previous movies,* and Luana Patten, a former Disney moppet, was cast in her first adult role in an unsuccessful attempt to continue her film career. The focus, though, was on Mitchum and on Peppard, who caught the eye of the critics although he reportedly annoyed Mitchum throughout the shooting because of his Actors' Studio techniques. Of Mitchum, director Minnelli had these thoughts: "Robert Mitchum, who snipes that the movie should have been called *Minnelli's Texas,* and says the sets got a lot of fan mail, knew the character of the father very well. He'd met many such men in Maryland, where Bob was a permanent resident. . . . Bob, who has an indolent image, could have walked through the part, but he didn't. . . . Throughout

*Peppard previously had acted on Broadway and in such films as *End As A Man* and *Pork Chop Hill.* Hamilton had made his screen debut in 1959 in *Crime and Punishment, U.S.A.*

the filming, Bob helped the young people enormously, and me too. He spoke from the viewpoint of a veteran actor—and star—and the young people were impressed." Minnelli also has pointed out: "He claims that he never sees his own pictures. I personally believe that when the truth comes out after his death, his shameful vice will be revealed. In some dark cellar, a celluloid cache will be discovered. It will be revealed as belonging to the late Robert Mitchum, and it won't be a year's supply of blue films. They'll be the pictures he made, which he would sneak in to see time and again."

The National Board of Review of Motion Pictures voted Mitchum as the year's best actor for his performance in both *Home from the Hill* and his next film, *The Sundowners,* which, in tandem, are regarded as examples of his finest work on the screen. "Pretty vigorous stuff," is what Paul V. Beckley wrote of the film in the *New York Herald Tribune.* "You feel an honest novel under its unusually sharp dialogue and the grim interplay among its happily contrasting characters. . . . Mitchum plays the father as a sturdy man's man, who divides his time between guns, a pipe, and other men's wives—he looks very much the part." The critic for *Time* thought that "the picture, rather crudely adapted from a vigorous first novel by William Humphrey, has a certain low-Faulknerian likeability," while John McCarten, in *The New Yorker,* found it "gamy nonsense . . . with all hands performing variations on sub-Mason-Dixon accents . . . the aging lecher of the piece is played by Robert Mitchum with his usual manly impassivity."

"There must be a point lurking somewhere," Bosley Crowther felt in *The New York Times,* "but where it is centered precisely in the long, rambling tale that is told, or what thought it is meant to focus, entirely eludes this reviewer. . . . For the most part, the whole thing is aimless, tedious and in conspicuously doubtful taste. Under Vincente Minnelli's direction, it is garishly overplayed." Henry Hart, editor of *Films in Review,* said: "This doesn't sound like something Vincente Minnelli should direct, but he did, and quite satisfactorily. I have no doubt Minnelli would have directed it better had the script been sounder. . . . Robert Mitchum once again proves he can act."

66
The
Sundowners

Warner Bros, 1960

THE CAST:

Ida Carmody, DEBORAH KERR; *Paddy Carmody*, ROBERT MITCHUM; *Venneker*, PETER USTINOV; *Mrs. Firth*, GLYNIS JOHNS; *Jean Halstead*, DINA MERRILL; *Quinlan*, Chips Rafferty; *Sean*, Michael Anderson, Jr.; *Liz*, Lola Brooks; *Herb Johnson*, Wylie Watson; *Bluey*, John Meillon; *Ocher*, Ronald Fraser; *Jack Patchogue*, Mervyn Johns; *Mrs. Bateman*, Molly Urquhart; *Bob Halstead*, Ewen Solon; and Dick Bentley, Gerry Duggan, Peter Carver, Leonard Teale, Alastair Williamson, Ray Barrett, Mercia Barden.

Producer, Gerry Blattner; *Director*, Fred Zinnemann; *Assistant Director*, Peter Bolton; *Screenplay*, Isobel Lennart; *Based on the Novel by* Jon Cleary; *Photography*, Jack Hildyard; *Music*, Dimitri Tiomkin; *Second Unit Director*, Lex Halliday; *Assistant Directors*, Peter Bolton and Roy Stevens; *Art Director*, Michael Stringer; *Editor*, Jack Harris. Technicolor. Running time: 141 minutes.

With Deborah Kerr in *The Sundowners*.

The role of Paddy Carmody, the hard-drinking, itinerant sheep drover or "sundowner" who cherishes the wanderlust life of Australia's outback is generally considered by Mitchum's fans to be his best. Sporting a brogue and a floppy hat, he gives an affectionate, exuberant performance complementing and complemented by the warm, loving portrayal by Deborah Kerr as his wife. No surprisingly, Mitchum has admitted: "All I did was feed her some lines. She did all the rest. She's really the one who can act.

Under the poetic direction of Fred Zinnemann, this motion picture that ranks among the finest "family" films of all time follows Paddy and Ida Carmody and their teen-aged son, Sean (Michael Anderson, Jr.), as they wander the bush in their horse-drawn wagon. Paddy, a drover, has no possessions, no home, only a full, rich, loving life with Ida. Lately, though, Ida and Sean have begun to yearn secretly to settle down. The idea of being stuck someplace, however, horrifies Paddy, and he continues his family's nomadic life

by taking the job of driving twelve hundred head of sheep four hundred miles west to Cawndilla, along with an extra drover: an easy-going, well-educated former English sea captain named Venneker (Peter Ustinov).

Their long trek is marked by a visit with the Batemans, former drovers who have settled down, and a dangerous "crown" forest fire they just manage to escape. After delivering their sheep, Ida persuades Paddy to let them all take job on the big Wattle Run station, hoping secretly to earn enough for a down payment on a farm. Paddy works as a shearer, Ida as a cook, and Sean as a tarboy. Venneker, having met Mrs. Firth (Glynis Johns), an attractive widowed hotel-keeper, stays on as a wool-picker. Ida finds her life at Wattle Run a happy one, but Paddy resents that she and Sean are spending so much time with friends they have acquired. When the shearing season ends, he insists they pack up and move on, and Venneker reluctantly takes leave of the lady who nearly succeeded in making him consider matrimony. They also take with them a race horse, named Sundowner, which Paddy had won gambling. En route, Sean gradually becomes an

With Deborah Kerr and Michael Anderson, Jr., in *The Sundowners*.

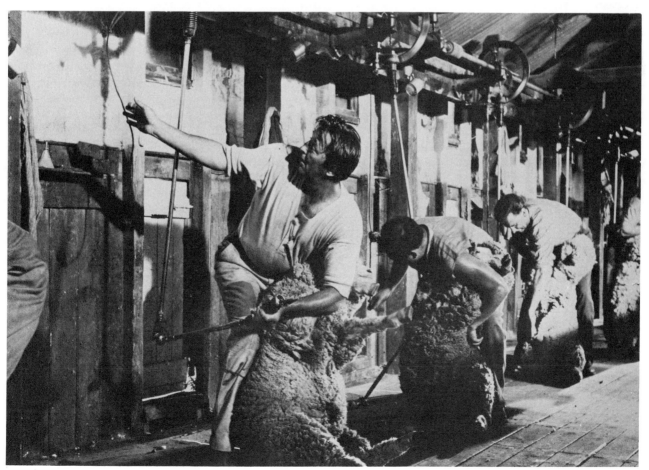

With players in *The Sundowners*.

accomplished jockey and Paddy decides to enter Sundowner at a small bush track. Sean scores an easy victory and, overjoyed, his father sees a new but still roving life ahead for them—going from track to track. Eventually, the Carmodys get enough money to buy a farm, only to have Paddy lose it all gambling. Ida and Sean are heartbroken, Paddy contrite. He agrees to sell Sundowner should he win the big race at Bulinga, but, though the horse wins, Ida cannot bring herself to allow Paddy to make the sacrifice. Then it is announced that Sundowner has been disqualified for interference and the sale is off. "There goes both our chances to be noble," Ida sighs. Happily the Carmodys drive away, Sundowner trailing their wagon. Behind them rides Venneker.

"Seldom does a movie capture the true spirit of family so well," critic Philip T. Hartung wrote in *Commonweal*. "Robert Mitchum, in what is perhaps his best performance, makes Paddy a likeable, carefree Irish-Australian." *Newsweek* said: "It's been a long time since moviegoers have been served as rich a slice of the human comedy. . . . Further, it effectively utilizes the acting services of an unlikely trio. . . . Robert Mitchum, Deborah Kerr and Peter Ustinov, whose styles have heretofore been notably dissimiliar, literally and figuratively, all speak the same language—in this case, Australian."

In *Films in Review,* editor Henry Hart called the film: "An almost perfect example of screen entertainment. . . . Robert Mitchum has grown as an actor, and in *The Sundowners* he projects a surprising variety of emotions, effortlessly. Mitchum deserves more critical attention than he has received. His forte is an ability to reveal how intellectually acute the merely instinctual intelligence can be." *Variety,* meanwhile, found *The Sundowners* "one of the year's finest films . . . a wonderfully warm, rich and compelling picture. . . . Mitchum's rugged masculinity is right for his part. His thespic range seems narrow, but that can be deceptive, for there are moments when he projects a great deal of feeling with what appears to be a minimum of effort. This may be the finest work he has done in films."

And in *Saturday Review,* Arthur Knight commented: "Most important . . . is the quality of performances that Zinnemann has obtained from every member of his large cast. They work together with the kind of insight into their own characters and an awareness of that character in its relation to all the others that can, in films, only be provided by a great director. Thanks to Zinnemann, *The Sundowners* is a picture that breathes humanity."

For *The Sundowners,* Deborah Kerr won an Academy Award nomination and was named Best Actress by the New York Film Critics (for the third time). Mitchum was chosen Best Actor of the Year by the National Board of Review of Motion Pictures for his roles in this film and *Home from the Hill.* Strangely, the part of Paddy Carmody is not one of Mitchum's favorites, and he once said that he only signed to make it because he knew Deborah Kerr would be the leading lady. When he was told she would like top billing, although he was entitled to refuse, Mitchum replied: "By all means. And you can design a twenty-four-foot sign of me bowing to her if you like."

A final word on *The Sundowners:* the Warner Bros. advertising campaign(s) were designed for three different situations—one for the action crowds, one for the family trade (with a cartoon kangaroo highlighting the ads and a montage showing the players buried near the bottom), and one playing up the nonexistent erotic angles with Kerr and Mitchum in a clinch similar to the famed shot of the actress with Burt Lancaster several years earlier win *From Here to Eternity.* The absurd ad-line to that third campaign: "The Sundowners strike fire when they touch!"

67
The Night Fighters

United Artists, 1960

THE CAST:

Dermot O'Neill, ROBERT MITCHUM; *Neeve Donnelly,* ANNE HEYWOOD; *Don McGinnis,* Dan O'Herlihy; *Jimmy Hannafin,* Cyril Cusack; *Sean Reilly,* Richard Harris; *Bella O'Neill,* Marianne Benet; *Ned O'Neill,* Nial MacGinnis; *Patrick O'Neill,* Harry Brogan; *Kathleen O'Neill,* Eileen Crowe; *Sgt. Crawley,* Geoffrey Golden; *Father McCrory,* Hilton Edwards; *Quinn,* Wilfrid Downing; *Malone,* Christopher Rhodes; *Corrigan,* Eddie Golden; *Tim,* Joe Lynch; *McIntyre Boys,* Jim Neylan and T. R. McKenna.

A D.R.M./Raymond Stross Production. *Producer,* Raymond Stross; *Director,* Tay Garnett; *Screenplay,* Robert Wright Campbell; *Based on the Novel A Terrible Beauty by* Arthur Roth; *Photography,* Stephen Dade; *Music,* Cedric Thorpe-Davie; *Music Director,* Dock Mathieson; *Art Director,* John Stoll; *Editor,* Peter Tanner. Running time: 88 minutes.

In the summer of 1959, producer Mitchum hired actor Mitchum to star with an all English and Irish cast in an "unexciting Irish war meller" (as *Variety* called it). Filmed in and around Dublin under the title *A Terrible Beauty* after Arthur Roth's source novel, the production dealt with such screenplay assets as Nazi saboteurs, World War II IRA intrigue, and the generations-old British-Irish conflict, but veered into the adventure-film mainstream rather than being a thoughtful case history of a revolutionary movement with inadequate practical or intellectual motivation. It turned up on the bottom half of double bills in New York City's neighborhood theaters the week before Christmas, 1960—between two other Mitchum films, giving the actor a rather high-profile December.

"Robert Mitchum blows the screen to kingdom come in 'The Night Fighters'!" screamed the ads for the film. "Mitchum runs wild with a red-hot machine-gun in his hands!" He plays Dermot O'Neill, a reluctant IRA terrorist, recruited by Don McGinnis (Dan O'Herlihy), a crippled fanatic who thinks the German invasion of Europe offers a perfect distraction for his IRA forces to attempt to expel the British. Engaging in a successful raid against a British ordinance depot, Dermot sees close friend Sean Reilly (Richard Harris) wounded and is forced to carry him to safety in the Irish Free State. Sean, though, attempts to get back to Northern Ireland and is captured and sentenced to ten years in prison. Urged by his fiancée, Neeve Donnelly (Anne Heywood), and his friend, Jimmy Hannafin (Cyril Cusack), who argues that aiding the Nazis against the British is siding with the greater of two evils, an embittered Dermot decides to quit the IRA and turns police informant. Captured by McGinnis, Dermot escapes with the help of his family and flees with Neeve. McGinnis, in pursuit, mistakes Dermot's trench-coated sister Bella (Marianne Benet) for Dermot and kills her. Her

With Anne Heywood in *The Night Fighters.*

With Anne Heywood and Richard Harris in *The Night Fighters.*

169

In *The Night Fighters*.

death is avenged by another brother, Ned (Niall MacGinnis), as Dermot and Neeve elude the IRA gunmen and board ship bound for Liverpool.

Typically, Mitchum himself has become the film's worst critic, noting: "I was offered one script, but when I got to Ireland I was handed another. What was I to do—pay off all the actors and take the loss? Or do it? I did it and now my obligation to Raymond Stross [with whom he previously had done *The Angry Hills*] is discharged. There is still an elemental force in the story. But it's like looking for a diamond that's been covered in sewage. You know it's there, but, man, does it smell!"

Eugene Archer, reviewing the film for *The New York Times*, thought that "the dramatic structure falters after establishing a promising situation in the early reels, and a brief lapse into unconvinc-ing melodrama at the end seriously limits the film's modest pretensions." Critic Archer on the star: "Robert Mitchum manages a brogue with reasonable facility, and a good supporting cast consistently suggest more than the script implies." In the *New York Herald Tribune*, Paul V. Beckley wrote: "*The Night Fighters* does not refer, as I assumed, to airplanes or jets, but stars Robert Mitchum in a reasonably exciting episode of Irish Republican Army fighting. . . . The viewpoint is anti-IRA, reflected in the incompetence and confusion of the undergroup group which Mitchum joins."

The *Variety* appraisal: "Mitchum etches an absorbing portrait through most of the picture, but, when the hero fails to be particularly heroic, the characterization languishes."

68
The Grass Is Greener

Grandon Productions/Universal, 1960

With Deborah Kerr and Cary Grant in *The Grass Is Greener*.

With Deborah Kerr in *The Grass Is Greener*.

THE CAST:

Victor Rhyall, CARY GRANT; *Hilary Rhyall*, DEBORAH KERR; *Hattie Durrant*, JEAN SIMMONS; *Charles Delacro*, ROBERT MITCHUM; *Trevor Sellers*, Moray Watson.

Producer/Director, Stanley Donen; *Screenplay*, Hugh and Margaret Williams (from their play); *Photography*, Christopher Challis; *Music*, Noel Coward; *Music Director*, Muir Mathieson; *Art Director*, Paul Sheriff; *Editor*, James Clark. Technirama and Technicolor. Running time: 104 minutes.

Stanley Donen's elegant *The Grass Is Greener* provided Robert Mitchum with a rather startling deparure from his usual roles—a sophisticated drawing-room comedy. It also gave the fourth-billed Mitchum a chance to work again with both Deborah Kerr and Jean Simmons (third time with

With Moray Watson and Cary Grant in *The Grass Is Greener.*

each lady). "At least I didn't have to grow a beard, fall off horses, or carry people around on my back," he later joked. "That's a hell of a change for me. I didn't have much to say, which is lucky as I can't remember the little I *do* have to say. And I had a girl at the side of the set who told me when to say 'Why?' or 'Really?' whenever Cary Grant came to the end of a speech."

The fluffy, veddy British, piece—really just a filmed stage comedy—deals with Victor Rhyall (Grant) and his wife Hilary (Deborah Kerr) who, pressed by the tax people, throw open the doors to their stately home to tourists at two shillings a head. "Here they come," Victor disgustedly sighs, "laughing and scratching, strewing little bits of sticky paper." One of the sightseers, Texas oilman Charles Delacro (Mitchum), invades the Rhyall's private apartment where he meets Hilary, and after a brief display of gallantry, wins her heart and takes her with him back to London.

Hattie Durant (Jean Simmons), a madcap family friend, tries to console Victor, but he is determined to rescue the marriage, and in order to play on his home ground, invites Charles back for the weekend. As in all civilized competitions, a duel is arranged under the watchful eye of Sellers (Moray Watson), the Rhyall butler. Victor misses his shot but is winged in the shoulder. The wound and some smoothly sympathetic talk are enough to win back Hilary, and Charles and Hattie are soon packed off together.

Critics as well as audiences were somewhat restrained about this ultra-English comedy that premiered in Manhattan on the day before Christmas, 1960. After viewing this soufflé about elegant folks of social London committing adultery and talking endlessly about it, Bosley Crowther decided: "Miss Kerr and Miss Simmons look attractive, and Mr. Grant and Mr. Mitchum try hard to create the illusion of being moved by love and passion. But they both appear mechanical and bored . . . gowns and scenery do not make a motion picture. Nor does talk." *Time* wrote that "whenever the script lapses, director Stanley Donen is right there with a cute shot. And the actors—with the lamentable exception of Mitchum, who does not seem to realize that the best way to play a cartoon American is simply to play himself—rescue scene after scene with a deft cliche of gesture or a delightful bit of business."

In the *New York Herald Tribune*, Paul V. Beckley chided: ". . . neither [Donen] nor his engaging cast can entirely dislodge their feet from the rather static drawing-room texture of the screenplay. It is hard to discover whether the film is recommending adultery or campaigning against it." Stanley Kauffmann of *The New Republic*

commented that "[it] has good performances by Cary Grant, Deborah Kerr and Jean Simmons, and the presence of Robert Mitchum."

And despite the film's powerhouse cast, even *Variety* turned thumbs down: "Weakest link in the romantic and comedic give-and-take is Mitchum. He's pretty sluggish on the comedy end and thoroughly unconvincing in his relationship with Miss Kerr, never really projecting the implied passion or even interest.

The critical consensus was that *The Grass Is Greener* on film remained pretty much the theatrical piece it had been when it opened in October 1959 on London's West End. Its cast then: Hugh Williams, Celia Johnson, Edward Underdown, Joan Greenwood, and, as the unconventional butler, Moray Watson.

69
The Last Time I Saw Archie

United Artists, 1961

With France Nuyen in *The Last Time I Saw Archie*.

THE CAST:

Archie Hall, ROBERT MITCHUM; *Bill Bowers*, JACK WEBB; *Peggy Kramer*, MARTHA HYER; *Cindy Hamilton*, FRANCE NUYEN; *Pvt. Sam Beacham*, Louis Nye; *Pvt. Billy Simpson*, James Lydon; *Pvt. Frank Ostrow*, Del Moore; *Pvt. Russell Drexel*, Joe Flynn; *Captain Little*, Don Knotts; *Col. Edwin Martin*, Richard Arlen; *M/Sgt. Stanley Erlenheim*, Robert Strauss; *Sgt. Malcolm Greenbriar*, Harvey Lembeck; *Lola*, Claudia Barrett; *Daphne*, Theona Bryant; *Carole*, Elaine Davis; *Patsy Ruth*, Marilyn Burtis; *Corporal*, James Mitchum; *Chuck (bartender)*, Gene McCarthy; *Gen. Williams*, Howard McNear; *Lt. Oglemeyer*, John Nolan; *2nd Lieutenant*, Martin Dean; *Officer*, Robert Clarke; *Miss Willoughby*, Nancy Kulp; *Soldiers*, Bill Kilmer, Phil Gordon, Dick Cathcart.

A Mark VII Ltd./Manzanita/Talbot Production. *Producer/Director*, Jack Webb; *Screenplay*, William Bowers; *Photography*, Joseph MacDonald; *Music*, Frank Comstock; *Art Director*, Field Gray; *Special Effects*, A. P. Pollard; *Assistant Director*, Chico Day; *Editor*, Robert Leeds. Running time:98 minutes.

With Jack Webb in *The Last Time I Saw Archie.*

With Jack Webb in *The Last Time I Saw Archie.*

The Last Time I Saw Archie, a wacky service comedy, continued Mitchum's efforts to demonstrate his abilities beyond his usual somber tough-guy image, with the star, as the title character, an inveterate con-man who finds himself in an Air Force unit for overaged civilian pilots. Mitchum made the film for his new production company, Talbot Productions, teaming with Jack Webb's Mark VII Ltd. It was written by William Bowers, based, apparently on his days in uniform. "Line for line," wrote *Variety,* "Bowers has cooked up a witty script, and take for take, director Jack Webb has seasoned it with an alert humor. But, in concert, the film does not jell, the running parts do not keep the machine humming along smoothly." And despite the first shock of discovering that both Mitchum and Webb really do have a feel for high comedy, *The Last Time I Saw Archie* never quite succeeded in capturing an idea that probably looked great on paper.

The first time we see Archie Hall (Mitchum) is

during the waning months of World War II when he and buddy Bill Bowers (Webb), a former Hollywood scriptwriter, are drafted into the Air Force to ferry aircraft and transport supplies. Archie is a born goldbrick, swaggering around the base with a clipboard under his arm. Eventually, he cons Duty Sergeant Malcolm Greenbriar (Harvey Lembeck) into giving him and Bowers permanent passes, and the two spend most of their time off base in the company of Peggy Kramer (Martha Hyer) and Cindy (France Nuyen). Master Sergeant Stanley Erlenheim (Robert Strauss) believes that Cindy is the girlfriend of Colonel Martin (Richard Arlen), the base commander, and this fact, together with the simple-minded Greenbriar's suspicions, convince the two sergeants that Archie is really a G-2 general in disguise.

Ultimately it becomes apparent to Archie that Cindy is really a spy, but when she turns out to be actually the opposite—a lure to catch the real spy ring—Archie convinces the colonel that he deserves a medal. Discharged, he goes to Hollywood with Bill, who gets back his old job and wangles one for his army buddy, too. The last time scriptwriter Bowers sees Archie, his ambitious friend has become head of the studio with an eye on the White House.

"I liked the role and I liked the picture," Mitchum has said. "And why not? I got $400,000 for working four weeks and had a week off between Christmas and the New Year to go home to the farm." On working with Webb (as producer, director, and costar), Mitchum noted: "Once you're committed, you have to submit to a style. And Jack's technique in direction is something—nobody ever gets to finish a sentence. It's a perilous prospect to play around in comedy—all situation comedy—because you're trespassing on the area of farce and that can spell doom. But he works. Man, how he works!"

Variety concluded that "thanks to the casting and the playing, the picture has its rewards. . . . Mitchum displays comic poise and solidity in the lead." And A. H. Weiler, in *The New York Times*, felt that "Archie and his colleagues prove to be as mobile as a glacier while being as colorful in speech as a top kick bawling out a hapless yardbird. . . . Mr. Mitchum wanders through this farce with the speed and elan of a poet dreaming of Nirvana." Britain's *Monthly Film Bulletin* offered a somewhat better notice: "Surprisingly, Robert Mitchum, obviously enjoying the role, makes quite a character of Archie, refusing to sentimentalize the fundamental amorality of the overage wide boy. And in spite of the static treatment and glaring weaknesses, the theme itself is still sufficiently intriguing to hold the interest."

The Last Time I Saw Archie marked the second time Mitchum worked with his son, Jim, who had a small role as a corporal—outranking his dad. The film also reunited Robert Strauss and Harvey Lembeck, who had done so much toward making *Stalag 17* a success several years earlier on both stage and screen.

70
Cape Fear

Universal, 1962

THE CAST:

Sam Bowden, GREGORY PECK; *Max Cady*, ROBERT MITCHUM; *Peggy Bowden*, Polly Bergen; *Nancy Bowden*, Lori Martin; *Mark Dutton*, Martin Balsam; *Dave Grafton*, Jack Kruschen; *Charles Sievers*, Telly Savalas; *Diane Taylor*, Barrie Chase; *Garner*, Paul Comi; *Judge*, Edward Platt; *Officer Marconi*, John McKee; *Deputy Kersek*, Page Slattery; *Officer Brown*, Ward Ramsey; *Dr. Pearsall*, Will Wright; *Waitress*, Joan Staley; *Dr. Lowney*, Mack Williams; *Lt. Gervasi*, Thomas Newman; *Pianist*, Bunny Rhea; *Betty*, Carol Sydes; *Vernon*, Alan Reynolds; and Herb Armstrong, Al Silvani, Paul Levitt, Norma Yost, Allan Ray, Jack Richardson.

A Melville/Talbot Production. *Producer*, Sy Bartlett; *Director*, J. Lee Thompson; *Screenplay*, James R. Webb; *Based on the Novel The Executioners by* John D. MacDonald; *Photography*, Sam Leavitt; *Music*, Bernard Herrmann; *Art Directors*, Alexander Golitzen and Robert Boyle; *Editor*, George Tomasini. Running time: 105 minutes.

With John D. MacDonald's novel, *The Executioners,* as his source, director J. Lee Thompson molded a moody tale of controlled sadism for a pair of superstars, Gregory Peck and Robert Mitchum, and their respective production outfits, Melville and Talbot. Once again, Mitchum essayed one of his psycho portrayals, with the result that *Cape Fear* provided a graphic shock to unsqueamish moviegoers in the prerating early sixties.

Mitchum is Max Cady, an ex-convict who sets out to avenge his six-year prison term by destroying small-town lawyer Sam Bowden (Peck), whose testimony had put him behind bars. Bowden tries to get police chief Mark Dutton (Martin Balsam) to run Cady out of town, but the latter is careful to stay within the law and even hires lawyer Dave Grafton (Jack Kruschen) to protect his civil liberties. Chief Dutton tells Bowden that his hands are tied, and Bowden is forced to hire a private detective, Charles Sievers (Telly Savalas), as Cady quietly continues his campaign of terror against Bowden, his wife, Peggy (Polly Bergen), and daughter, Nancy (Lori Martin).

With Barrie Chase in *Cape Fear.*

While Sievers is trying to get B-girl Diane Taylor (Barrie Chase) to admit that it had been Cady who beat her up, Cady is off poisoning the Bowden's dog. He scares Peggy and menaces Nancy, but refuses to be bought off. Finally, Bowden decides to take the law into his own hands, laying a trap for his pursuer. Cady is lured to Bowden's houseboat hideaway late one night where he attacks Peggy, but Nancy is his real goal. She escapes, however, as Bowden shows up to take on Cady in a murderous fight in the river, overpowering him at last and once more sending him to prison.

Despite Mitchum's brutal actions as Max Cady, there is little real insight into his behavior. His character is never really developed; it is just there, looming large and frightening all in sight. *Cape Fear* was, as Arthur Knight saw it in *Saturday Review,* "an old-fashioned, suspenseful melodrama that has no purpose beyond scaring the daylights out of you. . . . As the vengeful killer, Mitchum proves again that, given the opportunity, he can be a resourceful and expressive performer. His heavy-lidded eyes and petulent mouth here convey a depth of evil that is truly frightening."

Variety felt: "As a forthright exercise in cumulative terror, *Cape Fear* is competent and visually polished. . . . It achieves a goodly amount of suspense in the earnest but unstylish telling, yet the plot is always on the surface. . . . Granting the

With Lori Martin in *Cape Fear.*

With Gregory Peck in *Cape Fear*.

shallowness of his motivation, Mitchum has no trouble being utterly hateful. Wearing a Panama fedora and chomping a cocky cigar, the menace of his visage has the hiss of a poised snake." And *Time* noted: "Mitchum, as usual, makes a nice shiny reptile, and it's gory good fun to watch Peck cut him up into handbags."

Paul V. Beckley, critic for the *New York Herald Tribune*, spoke of *Cape Fear* as "a tour-de-force, reminiscent of *The Desperate Hours*, a study in terror that verges on the horror genre. . . . Mitchum's performance sets a new high—or low— in villains." Beckley hedged, though, feel-

ing that "If one can relax in spite of the brutality, sadism and melodramatic absurdity, one can appreciate the nonchalant excellence of Mitchum's acting, but otherwise it falls into the pattern of a masochistic exercise."

While Britain's *Monthly Film Bulletin* noted: "Mitchum, with bared chest and curling lip, obviously enjoys himself hugely suggesting Cady's way out depths of perverse brutality," Bosley Crowther was saying in *The New York Times*: "Menace quivers in the picture like a sneaky electrical charge. And Mr. Mitchum plays the villain with the cheekiest, wickedest arrogance and the most relentless aura of sadism that he has ever managed to generate." Crowther called the film "a pitiless shocker . . . a cold-blooded, calculated build-up of sadistic menace and shivering dread is accomplished with frightening adroitness."

Dorothy Masters's three-and-one-half star notice in New York's *Daily News* pointed out that "With the help of a dramatic scripts, dynamic direction and chilling dialogue, Robert Mitchum makes [the villain] an animal as terrifying and loathesome as the menace he portrayed in *The Night of the Hunter*," while Rose Pelswick wrote in her review in the *New York Journal-American*: "Mitchum, playing what is probably the season's most menacing screen character, gives a chillingly effective performance."

71
The Longest Day
20th Century-Fox, 1962

THE CAST:

Lt. Col. Benjamin Vandervoort, JOHN WAYNE; *Brig. Gen. Norman Cota,* ROBERT MITCHUM; *Brig. Gen. Theodore Roosevelt,* HENRY FONDA; *Brig. Gen. James M. Gavin,* ROBERT RYAN; and (Americans) Rod Steiger, Robert Wagner, Richard Beymer, Mel Ferrer, Jeffrey Hunter, Paul Anka, Sal Mineo, Roddy McDowall, Stuart Whitman, Steve Forrest, Eddie Albert, Edmond O'Brien, Fabian, Red But-

tons, Tom Tryon, Alexander Knox, Tommy Sands, Ray Danton, Henry Grace, Mark Damon, Dewey Martin, George Segal, John Crawford, Ron Randell, Nicholas Stuart, John Mellon, Fred Dur, Peter Helm; (British) Richard Burton, Kenneth More, Peter Lawford, Richard Todd, Leo Genn, John Gregson, Sean Connery, Jack Hedley, Michael Medwin, Norman Rossington, John Robinson, Patrick Barr, Leslie Phillips, Donald Houston, Frank Finlay, Lyndon Brook, Bryan Coleman, Neil Callum, Trevor Reid, Simon

Lack, Louis Mounier, Sian Phillips, Richard Wattis, Christopher Lee; (French) Irina Demich, Bourvil, Jean-Louis Barrault, Christian Marquand, Arletty, Madeleine Renaud, Georges Riviere, Jean Servais, Georges Wilson, Fernand Ledoux, Maurice Poli, Alice Tissot, Jo D'Avray; (Germans) Curt Jurgens, Werner Hinz, Paul Hartmann, Gert Frobe, Hans Christian Blech, Wolfgang Preiss, Peter Van Eyck, Heinz Reincke, Richard Munch, Ernest Schroeder, Karl Meisel, Heinz Spitzner, Robert Freytag, Til Kiew, Wolfgang Luckschy, Wolfgang Buttner, Ruth Housemeister, Michael Hinz, Paul Roth, Hartmuck Reck, Karl John, Dietmar Schonherr, Reiner Penkert, Eugene Deckers.

Producer, Darryl F. Zanuck; *Associate Producer,* Elmo Williams; *Directors,* Andrew Marton, Ken Annakin, Bernhard Wicki (and uncredited, Darryl F. Zanuck); *Screenplay,* Cornelius Ryan, based on his novel; *Addition Episodes Written by* Romain Gary, Jack Jones, David Pursall, and Jack Seddon; *Photography,* Jean Bourgoin, Henri Persin, and Walter Wottitz; *Helicopter Photography,* Guy Tabary; *Music,* Maurice Jarre; *Title Song,* Paul Anka; *Art Directors,* Ted Aworth, Leon Barsacq, and Vincent Korda; *Assistant Directors,* Bernard Farrel, Louis Pitzele, Gerard Renateau, and Henri Sokal; *Editor,* Samuel E. Beetley. CinemaScope. Running time: 180 minutes.

In *The Longest Day.*

Monumental is the term that most aptly describes *The Longest Day,* a surging epic of the Normandy invasion on June 6, 1944, and the apogee of Darryl F. Zanuck's career as a moviemaker. Despite the distraction of countless familiar faces in key roles, *The Longest Day* succeeded because of its overpowering sweep and dimension, with authenticity stamped all over it. It was Zanuck himself who decided to go with names when it came to the casting. "I wanted the audience to have a kick," he later explained. "Every time a door opened, it would be a well-known personality." The role of Brig. Gen. Norman Cota, commander of the 29th Infantry, originally was to have been played by John Wayne (who, instead, became Lt. Col. Benjamin Vandervoort, the 82nd Airborne officer whose broken ankle failed to prevent his participation in the invasion). Robert Mitchum finally was chosen to be Cota—tough, resolute, and caring, leading his men up the path from Omaha Beach after breaching the Vierville roadblock.

During the filming of *The Longest Day,* Mitchum again the made the front pages, when the United Press released a story that he had complained that some of the G.I.'s borrowed from the U.S. Army in Germany had been afraid to board a landing craft in stormy seas during a big action scene. He was quoted as saying: "It was raining, the wind was blowing and the sea was rough, and these troops were afraid to board. I had to hop aboard

first myself with some other actors and stuntmen before they gave in." Mitchum's pungent remarks astonished 20th's front office, and he was persuaded to more or less retract them. The papers then had him saying: "I have the highest respect and admiration for the soldiers. To quote me as saying the men were afraid is bordering on the ridiculous. I became good friends with these men during our work, and this story is insulting to me and the men." Later he added: "The worst thing is people will believe I said all those things. Americans believe if something appears in print it must be true, as opposed to the British who read something and throw it away because they know it isn't true."

Bosley Crowther spoke in his review in terms generally representative of his fellow critics: "Just as Cornelius Ryan put into vivid words the sweeping drama of the Normandy invasion in his book, Darryl F. Zanuck and a large team of associates have made that drama surge again upon the screen in a three-hour film. ... No character stands out particularly as more significant or heroic than anyone else. John Wayne is nobly rugged as Colonel Vandervoort [and]

With Darryl F. Zanuck on the set of *The Longest Day*.

In *The Longest Day*.

Robert Mitchum is tough as General Cota." Hollis Alpert wrote in *Saturday Review:* "There are individual performances that stand out because they seem right, among them Robert Mitchum's as General Cota." And *Variety's* reviewer felt that "the forty-three stars all deliver resoundingly [but] special pats are due to John Wayne, Robert Mitchum and to Red Buttons."

The Longest Day was nominated for a Best Picture Oscar and won Academy Awards for its photography and special effects.

72
Two for the Seesaw

Mirisch Company/United Artists, 1962

THE CAST:

Jerry Ryan, ROBERT MITCHUM; *Gittel Mosca,* SHIRLEY MacLAINE; *Frank Taubman,* Edmond Ryan; *Sophie,* Elisabeth Fraser; *Oscar,* Eddie Firestone; *Mr. Jacoby,* Billy Gray.

A Mirisch Company/Argyle Enterprises/Talbot Productions—Seven Arts Production. *Producer,* Walter Mirisch; *Director,* Robert Wise; *Screenplay,* Isobel Lennart; *Based on the Play by* William Gibson; *Photography,* Ted McCord; *Music,* Andre Previn; *Art Director,* Boris Leven; *Costumes,* Orry-Kelly; *Editor,* Stuart Gilmore. Panavision. Running time: 119 minutes.

With Shirley MacLaine in *Two for the Seesaw.*

In comments rather atypical of Mitchum, the actor actually admitted satisfaction with his performance in *Two for the Seesaw,* and smarted under the critical evaluations of his portrayal of Jerry Ryan, the harried lawyer from Omaha who drifts into a romantic affair with a kooky girl from the Bronx. When he originally had been asked to co-star in the Robert Wise film, Mitchum repeatedly refused, feeling that romantic indecision was not a quality he projects well. Later, he launched into a rare criticism of reviewers after reading their appraisals of his work in the movie: "The toughest chore in show business is trying to please them when an actor appears in a film or a stage play. No matter what you do, it's wrong as a sow's ear in a silk purse factory, especially to New York critics, who are guilty of intellectual snobbery. With them nothing can be done in Hollywood or anywhere else as well as in their home town, it seems."

Two for the Seesaw, a Broadway hit of 1958 when it starred Henry Fonda and Anne Bancroft (and in the early 1970s as the musical *Seesaw* with Ken Howard and Michele Lee), first had been announced as a movie vehicle for Elizabeth Taylor and Paul Newman, under Delbert Mann's direction. Eventually it fell to Mitchum and Shirley MacLaine and director Robert Wise, who did his

With Shirley MacLaine in *Two for the Seesaw*.

With Shirley MacLaine in *Two for the Seesaw*.

best to open up the two-character William Gibson play. Omaha lawyer Jerry Ryan (Mitchum), on the brink of divorce, comes to Manhattan emotionally bankrupt. Following a period of seclusion, he meets Gittel Mosca (Shirley MacLaine), a would-be dance instructor from the Bronx, at a Greenwich Village party. She helps him shake off his loneliness and the two drift into an affair. Jerry renews his law practice, using some of his salary to set up Gittel with a little dance studio. He continues, however, to be upset by the slightest thought of his wife, and Gittel, becoming morose, takes up once again with an old boyfriend. Waiting for Gittel to return from a party one night, Jerry accuses her of being unfaithful. A violent arguement ensues and Gittel ends up in the hospital with a stomach ulcer. After recovering, she suggests that they marry when his divorce becomes final. When Jerry tells her that it already has come through, Gittel realizes that he never has really left Nebraska. She ends the affair and Jerry decides to return to Omaha. Before leaving Manhattan, he calls Gittel to tell her how much she has meant to him. Before he hangs up, he says the words Gittel has waited to hear, "I love you."

"The basic flaws appear to be the play's innate talkiness and the unbalance of the two-way 'Seesaw,' " *Variety* concluded. "The selection of Robert Mitchum proves not to have been a wise

one and the strong attraction Gittel is supposed to feel for Jerry becomes less plausible because of Mitchum's lethargic, droopy-eyed enactment." Brendan Gill felt similarly in *The New Yorker:* "Mitchum—plump, hard-boiled, and looking more disbarred than domestically harried—is altogether out of place. Indeed, the perfection of the miscasting prompts one to speculate on how wonderful Miss MacLaine might have been as a sensitive girl from Omaha and how wonderful Mitchum might have been as a tough guy from the Bronx."

Newsweek wrote: "Mitchum, rigid to begin with, plays in the movie as if he were wearing tight shoes," and, in the *New York Herald Tribune*, Paul V. Beckley commented that "Mitchum is out of place . . . because the man the camera shows us is not a man likely to be involved in this particular situation. You really can't believe he would stand around so long with his thumb in his mouth." Alton Cook agreed in the *World Telegram and Sun:* "Mitchum radiates too imperious a character to have patience for this prolonged and futile discussion. One feels such a man would quickly have told the girl to shut up and git—and git fast."

One of the more favorable reviews came from Wanda Hale, who gave the film three-and-one-half stars in the New York *Daily News* and acknowledged that "It's enough to say that any picture is better for having Robert Mitchum in it."

73
The List of
Adrian
Messenger

Universal, 1963

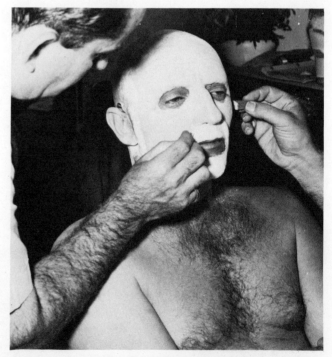

Being made up for *The List of Adrian Messenger.*

THE CAST:

Anthony Gethryn, GEORGE C. SCOTT; *Lady Jocelyn Bruttenholm*, DANA WYNTER; *Marquis of Gleneyre*, Clive Brook;

Mrs. Karoudjian, Gladys Cooper; *Sir Wilfred Lucas,* Herbert Marshall; *Raoulle Borg,* Jacques Roux; *Adrian Messenger,* John Merivale; *Anton Karoudjian,* Marcel Dalio; *Inspector Pike,* Bernard Archard; *Derek,* Walter Anthony Huston; *Carstairs,* Roland DeLong; *Mrs. Slattery,* Snita Sharp-Bolster; *Inspector Seymour,* Alan Caillou; *Lord Ashton,* John Huston; *Countryman,* Noel Purcell; *Sgt. Flood,* Richard Peel; *Lynch,* Bernard Fox; *Whitel* Nelson Welch; *Hunt Secretary,* Tim Durant; *Nurse,* Barbara Morrison; *Studen Nurse,* Jennifer Raine; *Maid,* Constance Cavendish; *Orderly,* Eric Heath; *Stewardesses,* Anna Van Der Heide and Delphi Lawrence; and *Halian,* TONY CURTIS; *George Brougham,* KIRK DOUGLAS; *Woman,* BURT LANCASTER; *Jim Slattery,* ROBERT MITCHUM; *Gypsy Stableman,* FRANK SINATRA.

A Joel Production. *Producer,* Edward Lewis; *Director,* John Huston; *Screenplay,* Anthony Veiller; *Based on the Novel by* Philip MacDonald; *Photography,* Joe MacDonald; *Music,* Jerry Goldsmith; *Art Directors,* Alexander Golitzen, Stephen Grimes, and George Webb; *Editors,* Terry Morse and Hugh Fowler. Running time: 98 minutes.

This well-made suspense thriller was gimmicked up with several noted film personalities in heavily disguised bit parts, and reunited Robert Mitchum, as one of the "guests," with director John Huston. Huston's novel touches baffled some movie goers and annoyed others whose fascination with the purely mystery elements of the film irritatingly was interrupted by staged appearances of red herrings, played by Frank Sinatra, Burt Lancaster, Tony Curtis, and Mitchum. Kirk Douglas, whose company produced the movie, originally had the lead in *The List of Adrian Messenger,* but he stopped production, gave his starring role to George C. Scott, and joined his buddies in disguise (he also played an integral part in the story) in what seemed on paper to be a surefire commercial ploy.

The taut thriller begins at a tea party where Anthony Gethryn (Scott), a retired British intelligence officer, is persuaded by his friend, Adrian Messenger (John Merivale), to locate eleven people. During the investigation, though, Messenger is killed, and Gethryn subsequently discovers that all of the people on Messenger's list also have met with mysterious accidents. Convinced that twelve murders have been committed, Gethryn enlists the aid of Scotland Yard and learns that one of the suspects is a master of disguises whose identity is altered for each murder. Gethryn finally pieces together facts that all of his victims had been POWs in Burma and that their killer had informed the enemy of his comrades' escape plans. Because of his new-found social and professional prominence, the

In *The List of Adrian Messenger.*

killer now had felt it necessary to eliminate those who might expose his past treachery. During a foxhunt, Gethryn confronts the culprit, who comes to a violent end, dying in one of his own traps while attempting to escape.

The whodunit then was tagged with an epilogue as Lancaster, Curtis, Sinatra, and Mitchum pealed off their putty-mask disguises and took their bows.

"A fine first-class mystery-murder suspense thriller to delight aficionados and offer movie buffs a couple of added jolts as an encore," wrote critic Judith Crist in the *New York Herald Tribune.* "Five actors are listed without character names and the producers demand that you spot them for yourselves. Well, Kirk Douglas reveals himself early on, with no discredit, giving an excellent display of unexpected versatility. You may, as I did, find Robert Mitchum and have your suspicion about Frank Sinatra—but Burt Lancaster and Tony Curtis do indeed defy detection."

Variety found the movie "a bizzare, but curiously irritating film experience. Discerning picturegoers will be annoyed to see distracting casting excesses mar a basically enthralling murder mystery otherwise executed with considerable vitality by director John Huston. . . . This casting brainstorm regretably turns out to be an

As one of the five "guests" in *The List of Adrian Messenger*.

artistic nuisance. Some of the acting is first rate [and] of the five stars who 'guest,' Kirk Douglas has the major assignment and carries if off colorfully and credibly. Only Mitchum is easily recognizable beneath the facial stickum."

Stanley Kauffmann felt in *The New Republic* that "the 'bonus' device of having five stars play small parts in rubber masks is feeble cleverness. They don't 'play' anything—five assistant electricians could have worn the masks. Besides, they must have looked to the other actors, as they look to us, like five fellows in rubber masks."

For the record, Robert Mitchum appears as a crippled pensioner in a wheelchair.

74
Rampage

Warner Bros.-Seven Arts, 1963

In *Rampage.*

THE CAST:

Harry Stanton, ROBERT MITCHUM; *Anna,* ELSA MARTINELLI; *Otto Abbot,* JACK HAWKINS; *Talib,* Sabu; *Chep,* Cely Carrillo; *Schelling,* Emile Genest; *Salki Chief,* Stefan Schnabel; *Baka,* David Cadiente.

A Talbot Production. *Producer,* William Fadiman; *Director,* Phil Karlson; *Screenplay,* Robert I. Holt and Marguerite Roberts; *Based on the Novel by* Alan Caillou; *Photography,* Harold Lipstein; *Music,* Elmer Bernstein; *Title Song,* Elmer Bernstein and Mack David; *Art Director,* Harold Blumenthal; *Gowns,* Oleg Cassini; *Editor,* Gene Milford. Technicolor. Running time: 98 minutes.

Robert Mitchum lent his good name and money to the jungle hokum called *Rampage,* a triangle melodrama in pith helmets and jodhpurs, "an inept blend of cliche and purience," *Variety* wrote, "one for the fellow who claims 'they don't make movies like they used to' . . . the scenario is crammed with contrived situations and hollow, pretentious dialog."

Mitchum, making the film for a lark and a vacation in Hawaii with his family, stars as Harry Stanton, an international trapper commissioned by a German zoo to catch a rare half tiger/half leopard. Accompanying him to the Malay jungle of the story is Otto Abbot (Jack Hawkins), a noted big-game hunter familiar with the territory. An unbridgeable difference between the trapper and the hunter is further widened when Abbot insists that his mistress, Anna (Elsa Martinelli), join them. Under the stewardship of Talib (Sabu), "head boy" of the trackers and beaters, the group is led to a mountain cave where the animal is trapped. Stanton prepares to net the big cat, but Abbot almost ruins things by entering the cave armed only with a blazing torch. Badly mauled, he is rescued by Stanton.

The safari completed, Stanton, Abbot, and Anna return to Germany, and Anna tearfully informs the unbelieving Abbot that she is in love with Stanton. Abbot vengefully lures Stanton into a railroad baggage car and uncages the tiger/leopard, leaving Stanton to his supposed death. Stanton is saved, though, when the van doors are opened and the cat leaps from the train into a

185

With Elsa Martinelli in *Rampage*.

With Elsa Martinelli in *Rampage*.

waiting crowd. Stanton and Anna, both armed, track the beast to a nearby rooftop and discover that Abbot already is there, rifle in hand. He attempts to shoot Stanton but is killed by the snarling beast. It is Anna who finally shoots the animal as it stands over Abbot's dead body.

"Fooey," Howard Thompson wrote in *The New York Times*. "Only a tiger—and *Rampage* has a couple of tawny beauties—could lick the wooden script and absurd dialogue of this feeble melodrama." In the *New York Herald Tribune*, Judith Crist said: "Sex, in fact, louses up what might have been a pretty exciting wild-game hunt involving some mighty handsome animals. But some equally handsome humans get so involved in a silly and dull little melodrama in the course of it that the big cats prowl, growl, and claw to small effect."

In *Time*, these words: "Animal crackers, as Hollywood plays the game, is a pleasant, simple-minded pastime that offers few surprises. This time around, Mitchum & Company see the usual things, say the usual things, do the usual things." Britain's *Monthly Film Bulletin* joked: "One of the remarkable things about *Rampage* is that it is possible to see animals act badly.... It is also quite an achievement to make a film about wild animals and make it dull."

Mitchum's own description of *Rampage:* "What's it all about? It's a lot of dancing girls, banjo playing and bull. There are these two guys on the make for this broad, see, but there's a man-eating tiger in the way, so one of them has to kill it or something . . . and all that jazz." His summation was remarkably succinct.

75
Man in the Middle

20th Century-Fox, 1964

THE CAST:

Lt. Col. Barney Adams, ROBERT MITCHUM; *Kate Dauray,* FRANCE NUYEN; *General Kempton,* Barry Sullivan; *Maj. John Kensington,* Trevor Howard; *Lt. Winston,* Keenan Wynn; *Dr. Kaufman,* Sam Wanamaker; *Col. Archer Burton,* Alexander Knox; *Lt. Morse,* Gary Cockrell; *Lt. Bender,* Robert Nicholls; *Col. Shaw,* Michael Goodliffe; *Sgt. Jackson,* Errol John; *Major Smith,* Paul Maxwell; *Capt. Gunther,* Lionel Murton; *Col. Thompson,* Russell Napier; *Capt. Dwyer,* Jared Allen; *Col. Mayburt,* David Bauer; *Major Wycliff,* Edward Underdown; *Major Poole,* Howard Marion; *Staff Sgt. Quinn,* William Mitchell; *Capt. Zimmerman,* Al Waxman; *Cpl. Burke,* Glenn Beck; *Cpl. Baxter,* Frank Killibrew; *Lieutenant at Sikri,* Edward Bishop; *Major Clement,* Terence Cooper; *Major Hennessey,* Graham Skidmore; *Col. Burnside,* Terry Shelton; *Col. Winovich,* Paul Bromley; *Col. Kelly,* Alistair Barr; *Major McCabe,* Brian Vaughn; *Major Cummings,* Julian Burton.

A Talbot/Pennebaker Production. *Executive Producer,* Max E. Youngstein; *Producer,* Walter Seltzer; *Director,* Guy Hamilton; *Screenplay,* Keith Waterhouse and Willis Hall; *Based on the Novel The Winston Affair by* Howard Fast; *Photography,* Wilkie Cooper; *Music,* Lionel Bart; *Music Director,* John Barry; *Art Director,* John Howell, *Editor,* John Bloom. CinemaScope. Running time: 94 minutes.

Mitchum's earnest performance as Lt. Col. Barney Adams in *Man in the Middle*, taken from Howard Fast's interesting courtroom novel, *The Winston Affair,* and the resourceful acting of a lengthy cast of primarily British players failed somehow to ignite this potentially charged confrontation drama—sidetracked slightly by an extraneous romantic interlude between Mitchum and France Nuyen. The story deals with the court-martial of an American lieutenant (Keenan Wynn, astonishingly good as a psychopath) who murders a British sergeant before eleven eyewitnesses, and is then defended by an American colonel (Mitchum) who has been told that, in the interest of Allied unity, his client will be found guilty and executed.

Lieutenant Winston's actions had been, in his eyes, punishment for his victim's defiling the white race by consorting with native women. Because the murder has caused terrible friction

With France Nuyen in *Man in the Middle*.

With Sam Wanamaker in *Man in the Middle*.

In *Man in the Middle*.

between the British and the Americans, Barney Adams is instructed by General Kempton (Barry Sullivan) to put up an intelligent but unsuccessful defense so that the conviction will have no loopholes when the defendant goes to the gallows. Barney then learns that Winston had been diagnosed as a psycopath by Major Kaufman (Sam Wanamaker), but that report was suppressed by his superior, Colonel Burton (Alexander Knox), who is anxious to have Winston convicted. Barney persuades Kaufman to testify at the trial, but when Burton learns this, he transfers Kaufman to a distant hospital. Frustrated, Barney then induces British Major Kensington (Trevor Howard), the district medical officer with high qualifications than Burton, to describe Winston's illness. When Barney learns that Kaufman had been killed in a jeep accident on his way to the trial, he calls Kensington to the stand. As the latter gives his diagnosis to the court, Winston cracks and begins raving, proving his own insanity and saving his neck.

"The format of the courtroom drama has seldom been used to contain a less taut and engrossing test of justice than that perfunctorily displayed in *Man in the Middle*," critic Bosley Crowther said. "In addition to being slow and unconvincing, the show is also sluggishly played, especially by Robert Mitchum [who] comes on sleepwalking, grumbling and looking tough, and he stays more or less in that mood all the way through the film." The reviewer for *Time* felt: "Nothing is much better than all right in this black-and-white morality play. Mitchum plays Mitchum with laconic assurance, and a cast of veteran character actors is warmed up for a first-rate courtroom drama, a la *The Caine Mutiny*, that only makes it to second."

Variety thought that the film "starts off with no promise and concludes on a note of disappointment. . . . It's a pro job, of sorts, but a letdown. Mitchum's portrayal is a fair job of emoting, though the actor is looking pudgy in this outing." And Britain's *Monthly Film Bulletin* wrote: "The relative restraint and dryness of the playing of Robert Mitchum and Trevor Howard, and Keenan Wynn in Winston's lucid patches, sustain the narrative."

Mitchum's comments: "I think my part as Barney Adams was intriguing because he faced a real dilemma only he could solve. Whichever course he chose—justice or loyalty—in his defense of a self-confessed murderer, would bring him personal unhappiness. It's the sort of decision lots of people have had to face during a war."

76
What a Way To Go!

20th Century-Fox, 1964

THE CAST:

Louisa Foster, SHIRLEY MacLAINE; *Larry Flint,* PAUL NEWMAN; *Rod Anderson,* ROBERT MITCHUM; *Leonard Crawley,* DEAN MARTIN; *Jerry Benson,* GENE KELLY; *Dr. Victor Steffanson,* BOB CUMMINGS; *Edgar Hooper,* DICK VAN DYKE; *Painter,* Reginald Gardiner; *Mrs. Foster,* Margaret Dumont; *Trentino,* Lou Nova; *Baroness,* Fifi D'Orsay; *Rene,* Maurice Marsac; *Agent,* Wally Vernon; *Polly,* Jane Wald; *Hollywood Lawyer,* Lenny Kent; *Mrs. Freeman,* Marjorie Bennett; *Ned,* Christopher Connelly; *Girl on Plane,* Barbara Bouchet; *Lord Kensington,* Tom Conway; *Lady Kensington,* Queenie Smith; *Willard,* Anthony Eustrol; *Press Agent,* Phil Arnold; *Driscoll,* Richard Wilson; *Movie Executive,* Sid Gould; *Secretary,* Paula Lane; *TV Announcer,* Army Archerd; *Movie Star,* Tracy Butler; *Mr. Foster,* Anton Arnold; *Minister,* Roy Gordon; *Crawleyville Lawyer,* Burt Mustin; *Leonard Crawley (age 7),* Billy Corcoran; *Jonathan Crawley (age 5),* Jeff Fithian; *Geraldine Crawley (age 4),* Pamelyn Ferdin; *Doris,* Helene F. Winston; *Chester,* Jack Greenberg; *French Lawyer,* Marcelle Hillaire; *Lawyer,* Milton Frome.

An Apjac Production. *Producer,* Arthur P. Jacobs; *Director,* J. Lee Thompson; *Screenplay,* Betty Comden and Adolph Green; *Story,* Gwen Davis; *Photography,* Leon Shamroy; *Music,* Nelson Riddle; *Songs,* Betty Comden, Jule Styne, and Adolph Green; *Choreography,* Gene Kelly; *Art Directors,* Ted Haworth and Jack Martin Smith; *Costumes,* Edith Head; *Jewelry,* Harry Winston; *Editor,* Majorie Fowler. Cinema-Scope and DeLuxe Color. Running time: 111 minutes.

For this elaborate, visually stunning, multiepisode film spoof designed by Betty Comden and Adolph Green (originally, it is said, for Marilyn Monroe and, according to Mitchum, Frank Sinatra), Mitchum signed on as one of six leading men opposite Shirley MacLaine, contractually sharing top male billing with Paul Newman after MacLaine—with ads designed to have Mitchum and Newman alternately listed first. The story expensively and expansively tells of a poor little rich girl seeking only happiness but becoming increasingly wealthy as a series of rich husbands die bizarre deaths. Each episode with each spouse contains a fantasy-satire of some stock screen genre—a silent flick (with Dick Van Dyke), a subtitled French film (with Newman), a lush Ross Hunter-type takeoff (with Mitchum), a Busby Berkeley musical (with Gene Kelly).

Robert Mitchum is rugged Rod Anderson, husband No. 3, a tycoon whose neglect of his empire for Louisa (Shirley MacLaine) perversely has tripled his fortune. He has so much money that life with Louisa becomes one of those extravagant, super-deluxe dramas (a "Lush Budget Production") complete with gorgeous Edith Head wardrobes and sumptuous sets allowing him to bed down with Louisa in an enormous champagne glass. Rod eventually takes Louisa away from it all and retires to a farm where he is unceremoniously kicked to death by an angry bull he mistakenly attempts to milk.

"*What A Way To Go!* is five or six big, splashy movies rolled into one," *Time* commented. "It sets out to satirize the very things it seems head over heels in love with: moom pictures and the cult of

With Shirley MacLaine in *What A Way To Go!*

With Shirley MacLaine in *What A Way To Go!*

'success—money—success' . . . For all its talent and occasional forward thrust, *What A Way To Go!* never really gets anywhere."

Brendan Gill called the film in *The New Yorker* "a monotonously prolonged gag about sex and death, at which one isn't so much expected to die laughing as to laugh watching other people die," while Bosley Crowther decided that "the whole thing, alas, lacks wit and grace . . . the idea of death as a propellant of an embarrassment of riches just isn't droll. . . . J. Lee Thompson's direction has failed to coalesce a good film farce. It lets the whole thing flap wildly—and that's no way to make a film."

Surprisingly favorable was the notice given the film by *Newsweek*, which called it "one of those great old movie-movies Hollywood hardly seems to be able to make any more. Absolute nonsense it may be, but it is nonsense with style, with flair, and with appealing extravagance." Mitchum, too, had several uncharacteristically good words for the picture. "I'm actually working for nothing after taxes because I've made too many films this year," he jokingly told an interviewer, "but I was with J. Lee Thompson in *Cape Fear* and couldn't turn down the chance to work with him and Shirley again. The film is a far-out, crazy comedy. In one of the dream sequences, I bed down with Shirley in a champagne glass. I also have a run-in with a big bad bull, which is more like the things I'm used to doing in pictures."

77
Mister Moses
United Artists, 1965

THE CAST:

Joe Moses, ROBERT MITCHUM; *Julie Anderson,* CARROLL BAKER; *Robert,* Ian Bannon; *Reverend Anderson,* Alexander Knox; *Ubi,* Raymond St. Jacques; *Chief,* Orlando Martins; *Parkhurst,* Reginald Beckwith.

A Frank Ross/Talbot Production. *Producer,* Frank Ross; *Director,* Ronald Neame; *Screenplay,* Charles Beaumont and Monja Danischewsky; *Based on the Novel by* Max Catto; *Photography,* Oswald Morris; *Music,* John Barry; *Art Director,* Syd Cain; *Editor,* Peter Wetherly. Panavision and Technicolor. Running time: 113 minutes.

In *Mister Moses.*

The film version of Max Catto's contemporary novel paralleling the biblical story of Moses put Robert Mitchum back in the jungle. This time, however, the tale was literate, the script lighthearted. Mitchum obviously relished doing his part although he looked less comfortable astride an elephant than on horseback in the Old West. *Mister Moses* opens with Joe Moses, quack doctor and diamond smuggler, being heaved into the river by some discontented African natives. Rescued downstream in some bulrushes by Julie Anderson (Carroll Baker), daughter of a local missionary (Alexander Knox), Moses finds himself in a small village that is to be flooded upon completion of a new dam. The local natives, though, have refused to leave because they cannot take their animals with them.

The District Commissioner (Ian Bannen) is prepared to use force when the native chief (Orlando Martins), impressed by one of Joe Moses's impromptu magic shows, announces that Moses will lead the tribe to their promised land. By threatening to report his smuggling activities, Julie persuades Moses into agreeing to guide the villagers. During the long trek across Africa,

With Carroll Baker in *Mister Moses*.

Moses has trouble with Ubi (Raymond St. Jacques), the American-educated tribesman who resents the white man's influence. By getting the sluice gates open so the tribe can cross the dam that has brought the journey to a temporary halt, Moses "parts" the waters. But while he is away briefly, Ubi attempts to expose him as a false prophet and leads his tribe in a ritual dance, destroying the Commissioner's helicopter. Ultimately, Ubi, accidentally ringing himself with fire, perishes in the flames. When the trek eventually ends, Moses is allowed to escape by the Commissioner, who has learned of his smuggling activities. As Mr. Moses heads for the bush, Julie hurries after him.

Stanley Kauffmann, critic for *The New Republic*, wrote: "The picture is sustained by Robert Mitchum in the title role. From time to time in the past, he has given acting performances; here he is simply present—paunchy, casual, obviously tolerant of the plot, but screen-fillingly present. When he opens his eyes after being knocked out near the beginning, looks up at the girl whom he

With Carroll Baker in *Mister Moses*.

has never seen before, and quickly induces her to lie to her fiance about him, we believe at once in her acquiescence."

In *Commonweal,* reviewer Philip T. Hartung felt that "director Ronald Neame, who handles his very large, almost unwieldy cast well, has also guided Mitchum in one of the best performances of his career."

Less enthusiastic was Judith Crist, who inscribed in the *New York Herald Tribune* that "*Mister Moses* is strictly for the bulrushes . . . an archaic rehash of every oldie about the childlike superstitious natives who need a great white father to lean them and the gin swiller who's conned into the leadership bit by the missionary's virginal daughter. . . . Mitchum gives no indication of stirrings or anything else from beginning to end."

Time observed that "Mitchum . . . conducts his exodus with the holier-than-thou sneer of a rascal who interprets Mosaic law as the survival of the fittest [and] looks most comfortable when he climbs aboard an elephant called Emily." *Monthly Film Bulletin* noted simply that "not surprisingly, the people who come out of it best are Robert Mitchum and Carroll Baker, who never really attempt to be anything other than their uncomplicated Hollywood selves."

78
The Way West
United Artists, 1967

THE CAST:

Sen. William J. Tadlock, KIRK DOUGLAS; *Dick Summers,* ROBERT MITCHUM; *Lije Evans,* RICHARD WIDMARK; *Rebecca Evans,* Lola Albright; *Johnnie Mack,* Michael Witney; *Sam Fairman,* Stubby Kaye; *Mercy McBèe,* Sally Field; *Amanda Mack,* Katherine Justice; *Brownie Evans,* Michael McGreevey; *McBee,* Harry Carey, Jr.; *Mrs. McBee,* Connie Sawyer; *Mrs. Fairman,* Elisabeth Fraser; *Michael Moynihan,* William Lundigan; *Turley,* Paul Lukather; *Masters,* Roy Barcroft; *Col. Grant,* Patric Knowles; *Hank,* Ken Murray; *Little Henry,* John Mitchum; *Calvelli,* Nick Cravat; *Saunders,* Roy Glenn; *Mrs. Moynihan,* Anne Barton; *Mrs. Masters,* Eve McVeagh; *Mrs. Turley,* Peggy Stewart; *Billy Tadlock, Jr.,* Stefan Angrim; *Indian Leader,* Michael Lane; *Indian Warrior,* Michael Heep.

A Harold Hecht Production. *Producer,* Harold Hecht; *Producer,* Andrew V. McLaglen; *Screenplay,* Ben Maddow and Mitch Linderman; *Based on the Novel by* A. B. Guthrie, Jr.; *Photography,* William H. Clothier; *Music,* Bronislaw Kaper; *Art Director,* Ted Haworth; *Editor,* Otho Lovering. Panavision and DeLuxe Color. Running time: 122 minutes.

In *The Way West.*

In his 1950 Pulitzer Prize-winning novel, *The Way West,* A. B. Guthrie described in epic form one of the world's great migrations. Director Andrew V. McLaglen, hoping to emulate his idol (and godfather), John Ford, used the book to create a western spectacular with three veteran cowboy

With Kirk Douglas and Richard Widmark in *The Way West.*

actors—Kirk Douglas, Robert Mitchum, and Richard Widmark—leading a huge cast of performers in buckskins and calico. Unfortunately, the scope of the film was too broad and encompassed enough plots, as one critic observed, to sustain a full year's television soap opera.

Robert Mitchum was engaged to play Dick Summers, a tough, embittered trail scout with failing eyesight, who reluctantly accepts the job of pointing the way West for the pioneers. Most of the footage, though, went to Kirk Douglas as Senator William J. Tadlock, the sadistic leader who dreams of a new Jerusalem, and Richard Widmark as Lije Evans, a dirt farmer with "Oregon fever." Others in the party: Lije's wife, Rebecca (Lola Albright); newlyweds Johnnie Mack (Michael Witney) and his neurotic bride, Amanda (Katherine Justice); and the slovenly, flirtatious Mercy McBee (Sally Fields). Tadlock proves to be a stern disciplinarian and a hard taskmaster. One night, young Johnnie Mack, frustrated by his frigid wife, gets drunk and seduces Mercy McBee, and then accidentally kills the son of a Sioux chieftain. Rather than risk delay by defying the Sioux, Tadlock hangs the lad. When it is later learned that Mercy is carrying Johnnie's child, Lije's son, Brownie (Michael McGreevey), offers to marry her.

Tadlock subsequently causes the death of his own son in a buffalo stampede. Griefstricken, he so despises his own weakness that he orders his Negro slave to whip him. In time, the emigrants weary of the hardships and consider changing course for California. Discovering later that Tadlock had faked a smallpox scare to avoid this, Lije Evans assumes command. Under Dick Summers's guidance and Lije's determination, the

wagon train eventually nears its destination, with only a precipitous chasm between the settlers and their goal. Tadlock, however, is permitted to supervise the lowering of the people, animals and dismantled wagons down the ravine. One by one they go, but when Tadlock takes his turn, the crazed Amanda Mack cuts his rope and he plunges to his death. After his grave has been dug, the remnants of the party set off down the Columbia River. Only Dick Summers remains behind, silently watching the settlers fade into the distance.

"It is hard to believe that anybody could have made such a hackneyed hash of that fine A. B. Guthrie novel," Bosley Crowther wrote in *The New York Times.* "It makes an old Western fan want to scream. . . . Robert Mitchum, droopy-eyed and surly, as though peeved at having to wear that Indian hat, views the whole silly business with contempt." *Time* said: "From the beginning, *The Way West* is off on the wrong trek. As was common in the taming of the frontier, there is a great waste of natural resources—in this case, Robert Mitchum, Kirk Douglas, Richard Widmark and Lola Albright. All are solid professional performers who deserve to travel first-class next time they journey West."

In *Commonweal,* Philip T. Hartung concluded: "To judge by *The Way West,* American Western makers are not only lagging, but are repeating

In *The Way West.*

themselves with cliches of years ago and have even lost their touch with them." *Variety* called the film "dull" and "disappointing," observing that: "The project probably looked good on paper, but washed out in scripting, direction and pacing. . . . Mitchum, evidently aware of the script vapidity, didn't try too hard."

Harshest was the critique of Brendan Gill in *The New Yorker,* who called the film "one of the worst movies of this or any season, and would obviously have been much less bad if there had been much less of it to *be* bad . . . the acting in *The Way West* is a match for the script."

79
El Dorado

Paramount, 1967

THE CAST:

Cole Thornton, JOHN WAYNE; *J. P. Harrah,* ROBERT MITCHUM; *Mississippi,* James Caan; *Maudie,* Charlene Holt; *Joey MacDonald,* Michele Carey; *Bull Thomas,* Arthur Hunnicutt; *Bart Jason,* Edward Asner; *Kevin MacDonald,* R. G. Armstrong; *Doc Miller,* Paul Fix; *Nelse McLeod,* Christopher George; *Luke MacDonald,* Johnny Crawford; *Saul MacDonald,* Robert Rothwell; *Matt MacDonald,* Adam Roarke; *Jared MacDonald,* Chuck Courtney; *Milt,* Robert Donner; *Pedro,* John Gabriel; *Jason's Foreman,* Jim Davis; *Maria,* Marina Ghane; *Saul's Wife,* Anne Newman; *Matt's Wife,* Diane Strom; *Jared's Wife,* Victoria George; *Dr. Donavan,* Anthony Rogers; *Swedish Gunsmith,* Olaf Wieghorst; *Rosa,* Rosa Turich; and Ralph Volkie, Danny Sands, Buzz Henry, Deen Pettinger, Lee Powell, Enrique Contreras, Riley Hill, John Strachen, Mike Letz, Betty Graham, Richard Andrade, Ruben Moreno, Robert Shelton, Linda Dangcil, Dean Smith, Nacho Galindo, Myrna MacMurray, Bonnie Charyl Josephson, Joe Garcio, John Mitchum, Christopher West, Frank Leyva, Charlita, Rodolfo Hoyos, Don Collier, William Albert Henry.

A Howard Hawks Production. *Producer/Director,* Howard Hawks; *Screenplay,* Leigh Brackett; *Based on the Novel The Stars in Their Courses by* Harry Brown; *Photography,* Harold Rosson; *Music,* Nelson Riddle; *Art Directors,* Hal Pereira and Carl Anderson; *Editor,* John Woodcock. Technicolor. Running time: 126 minutes.

"It's the Big One with the Big Two!" was the line that highlighted Paramount's ads for Howard Hawks's brawling, colorful western that teamed (for the only time) John Wayne and Robert Mitchum, both at top form as aging cowboys who,

With John Wayne in *El Dorado.*

as one writer put it, have grown old and crippled together and find comfort in each other's discomfort. Basically a thinly disguised copy of Hawks's 1959 *Rio Bravo,* the film has Wayne as a two-fisted hired gunslinger and Mitchum as his one-time companion, now a drunken sheriff mooning over a lost love. Hawks and his screenwriter, Leigh Brackett, started out with an adaptation of Harry Brown's solemn, ultraviolent novel, *The Stars in Their Courses,* but became disenchanted with it and instead turned to their earlier *Rio Bravo,* incorporating many of the same elements and characters into their new film. Wayne repeated his original part, Mitchum did the Dean Martin role, James Caan went in for Ricky Nelson,

In *El Dorado*.

With John Wayne and Paul Fix in *El Dorado*.

Arthur Hunnicutt for Walter Brennan, Charlene Holt for Angie Dickinson. Then, taking the standard western saga—the gunfighter and the lawman teaming to prevent a range war, Hawks also filled *El Dorado* with variations of scenes on which he long since had put his stamp: the toe-to-toe slugfest in which two old friends nearly beat each other insensible before discovering they are on the same side; two old-timers holding off the young upstarts and coming through unscathed no matter what the odds; the lighthearted relationship between a veteran gunman and his young rival. For Mitchum, *El Dorado* provided a wonderfully comic role as the paunchy, boozing sheriff, with quite a bit of footage devoted to the efforts of Wayne and others to sober him up with various foul-tasting concoctions.

In *El Dorado*, Cole Thornton (Wayne), hired as a gunslinger by cattle baron Bart Jason (Edward Asner) to keep the settlers in line, rides into town to see what his old friend, Sheriff J. P. Harrah (Mitchum), plans to do about it. Learning he had been hired to take part in a range war over water rights, Cole turns down Jason's job offer. Ambushed while returning from Jason's, Cole inadvertently shoots a settler's boy (Johnny Crawford). Before he can explain the fatal accident, he in turn is shot down by the boy's hot-headed sister (Michele Carey), but manages to make his way back to town. Nursed back to health by an old girlfriend, Maudie (Charlene Holt), now Harrah's flame, Cole is warned that he could face creeping paralysis in his arm.

Months later, after striking up a friendship with a young gambler named Mississippi (James Caan), Cole learns that professional gunslinger Nelse McLeod (Christopher George) has been hired to harass the ranchers and that old J. P. has gone on a long drunk after being jilted by Maudie. Cole and Mississippi ride back to El Dorado to sober up Harrah with a fiendish remedy—a liquid brew laced with gunpowder. With their help, Harrah takes hold of himself, returns to duty, and drives McLeod and his men out of town after jailing Jason. McLeod, though, returns with his gang, wounds Harrah in the leg and captures Cole when the bullet in his spine temporarily paralyzes his shooting hand; then he offers to swap Cole for Jason. Harrah and company then go after the gunslinger and his gang and wipe them out in a showdown in Maudie's saloon. Harrah, hobbling on a crutch, and Cole, nursing a useless right arm, smugly congratulate themselves about cleaning up the town.

With John Wayne and Arthur Hunnicutt in *El Dorado*.

Howard Thompson, in *The New York Times*, cheered *El Dorado* as "a tough, laconic and amusing Western that ambles across the screen as easily as the two veteran stars. The release is worth seeing if only for the casual, saddlesore expertise and ribaldry of these two leathery dudes [and] the taut guidance of Mr. Hawks. . . . Mr. Mitchum is simply wonderful as a whisky-sodden sheriff." *Time* wrote: "As the liquor-laden lawman, Mitchum is a perfect foil for Wayne. . . . At the fadeout, Wayne has been pinked in the knee, Mitchum in the high. With crutches as swagger sticks, they limp triumphantly past the camera—two old pros demonstrating that they are better on one good leg apiece than most of the younger stars on two."

In The *New York Post*, Archer Winsten observed: "A Howard Hawks Western, with big John Wayne and bow-legged Robert Mitchum, has got to be exactly what you expect. . . . It's a lucky thing that these two heroes are the stars

they are, for otherwise they wouldn't have a chance. . . . Let's just say that Wayne and Mitchum maintain their long established ways and director Howard Hawks knows his way around the action antics."

And while Britain's *Monthly Film Bulletin* enthused: "With Hawks, Wayne, Mitchum and scriptwriter Leigh Brackett all at the top of their form . . . . this is as good a Western as has been seen in years," Pauline Kael commented in *The New Republic* that "*El Dorado* combines Wayne and Mitchum, both looking exhausted. The director, Howard Hawks, is also tired, and like John Ford, he doesn't want to go on location."

Robert Mitchum's sole comment about *El Dorado:* "Great experience working for the first time with Duke Wayne."

In 1970, the Wayne/Hawks/Brackett combination did another twist on *Rio Bravo* and *El Dorado*, this time under the title *Rio Lobo*, with Wayne again playing the same lead character (called

Cord McNally, in this case), Mexican actor Jorge Rivero as the counterpart to Dean Martin/Robert Mitchum, Jack Elam standing in for Walter Brennan/Arthur Hunnicutt, and Robert Mitch-um's younger son, Chris, taking the Ricky Nelson/James Caan part. It was Howard Hawks's last film.

80
Anzio
(also called *The Battle for Anzio*)*
Columbia Pictures, 1968

With Peter Falk in *Anzio*.

THE CAST:

Dick Ennis, ROBERT MITCHUM; *Corporal Rabinoff*, Peter Falk; *Sergeant Stimler*, Earl Holliman; *Richardson*, Mark Damon; *Movie*, Reni Santoni; *Doyle*, Joseph Walsh; *Andy*, Thomas Hunter; *Cellini*, Giancarlo Giannini; *General Lesley*, Arthur Kennedy; *General Carson*, Robert Ryan; *General Marsh*, Anthony Steele; *General Starkey*, Patrick Magee; *General Howard*, Arthur Franz; *Emilia*, Elsa Albani; *Colonel Hendricks*, Wayde Preston; *Captain Burns*, Venantino Venantini; *Anna*, Annabella Andreoli; *Marshal Kesselring*, Wolfgang Preiss; *General Van MacKensen*, Tonio Selwart; *Diana*, Stefanella Giovannini; *Assunta*, Marcella Valeri; *Pepe*, Enzo Turco; *Raffaella*, Elisabeth Tompson; *Sniper*, Wolf Hollinger; *Neapolitan Street Hawker*, Dante Maggio; *Neapolitan Girls*, Vittoria Dal Verme, Giorgia Della Gusta, and Carmen Scrapitta; *English MP*, Tiberia Mitri.

A Dino De Laurentiis Production. *Producer*, Dino De Laurentiis; *Director*, Edward Dmytryk; *English Screenplay*, Harry A. L. Craig; *Based on the Novel Anzio by* Wynford Vaughan-Thomas; *Adaptation*, Frank De Felitta and Giuseppe Mangione; *Photography*, Giuseppe Rotunno; *Music*, Riz Ortolani; *Song* "This World Is Yours" by Riz Ortolani and Jerome Pomus; *Sung* by Jack Jones; *Art Director*, Luigi Scaccianoce; *Special Effects*, Walfrido Traversari; *Editors*, Alberto Gallitti and Peter Taylor. Panavision and Technicolor. Running time: 117 minutes.

With Arthur Kennedy and player in *Anzio*.

"Bob Mitchum Plays It Anti-War In 'Anzio' " read the headline over critic Wanda Hale's review in the New York *Daily News*. The film was the star's first "foreign" movie, i.e., made for an Italian

*Original Italian title: *Lo Sbarco di Anzio (The Anzio Landing)*.

With Earl Holliman in *Anzio*.

company with a basically European cast and crew. Mitchum alone had his name above the title, which, despite the ads, officially is *The Battle of Anzio,* and was reunited with director Edward Dmytryk* with whom he previously had made *Till the End of Time* (1946) and *Crossfire* (1947).

Mitchum stars as Dick Ennis, a battle-hardened journalist who lands with the Allied troops at Anzio on June 22, 1944. With a Ranger named Movie (Reni Santoni) and a Commando named Rabinoff (Peter Falk), Ennis drives all the way into Rome without confronting a single German. When they report that fact to General Lesly (Arthur Kennedy), he refuses to advance, suspecting an enemy trap, and instead concentrates on reinforcing his beachhead. Marshall Kesselring (Wolfgang Preiss), the German commander, takes advantage of this delay, and when Lesly

*Although Dmytryk is given official directing credit, Italian Film Production sources list veteran Duilio Coletti as director as well as author of the screenplay.

finally orders a raid on a strategic village, the Allied troops find the enemy awaiting. Ennis and others find themselves trapped behind the lines and stumble across a heavily fortified line that Kesselring is constructing.

After carefully working their way through the German lines, Ennis, Movie, and Sergeant Stimler (Earl Holliman) survive. (In one brief bit, Ennis plays dead in the middle of battle, lying on his back and smoking a cigarette, concluding, "They don't shoot at dead people.") Struggling back to the beach, they warn about the German's powerful Caesar Line enclosing the Allied position. Following a four month siege, the Anzio forces finally smash through the enemy lines and, after Lesly is relieved of command, they march victoriously into Rome. As he watches General Carson (Robert Ryan) play the conquering hero, Ennis turns away from the parade saddened and disillusioned by the incompetency that had led to so many deaths.

"*The Battle for Anzio* starts off on the wrong foot with a ludicrously irrelevant song [crooned by Jack Jones] behind the credits, and thereafter it hardly puts a foot right," critic David Wilson announced in Britain's *Monthly Film Bulletin*. And Vincent Canby, reviewing his first Mitchum movie for *The New York Times*, wrote that "Mitchum, who even here walks as if he'd just got off a horse, is the most unlikely war correspondent since Lana Turner covered the Japanese invasion of the Philippines in *Somewhere I'll Find You*.... Edward Dmytryk directed the movie with his usual style, which is so impersonal, so unimaginative, so predictable, so War Comics, as to be almost Hollywood Classic."

In the *New York Post*, Archer Winsten disagreed, noting that "the saga of these brave men led by the intrepid and knowledgeable Mitchum makes an exciting adventure in Hollywood's older tradition of war movies. . . . When you sit back and think about it, it does seem a bit thick to have Mitchum, hero of *G.I. Joe*, now equally heroic as an unarmed newspaper correspondent. But the part is well-written and well-acted." The reviewer for *Variety* stated, though, that "Anzio suffers from flat writing, stock performances, uninspired direction and dull pacing [and] Robert Mitchum stars in a cast that is far better in potential than in reality."

81
Five Card Stud
Paramount, 1968

THE CAST:

Van Morgan, DEAN MARTIN; *Jonathan Rudd,* ROBERT MITCHUM; *Lily Langford,* Inger Stevens; *Nick Evers,* Roddy McDowall; *Nora Evers,* Katherine Justice; *Marshall Al Dana,* John Anderson; *Mama Malone,* Ruth Springfield; *Little George,* Yaphet Kotto; *Sig Evers,* Denver Pyle; *Doc Cooper,* Whit Bissell; *Eldon Bates,* Ted DeCorsia; *Rowan,* Don Collier; *Mace Jones,* Roy Jenson; *Joe Hurley,* Bill Fletcher; *Stoney Burro,* Jerry Gatlin; *Fred Carson,* Boyd Morgan; *Frankie Rudd,* George Robotham.

A Hal Willis Production. *Producer,* Hal B. Wallis; *Associate Producer,* Paul Nathan; *Director,* Henry Hathaway; *Screenplay,* Marguerite Roberts; *Based on the Novel Glory Gulch by* Ray Gaulden; *Photography,* Daniel L. Fapp; *Music,* Maurice Jarre; *Title Song,* Maurice Jarre and Ned Washington; *Sung by* Dean Martin; *Art Director,* Walter Tyler; *Editor,* Warren Low. Technicolor. Running time: 103 minutes.

Reunited with director Henry Hathaway for the first time since *White Witch Doctor*, Mitchum portrays in *Five Card Stud* another murderous preacher who carries a pistol in a hollowed out Bible. Confronting costar Dean Martin at one point, he explains his calling: "Elected by God

and Mr. Colt. Samuel's his first name . . . sort of biblical." The film, adapted by Marguerite Roberts from Ray Gaulden's novel, *Glory Gulch*, is usually classified as a detective story in a western setting—or, as one critic saw it, Agatha Christie's *Ten Little Indians* gone sagebrush.

In *Five Card Stud* (his third film to open in Manhattan in as many weeks), Mitchum is a self-ordained minister who drifts into the Colorado gold rush town of Rincon and hangs his shingle outside the local church: "God's house—Jonathan Rudd, Caretaker." Shortly before, a poker game had ended when one of the players was found palming an ace. Professional gambler Van Morgan (Dean Martin) had been knocked out trying to save the stranger; the other five lynched the cheat. Morgan leaves town as the guntoting Rudd rides in, at about the same time as a houseful of girls, under the patronage of Lily Langford (Inger Stevens), offering shaves and haircuts in addition to other services. Within days, storekeeper Fred Carson (Boyd Morgan) is found smothered in his flour barrel and Stoney Burro (Jerry Gatlin), a cowpoke, strangled on

With Roddy McDowall in *Five Card Stud*.

With Dean Martin in *Five Card Stud*.

In *Five Card Stud*.

barbed wire. Both had been in on that fateful poker game. Little George (Yaphet Kotto), the bartender that night, goes to Denver to warn Morgan that someone may be out to kill every man who had held a hand.

Morgan rides back to town, and at a meeting of the survivors, Nick Evers (Roddy McDowall) suggests that the killer is an outsider and reveals he found fresh flowers on the grave of the lynched man. Later, Morgan discovers the next victim, Mace Jones (Roy Jenson), hanging from the church bell-rope. The whole town is now terrified, and a fourth victim is soon found: Joe Hurley (Bill Fletcher) has been strangled in the livery stable. Morgan continues to track the killer, only to find Little George knifed to death. This time, though, a clue was left behind, pointing to Rudd, whose brother had been the lynching victim. Rudd, it turns out, has been aided in his vengeance by Nick Evers. After Rudd discovers that his informer had been the ringleader at the hanging, however, he guns down Nick and goes after his last victim, Morgan. In the final shoot-out, Rudd is cut down by Morgan, who then rides off in search of another poker game.

Amid the various shootings, hangings, burnings, chokings, knifings, and frequent displays of fisticuffs, is woven a musical soundtrack laced, curiously, with a Russian sounding score by Maurice Jarre. The film also sports the inevitable title song, sung just as inevitably by Dean Martin.

In *The New York Times*, Vincent Canby noted that: "Since an audience knows from the beginning that Dean Martin cannot be the vengeance-seeking killer, what mystery the film possesses can be solved simply by interpreting the billing of the stars. Robert Mitchum is tough, laconic and quite good as the fire-and-brimstone preacher. . . . The almost continuous action of *Five Card Stud* is rough and explicit without in any way being tough or adult."

Archer Winsten, critic for the *New York Post*, called the film "a Western with five distinct advantages; to wit, Dean Martin at his most relaxed, Robert Mitchum at his, Roddy McDowall performing up a storm, director Henry Hathaway staging like the perfectionist he is, and a plot that not only boasts eleven killings but a working mystery as to the perpetrator of most of them."

And in *Monthly Film Bulletin*, reviewer Gavin Miller said: "Though marginally watchable, this is the sort of Western destined to sink without a trace beneath the surface of the mind after one leaves the cinema . . . the initial pleasure of seeing Mitchum repeat what might have been another *Night of the Hunter* quickly palls when we find that this hunter carries no wicked conviction, but, as they say, just models for it."

82
Villa Rides!
Paramount, 1968

THE CAST:

Pancho Villa, YUL BRYNNER; *Lee Arnold*, ROBERT MITCHUM; *Fierro*, CHARLES BRONSON; *Fina Gonzalez*, Grazia Buccella; *Urbina*, Robert Viharo; *Capt. Francisco Ramirez*, Frank Wolff; *General Huerta*, Herbert Lom; *Pres. Francesco Madero*, Alexander Knox; *Emilita*, Diana Lorys; *Don Luis Gonzalez*, Robert Carricart; *Colonel Fuentes*, Fernando Rey; *Lupita Gonzalez*, Regina de Julian; *Juan Gonzalez*, Antonio Ruiz; *Captain Herrera*, Andres Monreal; *Arnold's Girlfriend*, Jill Ireland; *Dave*, John Ireland.

Producer, Ted Richmond; *Director*, Buzz Kulik; *Screenplay*, Robert Towne and Sam Peckinpah; *Based on the Novel Pancho Villa by* William Douglas Lansford; *Photography*, Jack Hild-yard; *Music*, Maurice Jarre; *Art Director*, Ted Haworth; *Editor*, David Bretherton. Panavision and Technicolor. Running time: 125 minutes.

A rip-roaring adventure yarn, punctuated with a succession of battles, explosions, chases, and sadistic blood-lettings, all played against the well-worn Pancho Villa legend, presented Robert Mitchum as a gun-running aviator—the outsider who finds himself caught up in conflicting allegiances. Made in Spain by an American com-

With Robert Viharo, Yul Brynner, and Charles Bronson in *Villa Rides!*

pany, the film is snappily directed by Buzz Kulik from a screenplay by cult moviemaker Sam Peckinpah and writer Robert Towne (who subsequently made a name for himself with *The Last Detail* and *Chinatown* and Mitchum's later *The Yakuza*).

A bewigged Yul Brynner stars as Villa and Charles Bronson, on the eve of his superstar days, portrays one of Villa's sadistic lieutenants, who prides himself in gunning down three peasants with a single bullet. Mitchum is Lee Arnold, an American pilot who has been smuggling arms to General Huerta (Herbert Lom) in the latter's plot to seize the Mexican presidency. While waiting for his plane to be repaired following one of his missions, Arnold witnesses a brutal reprisal raid on a village loyal to Villa and his revolutionary government and soon finds himself a reluctant participant in Villa's movement—pressed into service at gunpoint as a one-man private air force.

With Charles Bronson and Grazia Buccella in *Villa Rides!*

203

With Yul Brynner in *Villa Rides!*

For Villa, Arnold first flies reconnaissance, and later drops bombs on enemy troops. Meanwhile, Huerta attempts to discredit Villa, unswervingly loyal to President Madero (Alexander Knox), by sending him on a suicide mission. In the assault on the heavily fortified insurrectionist city of Conejos, Villa's troops are decimated and abandoned by Huerta. With Arnold's aerial assistance however, Villa salvages a victory. Villa then is arrested by Huerta for disobeying orders. Huerta plans to remove Villa as a threat to his dictatorial ambitions by putting him before a firing squad.

Only the determined efforts of Villa's loyal Fierro (Charles Bronson) prevents the execution. Arnold, also imprisoned, blasts his way out of jail and escapes across the border to El Paso, where, sometime later, he is persuaded by Villa to help raise another army of liberation to overthrow Huerta, who has been installed as dictator.

Although an inscription among the credits, "Dedicated to Pancho Villa," was included by director Kulik (some say perversely), few critics lauded him for his screen tribute. A. H. Weiler commented in *The New York Times:* "Yul Brynner, Robert Mitchum, cavalry, politicos, and even the faint strains of 'La Cucaracha' fail to disguise the fact the *Villa Rides!* is simply a sprawling Western and not history [and] neither the imperturbable Mr. Mitchum, nor Mr. Brynner, as the stoically tough Villa . . . try to dig beneath the surface of the characters involved." In *New York Magazine,* Judith Crist admitted: "The violence goes beyond the shoot-'em-up routine . . . seldom have we watched Robert Mitchum get knocked down so often with so little effort . . . he's reached the point of seemingly counting to ten before talking, but considering the lines allotted him, a hundred would be a wiser figure."

Variety thought that the movie "is competently, if leisurely and routinely, directed by Buzz Kulik with the accent on violent death. . . . Mitchum, still a gutsy actor who commands attention just by being seen, takes the curse off some of the script by reacting in bewilderment to events." And reviewing in the New York *Daily News,* Kathleen Carroll gave the film two stars and said: "Robert Mitchum plays a Texas gunrunner who becomes Villa's one-man air force, apparently half asleep. One can't really blame Mitchum for dozing off. This is perhaps one of the most tiresome action movies on record."

83 Secret Ceremony

World Film Services Ltd./Universal, 1968

In *Secret Ceremony*.

THE CAST:

Leonora, ELIZABETH TAYLOR; *Cenci,* MIA FARROW; *Albert,* ROBERT MITCHUM; *Aunt Hannah,* Peggy Ashcroft; *Aunt Hilda,* Pamela Brown; *Dr. Stevens,* Michael Strong;* *Sir Alex Gordon,* Robert Douglas.*

A Paul M. Heller Production. *Producers,* John Heyman and Norman Priggen; *Director,* Joseph Losey; *Screenplay,* George Tabori; *Original Story,* Marco Denevi; *Photography,* Gerald Fisher; *Music,* Richard Rodney Bennett; *Music Director,* Marcus Dods; *Art Director,* John Clark; *Editor,* Reginald Beck. Technicolor. Running time: 109 minutes.

In Joseph Losey's bizarre psychological thriller, *Secret Ceremony,* Mitchum accepted special below-the-title billing! "I was in Mexico," Mitchum recalls, "and Losey got me on the phone. Could I do a certain kind of English accent? 'Hell, yes,' I told him. 'What do you want—north country, Cockney, Lancashire?' He told me he wanted a sort of transatlantic indifferent accent. I tried out a few on the phone and he asked me to play the role. They did some weird things with the script. They were in trouble when I got there, and I don't think I improved the situation any." He has only two or three scenes in the film, battling Elizabeth Taylor for Mia Farrow.

Written by George Tabori, the movie is based on a short story by Marco Denevi, an Argentinian civil service worker, who won $5,000 first prize for it in a magazine contest. When it got to television, however, it was somewhat cleansed for home viewing by having actors Michael Strong and Robert Douglas talk several connecting scenes to clear up its incoherency and changing Elizabeth Taylor's role from whore to seamstress. The theatrical version tells of a fading prostitute named Leonora (Taylor) who, one day, meets a sad-faced waif (Mia Farrow). Spotting a remark-

With Elizabeth Taylor in *Secret Ceremony.*

With Mia Farrow in *Secret Ceremony*.

able resemblance to her own deceased daughter, Leonora allows Cenci to take her home to a strange, opulent townhouse. There, Leonora learns that she, in turn, is almost the exact image of Cenci's dead mother; touched, she succombs to Cenci's wish that she live with her as her mother.

Though devoted to the childlike girl, Leonora also becomes fiercely possessive. Their harmony is disrupted, however, by a bearded stranger, Albert (Mitchum), who claims to be Cenci's stepfather and has been prowling around outside the girl's window for days. After Cenci then carefully makes it appear that she has been raped by Albert, Leonora takes the girl, feigning pregnancy, to a seaside hotel. Albert follows and tells Leonora that Cenci is a sexual psychotic who has repeatedly tried to seduce him. But when Leonora tries to force Cenci to face reality, the girl instead seeks out Albert on the beach, consummates her love for him, and then drives Leonora

away. Later, Leonora begs Cenci to resume their former relationship. Cenci, though, rejects her and swallows a lethal dose of sleeping pills. When Leonora and Albert meet in silence at Cenci's funeral, Leonora removes a knife and plunges it into Albert.

Mitchum later added an equally bizarre footnote: "Apparently after my ten days were finished, they took two scenes I was in and recast them with Elizabeth Taylor. You know that bathtub scene? In the script, I was in the bathtub with Mia—that scene where she's rubbing Elizabeth's back, licking her neck. In the script that was *my* back. Just after we made *Secret Ceremony*, lesbianism came in. Maybe that's why they reshot the scene. I'm no damned good as a lesbian. I'll play anything else, but not that."

Time wrote: "Confined to a few brief scenes, the bearded Robert Mitchum is little more than a cameo of a goat. The bloated, bejeweled Elizabeth

Taylor seems less a depleted call girl than a prosperous madam." *Variety* called the film "moody, leisurely developed and handsomely produced [and] the performances are generally good—Mia Farrow's via an emphasis on facial expressions, Elizabeth Taylor's via a salutary toning down of her shrieking-for-speaking tendencies, and Robert Mitchum's casual, solid projection."

In *Newsweek*, critic Raymond A. Sokolow found the movie "an ineffably silly story about nothing in particular except clothes and interior decoration. ... Mitchum looks like a highly credible satyr compared to [his costars'] lumbering antics." And in the New York *Daily News* was critic Wanda Hale's immortal line: "*Secret Ceremony* makes *Virginia Woolf* look like *Little Women*."

84
Young Billy Young

United Artists, 1969

With Angie Dickinson in *Young Billy Young.*

THE CAST:

Ben Kane, ROBERT MITCHUM; *Lily Beloit*, ANGIE DICKINSON; *Billy Young*, Robert Walker; *Jesse Boone*, David Carradine; *John Behan*, Jack Kelly; *Frank Boone*, John Anderson; *Charlie*, Paul Fix; *Doc Cushman*, Willis Bouchey; *Bell*, Parley Baer; *Gambler*, Bob Anderson; *Mexican Officer*, Rodolfo Acosta; *Evvie Cushman*, Deana Martin.

A Talbot/Youngstein Production. *Producer*, Max E. Youngstein; *Associate Producer*, J. Paul Papkin; *Director*, Burt Kennedy; *Screenplay*, Burt Kennedy; *Based on the Novel Who Rides with Wyatt by* Will Henry; *Photography*, Harry Stradling, Jr.; *Music*, Shelly Manne; *Title Song*, Shelly Manne and Ernie Sheldon; *Sung* by Robert Mitchum; *Art Director*, Stan Jolley; *Editor*, Otho Lovering. DeLuxe Color. Running time: 88 minutes.

The first of two westerns Mitchum made with director Burt Kennedy is a lackluster item that *Variety* might term "a standard oater." Made for his own Talbot Productions, it had him shepherding around the offspring of various screen veterans: Jennifer Jones's son, Robert Walker, in the title role; John Carradine's son, David (in his pre-*Kung Fu* days), playing an upstart young gunslinger; Dean Martin's daughter, Deana, as the love interest for Walker; and Bob Mitchum's

With Angie Dickinson in *Young Billy Young.*

With Robert Walker in *Young Billy Young.*

own son, Chris, as his film son during the flashbacks. Director Kennedy also wrote the screenplay, from Will Henry's novel, *Who Rides with Wyatt,* but kept the happenings light on the humor with which he had embellished previous westerns.

Somber was a more apt word for *Young Billy Young,* which opens with two young hired guns, Billy Young (Walker) and Jesse Boone (Carradine), returning from Mexico with a posse on their tail. When Billy's horse falls, Jesse abandons him, but he is rescued by Ben Kane (Mitchum). Kane is hunting for Frank Boone (John Anderson), who had killed Kane's son while making a jailbreak, and has accepted the marshal's job in Lordsburg as a way to get at Boone. In Lordsburg, dancehall girl Lily Belloit (Angie Dickinson) falls in love with Kane and warns him that town boss John Behan (Jack Kelly) and his associate, Frank Boone, are planning to kill him. Billy Young, having refused to become Kane's

deputy, changes his mind when Jesse, hired by Behan, tries to kill the new marshal. Kane arrests Jesse, at first unaware that he is Frank Boone's son. Then Kane realizes he has the decoy to make Boone confront him. Hoping to prevent a shooting, Billy frees Jesse, but when Boone and his men attack the jail, Kane locks Billy in a cell for his own protection and, in a desperate shootout, kills both Behan and Boone and recaptures Jesse. Kane then storms the saloon and carries off Lily, leaving Billy to mind the store as deputy marshal.

"The casual little Western," Howard Thompson said in *The New York Times,* "belongs in a television slot. It looks, plays and sounds exactly like an episode—a middling one—in a weekly series, running about an hour with time out for commercials. . . .The picture contains two casually expert performances by two professionals, namely Mitchum and young Walker." In the *New York Post,* reviewer Archer Winsten felt that

"[Mitchum] has never been more loftily, contemptuously confident. The whole show runs off like the 99th printing from the same stencil, but it's amazing how much of it Mitchum can make you believe anyway."

Less complimentary notices included Kevin Thompson's in his *Los Angeles Times* review, judging that Burt Kennedy "has allowed a leisurely pace to slip into downright lethargy, and this defect is compounded by a rather mechanical performance from Mitchum . . . the larger problem with the picture, however, is one of emphasis. Walker, a kind of surrogate son for Mitchum, does come of age under Mitchum's tough tutelage, but unfortunately, Kennedy shifts major attention to a cliche affair between Mitchum and perennial dance hall girl Angie

Dickinson." *San Francisco Chronicle* reviewer John L. Wasserman concluded that "the single distinction in *Young Billy Young* is that it is entirely without distinction—a conventional Western of 'B' stature . . . director-writer Burt Kennedy has made a completely straight-forward and tedious film about straight-forward and tedious people." And in the New York *Daily News* Ann Guarino wrote: "*Young Billy Young*, a routine Western, holds interest because of its cast. Robert Mitchum, still handsome, rides herd on the offspring of well-known actors."

Indeed, *Young Billy Young* will undoubtedly be remembered best for the fact that, in true Dean Martin fashion, Robert Mitchum warbles the title song over the film's credits.

85
The Good Guys and the Bad Guys

Warner Bros.—Seven Arts, 1969

With Lois Nettleton in *The Good Guys and the Bad Guys*.

THE CAST:

James Flagg, ROBERT MITCHUM; *Big John McKay,* GEORGE KENNEDY; *Waco,* David Carradine; *Carmel,* Tina Louise; *Mary Foster,* Lois Nettleton; *Grundy,* Douglas V. Fowley; *Ticker,* John Carradine; *Deuce,* John Davis Chandler; *Polly,* Marie Windsor; *Mayor Randolph Wilker,* Martin Balsam; *Howard Boyle,* Dick Peabody; *Mrs. Stone,* Kathleen Freeman; *Buckshot,* Jimmy Murphy; *Hawkins,* Garrett Lewis; *Engineer,* Nick Dennis; *Mrs. Pearce,* Dorothy Adams; *Reporter,* Governor David Cargo; *Townsman,* Buddy Hackett.

Executive Producer, Robert Goldstein; *Producers,* Ronald M. Cohen and Dennis Shryack; *Associate Producer,* Stan Jolley; *Director,* Burt Kennedy; *Screenplay,* Ronald M. Cohen and Dennis Shryack; *Photography,* Harry Stradling, Jr.; *Music,* William Lava; *Music Supervision,* Sonny Burke; *Song* "The Ballad of Marshal Flagg," William Lava and Ned Washington; *Sung* by Glen Yarbrough; *Art Director,* Stan Jolley; *Editors,* Howard Deane and Otho Lovering. Panavision and Technicolor. Running time: 98 minutes.

The various elements lacking in *Young Billy Young* were brought into focus for the second Robert Mitchum/Burt Kennedy western, a much more skillful blending of comedy and drama. *The Good Guys and the Bad Guys,* like Sam Peckinpah's unforgettable *Ride the High Country,* deals with a pair of old relics—two aging cowboys feeling both a sense of obsolescence and indignant scorn for the young ones who have taken their place.

The film is set in the new Old West—the early 1900s, when horses no longer have the main street to themselves. For twenty years, James Flagg (Mitchum) has been the marshal of Progress, but his talk of posses and outlaws now seem incongruous against the background of a modern town. Warned that his old adversary Big John McKay (George Kennedy) is headed for town with a mean-looking band of men, Flagg alerts

With Lois Nettleton and George Kennedy in *The Good Guys and the Bad Guys.*

Mayor Randolph Wilker (Martin Balsam) and proceeds to round up a posse. Instead, Wilker, pooh-poohing the emergency and wanting to play it safe in the upcoming election, retires Flagg. "They gave me a gold watch, a pat on the back, and a kick in the ass," he later complains.

Flagg, determined to settle an old score with McKay, sets out alone and finds his old enemy now simply an old-timer among a group of young outlaws led by Waco (David Carradine). When McKay refuses to gun down an unarmed Flagg, both men are left alone while the gang rides into Progress. Flagg and McKay soon start throwing punches and beat each other into exhaustion. They are found later and taken to the boarding house of Flagg's lady friend, Mary Foster (Lois Nettleton), where Flagg holds McKay prisoner.

Meanwhile, Waco and his men decide that the new bank looks too formidable and figure they'll rob the money while it is being unloaded from the train. Flagg, guessing what the gang has in mind, decides to board the train out of town and warn the engineer not to stop in Progress. McKay, now

his ally, accompanies him, but is recognized by the train's conductor, Tinker (John Carradine), who assumes that both he and Flagg are robbers and engages them in an outrageous gun battle. Meanwhile, the train cannonballs through Progress with the outlaws giving chase, and Wilker and the townspeople following by railroad handcar, on horseback, in wagons, and in sputtering automobiles, to help Flagg and McKay rout Waco and his gang. Flagg is then offered his badge again but refuses and leaves after advising his young replacement that he'll do all right as long as he learns to tell the good guys from the bad guys.

Critical notices for the lament for the Old West were, unfortunately, not as upbeat as they might have been. Best was Kathleen Carroll's report in the New York *Daily News:* "Mitchum and Kennedy are steamroller actors. At times, it seems that they don't play a part as much as they crush it. Yet they both have an easy-sell, genial quality that keeps you liking them all the while." Archer Winsten wrote in the *New York Post:* "The pic-

With Martin Balsam and Dick Peabody in *The Good Guys and the Bad Guys.*

ture's action is straight enough, but the characterizations and dialogue are much too broad when the actor's willing. . . . Mitchum restrains himself, but he can't keep the whole picture in line."

Most disappointed among the important papers was *The New York Times,* whose critic, Howard Thompson, complained: "There's nothing even mildly compelling about this anemic, fumbling and altogether aimless little exercise that soundly squanders some fetching color scenery and a trio of professionals like Robert Mitchum and two Oscar-winners, George Kennedy and Martin Balsam."

The western found a more receptive audience in Great Britain, and David Hutchison, writing in *Films and Filming,* called it "a skillful blending of comedy and drama in the best Burt Kennedy tradition . . . and the services of a talented cast combine to make a vastly enjoyable movie. . . . Burt Kennedy directs in fine style, expertly blending comedy and pathos as in the scene of Flagg's forceable retirement—aided by a fine piece of acting by Mitchum."

The Good Guys and the Bad Guys remains, to date, Mitchum's last western.

86
Ryan's Daughter

Metro-Goldwyn-Mayer, 1970

With Sarah Miles in *Ryan's Daughter*.

THE CAST:

Charles Shaughnessy, ROBERT MITCHUM; *Rosy Ryan*, SARAH MILES; *Father Collins*, TREVOR HOWARD; *Randolph Doryan*, CHRISTOPHER JONES; *Michael*, JOHN MILLS; *Tom Ryan*, Leo McKern; *Tim O'Leary*, Barry Foster; *McCardle*, Archie O'Sullivan; *Mrs. McCardle*, Marie Kean; *Moureen*, Yvonne Crowley; *Corporal*, Barry Johnson; *Driver*, Douglas Sheldon; *Paddy*, Philip O'Flynn; *Bernard*, Ed O'Callaghan; *Captain*, Gerald Sim; *Lanky Private*, Des Keogh; *O'Keefe*, Niall Toibin; *Moureen's Boyfriend*, Donal Meligan; *Constable O'Connor*, Brian O'Higgins; *Joseph*, Niall O'Brien; *Peter*, Owen O'Sullivan; *Sean*, Emmet Bergin; *Storekeeper*, May Cluskey; *Old woman*, Annie Dalton; *Policeman*, Pat Layde.

A Faraway Production for EMI. *Producer*, Anthony Havelock-Allan; *Associate Producer*, Roy Stevens; *Director*, David Lean; *Screenplay*, Robert Bolt; *Photography*, Freddie Young; *Music*, Maurice Jarre; *Assistant Directors*, Pedro Vidal and Michael Stevenson; *Second Unit Directors*, Roy Stevens (for the storm sequence) and Charles Frend; *Production Design*, Stephen Grimes; *Art Director*, Roy Walker; *Special Effects*, Robert MacDonald; *Second Unit Photography*, Denys Coop and Bob Huke; *Editor*, Norman Savage. Super Panavision 70 and Metrocolor. Running time: 206 minutes.

With Sarah Miles and Trevor Howard in *Ryan's Daughter*.

No Mitchum role better demonstrates his true versatility as an actor than that of Charles Shaughnessy, the gentle, diffident schoolteacher who marries *Ryan's Daughter*. His image-shattering performance in David Lean's over-blown romantic drama divided critics into various camps. One group hailed his portrayal as his finest; some ranked him among the truly great actors of the screen; others felt his was the only work 'in the film worth watching; and some dismissed him as being woefully miscast in his role.

Lean himself spent five years and many millions creating *Ryan's Daughter*. It was written by Lean's frequent collaborator, Robert Bolt, for Bolt's then-wife, Sarah Miles, ranks high in

With Sarah Miles in *Ryan's Daughter*.

Variety's list of all-time box-office champions, and remains one of MGM's perennial "filler" movies. Basically, it is a romantic triangle that unfolds amid the "troubles" in Ireland of 1915. Marrying a widowed schoolteacher (Mitchum) fifteen years her senior, Rosy Ryan (Sarah Miles) finds herself sexually frustrated at home and takes up with Randolph Doryan (Christopher Jones), a shell-shocked young British officer in command of a local garrison. Theirs is an ecstatic love affair that rapidly becomes the scandal of the village, and Rosy's husband is torn between leaving her and trying to nurse her through the affair. Father Collins (Trevor Howard), the local priest, admonishes her, and Michael (John Mills), the village idiot, fancies himself a potential suitor after observing how she moons over her crippled officer.

Meanwhile, a band of gunrunners, led by Tim O'Leary (Barry Foster), has been waiting for a promised arms shipment from Germany. When the cargo is endangered by a fierce storm, the entire village steals down to the beach to help with the rescue operation. On their way back, the villagers are confronted by Doryan's soldiers. Suspicion falls on Rosy as the betrayer because of her liaison with Doryan, and within hours of the arrests, she is dragged from her home, stripped, and shorn of her hair. Only the arrival of Father Collins prevents further violence.

Wandering the beach, Michael has collected the remains of the arms shipment and shows them to Doryan, who has learned that Rosy has returned to her husband. That night, the now distant Doryan commits suicide. Rosy and Michael decide to leave the village bound for Dublin and perhaps a reconciliation.

Ryan's Daughter remains a simple love story expanded cinematically to blockbuster proportions. Its plusses are the unusual casting of both

In *Ryan's Daughter*.

Robert Mitchum and the grotesquely made up John Mills (who won an Academy Award for his performance as the village idiot), the magnificent photography of Freddie Young (which also won an Oscar), and the stunning storm sequence, for which second-unit director Roy Stevens rightly is given credit.

Of Mitchum's performance in *Ryan's Duaghter*, these views represent the critical spectrum:

Roger Ebert, *Chicago Sun-Times:* "The performances largely survive the film's visual overkill. Robert Mitchum is splendid as the schoolteacher, and you realize once again what a fine actor he is. He's the only American in the cast,* yet paradoxically he seems the most Irish."

Judith Crist, *New York Magazine:* "One of the most satisfying films of the year. . . . Robert Mitchum, in his finest performance in many years, portrays the schoolteacher, a calm man of sentiment and devotion, devoid of sexual prowess, but aware of the kindness of loving."

Derek Malcolm, *The Guardian:* "Had it not been for the presence—and the word is absolutely apposite—of Robert Mitchum, I do not believe there would have been a film at all. Everyone else acts like Trojans. . . . Mitchum is simply and gloriously himself in spite of everything—one of the most powerful and expressive nonactors in the business. Even when off screen . . . he casts a shadow. It makes everyone else, not least David Lean, look small."

Pauline Kael, *The New Yorker:* "Mitchum is

*If one overlooks costar Christopher Jones.

trying to be unsexy and self-effacing; at first he just naturally livens up the movie, but then he becomes as dull as his role. . . . [He] has such immense camera presence not just because he's a natural and original actor but because his cynicism is there in the droopy eyelids and the great, reptilian face. To use him in a Herbert Marshall/John Forsythe-type role is to cancel him out. Sure we'd rather watch him than Forsythe, but Bolt and Lean ought to recognize that if they have to try to make a role more interesting by casting an actor against the grain, it's because of a failure in conception."

Vincent Canby, *The New York Times:* "Mr. Lean's casting of Mr. Mitchum as Rosy's nice, solemn, quite prissy husband is a terrible mistake. No matter how he tries—and he is a good, intelligent actor, Mr. Mitchum simply can't convince us that's less interesting than Mr. Jones' bland British major."

Louise Sweeney, *Christian Science Monitor:* "Robert Mitchum is cast counter to his screen image . . . it doesn't quite work, although it's a thoughtful performance."

Director David Lean has said: "I cast Mitchum as the weak schoolteacher precisely because he is such a strong personality." Mitchum himself calls the movie "really David's love affair with Ireland," and admits: "My performance was fine, but my character, my nature, lacked much definition. . . . It's a film I can talk about without embarrassment, but I don't know whether I'll be able to sit through it. I might get a cramp in my butt."

87
Going Home
Metro-Goldwyn-Mayer, 1971

THE CAST:

Harry K. Graham, ROBERT MITCHUM; *Jenny,* Brenda Vaccaro; *Jimmy Graham,* Jan-Michael Vincent; *Jimmy (aged 6),* Jason Bernard; *Ann Graham,* Sally Kirkland; *Bible Man,* Joe Attles; *Mr. Katz,* Lou Gilbert; *Bonelli,* Josh Mostel; *Betsy,* Barbara Brownell; *Ella,* Carol Gustafson; *Sailors,* David Wilson, Glenn Walken, Clay Watkins, and Bruce Kornbluth;

Angry Man, Louis Criscuolo; *Pleasant Man,* Richard Goode; *Hippie Girl,* Vicki Sue Robinson; *Pass Clerk,* Lawrence E. Bender; *Bowling Alley Drunks,* Tim Wallace and Jules Sicilia; *Malloy,* George Mathews; *Real Estate Lady,* Mary Louise Wilson; *Lady in Nursery,* Ann Thomas; *Sergeant,* George DiCenzo; *Mother at Prison,* Hope Clarke; *Portman,* William K. Leech; *Nightclub Entertainers,* Lynn Terry and Ben Terry; *Waitress,* Shari Marcell; *Friends at Beach,* Hank Luba, Edward

Steinfeld, Jack C. Harper, and Ginny Heller; *Girl at Trailer Park*, Paula Swart; *Mechanic*, William R. Tebbs; *Girl at Prison*, Carol Wilkerson; *Girl at Party*, Winkie Miller; *Bowler*, Robert Rinier.

A Herbert B. Leonard/Talbot Production. *Producer/Director*, Herbert B. Leonard; *Associate Producers*, Stanley Neufeld and Nicky Blair; *Screenplay*, Lawrence B. Marcus; *Photography*, Fred Jackman; *Music*, Bill Walker; *Assistant Directors*, Howard W. Koch, Jr., and Don Klune; *Action Sequences Coordinator*, Max Kleven; *Art Director*, Peter Wooley; *Editor*, Sigmund Neufeld. Metrocolor. Running time: 97 minutes (originally 118 minutes).

Mitchum returned to films following the surprisingly brief "retirement" he had announced after making *Ryan's Daughter*, and starred in an offbeat, original drama, *Going Home*, which unfortunately fell under the shears of a new management team then assuming control of MGM. The film, marking the directorial debut of television producer Herbert B. Leonard, confirmed further the growing appreciation among even the most jaded critics of Mitchum's abilities as an actor.

Going Home opens with a brutal, drunken killing by Harry K. Graham (Mitchum) of his wife Ann (Sally Kirkland), as witnessed by their six-year-old son. Harry is sent to prison and the boy is shunted from orphanage to foster homes. Years later, nineteen-year-old Jimmy Graham (Jan-Michael Vincent) sets out to find his father, motivated by a mixture of love and hatred and groping for his root. Learning that his father has been paroled and is living in a New Jersey seaside resort, Jimmy hitchhikes to the shoddy town and finds that Harry is intent on breaking away from the past and making a new life for himself. He works as a handyman and is courting a nice, earthy divorcée, Jenny (Brenda Vaccaro). After an initially strained reunion, a now mellower Harry invites his son to move in with him and Jenny, and the father and son try to find a common basis for a relationship.

Jimmy's frustration and hostility intensify, however, and he tries to provoke Harry into a confrontation, first by reporting his father's presence to the local police and later by scrawling on the wall of a gas station rest room, "Beware of Harry Graham who killed his wife." Jenny becomes annoyed at Jimmy's taunting gestures and orders him away from Harry. He retaliates by raping her and then, distraut, drives off to his dead mother's house, which he finds has become a bordello. He telephones Harry from the house and begs for a confrontation. When Harry arrives

With Sally Kirkland in *Going Home*.

With Jan-Michael Vincent in *Going Home*.

215

With Brenda Vaccaro in *Going Home*.

and hears his son's confession, he beats the boy to the ground but refrains from losing his temper completely. Jimmy still pleads to know why Harry had killed his mother. "I was drunk," Harry tells him. Jimmy then wants to know what happens next. Before driving off, Harry says, "*You* get to be twenty."

"If an actor has any screen presence at all, his ego usually shows; you know he thinks well of himself," Pauline Kael wrote in *The New Yorker*. "Robert Mitchum has that assurance in such large amounts that he seems almost a lawless actor.... There's no other powerhouse like Mitchum. This great bullfrog with the puffy eyes and the gut that becomes an honorary chest has been in movies for almost thirty years, and he's still so strong a masculine presence that he knocks younger men off the screen.... He can barrel his way through, as he does in *Going Home*, even when the role isn't worth playing."

Roger Ebert, critic for the *Chicago Sun-Times*, felt that "*Going Home* is a fairly awful melodrama that's worth seeing primarily for the presence of Robert Mitchum. ... Someone was remarking the other day that Mitchum had never been in a really great film ... he's been in some good films but nothing really great. Yet he remains the favorite movie star of a lot of people (myself probably included) and he is able to make a bad movie interesting."

Variety called the movie "a most unusual and intriguing contemporary melodrama [and] Robert Mitchum in an offbeat role gives an excellent performance ... one of his finest achievements. ... [He] presents a characterization that combines a wide range of acting talents. It would be proper in the next couple of months for his fellow performers to take note of this film. Very few of his contemporaries, and fewer of his followers, have even ventured so far and so effectively from a cliche screen image."

Wanda Hale hailed in the New York *Daily News:* "Mitchum's extraordinary performance of an ordinary man is one of the best performances of the year . . . one of the best things Robert Mitchum has ever done, pro through and through." And Archer Winsten described the film as "a tribute to the performance and personality of Mitchum."

On the negative side, Vincent Canby reported in *The New York Times* that *Going Home* is "an exceedingly nasty movie . . . more objectionable, more pervicious, than other much dumber movies because it appears to have some surface intelligence. . . . Mitchum has reached that point in his career where he doesn't seem to act as much as inhabit whatever film he's in, whatever role he's playing." Arthur Cooper, reviewing for *Newsweek*, found *Going Home* "a dreary film that wastes commendable performances by Robert Mitchum and Brenda Vaccaro. . . . Mitchum looks weary and exhausted—he seems to know he has as much chance in this movie as a man trying to bowl duck pins with a dried pea." And Jay Cocks, in *Time*, felt: "Mitchum is somnolent as usual. It is often said that Mitchum is a fine actor who has seldom had a role to really challenge him. He has been extraordinary at least twice: as the deranged preacher in Charles Laughton's *The Night of the Hunter* and as the inebriated deputy in Howard Hawks' *El Dorado*. In his multitude of other roles, he has mostly looked sullen and talked tough; one has the sense, watching him, that he thinks acting is a hell of a way for a man to earn a living."

It was a *Time* report that exposed MGM president James Aubrey's decision to lop twenty-one minutes from the film, toning down the climactic rape sequence and deleting a nude scene involving Jan-Michael Vincent and Sylvia Miles, as a frustrated housewife. Director Herbert B. Leonard then took out trade ads denouncing the studio's treatment and claimed that "[Aubrey] unilaterally and arbitrarily raped the picture."

88
The Wrath of God

Metro-Goldwyn-Mayer, 1972

With Ken Hutchison and Victor Buono in *The Wrath of God.*

THE CAST:

Van Horne, ROBERT MITCHUM; *Tomas De La Plata,* FRANK LANGELLA; *Senora De La Plata,* RITA HAYWORTH; *Colonel Santilla,* John Collicos; *Jennings,* Victor Buono; *Emmet Keogh,* Ken Hutchison; *Chela,* Paula Pritchett *Jurado,* Gregory Sierra; *Moreno,* Frank Ramirez; *Nacho,* Enrique Lucero; *Cordona,* Jorge Russek; *Antonio,* Chano Urueta; *Pablito,* Jose Luis Parades; *Senora Moreno,* Aurora Clavel, *Delgado,* Victor Eberg; *Tacho,* Pancho Cordova; *Diaz,* Guillermo Hernandez.

A Ralph Nelson Film for Rainbow Productions and Cineman Films. *Executive Producer,* Peter Katz; *Producer/Director,* Ralph Nelson; *Associate Producer,* William S. Gilmore, Jr.; *Screenplay,* Ralph Nelson; *Based on the Novel by* James Graham; *Photography,* Alex Phillips, Jr.; *Music,* Lalo Schifrin; *Assistant Directors,* Mario Cisneros and Jerry Ziesmer; *Art Director,* John S. Poplin, Jr.; *Special Effects,* Federico Farfan; *Editors,* J. Terry Williams, Richard Bracken, and Albert Wilson. Panavision and Metrocolor. Running time: 111 minutes.

With Rita Hayworth and Gregory Sierra in *The Wrath of God.*

As in both *The Night of the Hunter* and *Five Card Stud,* Robert Mitchum once again portrayed a self-styled arms-toting preacher in *The Wrath of God,* a solid action adventure played initially tongue-in-cheek but later filled increasingly with violent symbolism. Set during a Latin American rebellion of the late 1920s, it boils down to a variant on the standard western, with a rugged renegade priest standing in for the lonesome cowboy hero here and mythical south-of-the-border rebels for the villainous cattlemen. Mitchum, machine gun ablaze, dominated the film's ad campaign and was accorded sole, above-the-title billing. The movie, his first for director Ralph Nelson, reunited him with Rita Hayworth (as an evil tyrant's still-beautiful mother).

The Wrath of God finds three foreigners involved in a Central American revolution. Irishman-on-the-run Emmet Keogh (Ken Hutch-

ison) is tricked by British profiteer Jennings (Victor Buono) into running bootleg whisky across the border. After rescuing Chela (Paula Prichett), a mute Indian girl, Keogh encounters Father Van Horne (Mitchum), a defrocked, cigar-chomping priest who carries a pistol in his Bible, a knife in his crucifix, and a tommygun in the back seat of his roadster. Captured by Colonel Santilla (John Collicos), the foreign trio are told that in return for their freedom, they must assassinate Tomas de la Plata (Frank Langella), the mentally unbalanced feudal overlord of the tiny village of Mojada.

Keogh and Jennings infiltrate the village disguised as mining engineers, while Van Horne ingratiates himself with the peasants by performing the various sacraments denied them by the tyrannical de la Plata. For this the overlord has the priest taken into custody and strapped with

With Frank Langella in *The Wrath of God*.

In *The Wrath of God*.

barbed wire to a stone cross. Finally, Senora de la Plata (Rita Hayworth) admits to her son's madness and mortally wounds him. In the ensuing battle, Van Horne and Jennings both die, but Keogh survives when Chela warns him about an assassin's bullet.

Critics and moviegoers alike were mystified by whatever message writer/director Ralph Nelson was trying to convey. "Ralph Nelson," Judith Crist concluded in *New York Magazine*, "feels apparently there's gold to be mined via Robert Mitchum as an embittered priest turned hard-drinking, roistering conman in the guise of priest," but found the film yielded only "intolerable nonsense right off the cliche assembly line." Critic Kevin Thomas thought, in the *Los Angeles Times*, that "*The Wrath of God* is trash ... a hypocritical, brutalizing cartoon of a film, [it] makes fun of much of the very violence it ostensibly deplores."

Kathleen Carroll wrote in the New York *Daily News:* "Mitchum, as usual, shows his boredom. Delivering lines with all the emotion of a punch-drunk fighter, he makes you aware he considers the whole thing beneath him." And in *The New*

York Times, reviewer Roger Greenspun considered that "with so much junk in one pile, it would be sad indeed if there weren't a little quality at the edges. And as in all the Ralph Nelson films I have ever seen, that quality rests in the exuberance of the performance. . . . The cast is most excellent. Not only Mitchum and the fine Ken Hutchison . . . but also the countless revolutionaries who die like flies, or praise the Lord, or even dance in the streets when the crazy screenplay calls for it."

In the *Chicago Sun Times*, Roger Ebert observed that "there are a lot of things hard to figure out about *The Wrath of God*," but called the film "a simple, dashing tale told for sheer fun."

Mitchum's best notice this time out came from *Variety*, which said: "Very few film players can project the necessary toughness/tenderness which Mitchum herein has been able to do. . . . While [he] is one of the few remaining established male starts to have the guts to essay a broad spectrum of roles—not always successfully—in his long career, the casting here is relatively close to his primary image among audiences of all ages [and] his presence is felt throughout."

89
The Friends of Eddie Coyle

Paramount, 1973

With Jane House in *The Friends of Eddie Coyle*.

THE CAST:

Eddie Coyle, ROBERT MITCHUM; *Dillon*, Peter Boyle; *Dave Foley*, Richard Jordan; *Jackie Brown*, Steven Keats; *Scalise*, Alex Rocco; *Artie Van*, Joe Santos; *Waters*, Mitchell Ryan; *Partridge*, Peter MacLean; *Manager of Second Bank*, Kevin O'Morrison; *Vernon*, Marvin Lichterman; *Nancy*, Carolyn Pickman; *The Man's Contact Man*, James Tolkan; *Andrea*, Margaret Ladd; *Pete*, Matthew Cowles; *Sheila Coyle*, Helena Carroll; *Wanda*, Jane House; *The Kid*, Michael McCleery; *Phil*, Alan Koss; *Webber*, Dennis McMullen; *Mrs. Partridge*, Judith Ogden Cabot; *Pale Kid*, Jan Egleson; *The Beard*, Jack Kehoe; *Moran*, Robert Anthony; *Ames*, Gus Johnson; *Sauter*, Ted Maynard; *Ferris*, Sheldon Feldner.

Producer, Paul Monash; *Director*, Peter Yates; *Screenplay*, Paul Monash; *Based on the Novel by* George V. Higgins; *Photography*, Victor J. Kemper; *Music*, Dave Grusin; *Assistant Directors*, Peter Scoppa and Sal Scoppa; *Art Director*, Gene Callahan; *Editor*, Pat Jaffe. Panavision and Technicolor. Running time: 102 minutes.

In his finely-etched portrait of an aging, small-time hood named Eddie Coyle, Robert Mitchum offered another remarkable acting lesson. The film, directed on location in Boston and vicinity by Peter Yates, interlocked a character study of a tired, old-line gunrunner trying to provide for his wife and children, and a conventional caper movie about an intricately planned and executed bank robbery.

The "friends" of the title are Eddie's contacts in the underworld and various partners in crime. Aware that time is running out for him, Eddie grinds out a living on the fringes of the underworld, doing free-lance dirty work—selling guns, running contraband across state lines—to keep his family from going on welfare. Facing imminent sentencing for a New Hampshire arrest, he sees a way to possibly beat the rap by doing some informing to the federal agents. Both Eddie and his "friend," Dillon (Peter Boyle), an ex-con bartender, deal with treasury agent Dave Foley

(Richard Jordan), an ambitious young investigator. To Eddie, he promises a favorable word to the court; to Dillon, the deal is strictly cash.

Eddie works as a middle-man in the gun business, buying from Jackie Brown (Steven Keats), a brash, wary newcomer, and selling to Scalise (Alex Rocco), leader of a gang of bank robbers. When Jackie arranges to sell machine guns to two young dropouts, Eddie warns Foley, whose agents nab Jackie. Foley then tells Eddie that his chances with the court will be better if he continues to cooperate, and Eddie decides to betray Scalise. But Scalise and his gang are picked up on someone else's tip, though the underworld still thinks Eddie is the squealer. A contract for his execution is passed on to Dillon, who invites Eddie to a hockey game, gets him drunk, and then professionally murders him. At their next meeting, Foley thanks Dillon for the tip leading to Scalise's arrest, and promises not to pressure for information about Eddie Coyle's killing.

"There's more than mere looks to Robert Mitchum's performance as Eddie Coyle," Richard Schickel wrote in *Time*. "Now, at last, Mitchum achieves a kind of apothesis. . . . Self-consciously, with an old pro's quiet skills, Mitchum explores all of Coyle's contradictory facets. At 56, when many of his contemporaries are hiding out behind the remnants of their youthful images, he has summoned up the skill, the courage to demonstrate a remarkable range of talents." *Variety* called the movie "superior underworld melodrama" and said that "Mitchum is one of the more underrated actors in films, to the extent that his recent forays into unusual characterizations have been grossly overlooked by his peers. His latest role herein is another excellent achievement." And William Wolfe, cri-

With Peter Boyle in *The Friends of Eddie Coyle*.

With Steven Keats in *The Friends of Eddie Coyle*.

tic for *Cue,* decided that "Robert Mitchum gives his best performance in years as Coyle."

Judith Crist found the film "a disappointment [though] Robert Mitchum, as Coyle, gives, for example, a taut, terse portrait of a tired, aging hood," while Jerry Oster, reviewing *The Friends of Eddie Coyle* for the New York *Daily News,* concluded of Mitchum: "He must be tired. And worse, he seems to have infected his colleagues with his lack of enthusiasm, for this is his most listless movie."

Mitchum's own appraisal was, as expected, self-deprecating: "When I was getting ready for this picture, I went to the barber to get an Eddie Coyle sort of haircut. I told him to cut it short but not too short. If someone says I give a good performance, you just tell them it's the haircut."

90
The Yakuza
Warner Bros., 1975

With Brian Keith in *The Yakuza.*

THE CAST:

Harry Kilmer, ROBERT MITCHUM; *Tanaka Ken,* TAKAKURA KEN; *George Tanner,* BRIAN KEITH; *Oliver Wheat,* Herb Edelman; *Dusty,* Richard Jordan; *Tanaka Eiko,* Kishi Keiko; *Tono Toshiro,* Okada Eiji; *Goro,* James Shigeta; *Kato Jiro,* Kyosuke Mashida; *Spider,* Go Eiji; *Hanako,* Christina Kokubo; *Louise Tanner,* Lee Chirillo; *Boyfriend,* M. Hisaka; *Tanner's Bodyguard,* William Ross; *Tono's Bodyguard,* Akiyama; *Goro's Doorman,* Harada.

Executive Producer, Shundo Koji; *Producer/Director,* Sidney Pollack; *Co-Producer,* Michael Hamilburg; *Screenplay,* Paul Schrader and Robert Towne; *Story,* Leonard Schrader; *Photography,* Okazaki Kozo and (American sequences) Duke Callaghan; *Music,* Dave Grusin; *Art Director,* Ishida Yoshiyuki; *Second Unit Director and Production Design,* Stephen Grimes; *Assistant Directors,* D. Michael Moore and Mike Abe; *Special Effects,* Richard Parker and Kasai Tomoo; *Editors,* Frederic Steinkamp, Thomas Stanford, and Don Guidice. Panavision and Technicolor. Running time: 112 minutes.

The Yakuza was an ambitious attempt to introduce to international audiences a Japanese film genre that transposed the strict ethical codes and violence of samurai movies into a modern setting. The Yakuza—accent on the first syllable—are roughly the Japanese equivalent of the Mafia, although this pictorially striking American-Japanese co-production unsuccessfully tried to sort out the interlacing of organized crime, Oriental ritual, and interracial romance to offer a

With Takakura Ken in *The Yakuza.*

With Kishi Keiko in *The Yakuza*.

traditional gangster film of universal appeal.

Robert Mitchum was accorded solo billing above the title, while international movie fans were introduced to Takakura Ken, one of Japan's leading stars and his country's equivalent to Mitchum. The nearly ten million dollars said to have been invested in this project seemed a gross overpayment judging by the final product, although Mitchum probably took a large salary and apparently two complete screenplays were purchased ($300,000, according to *Newsweek*, went to Paul Schrader for his scenario from his brother's original story, and thousands more to Robert Towne for his rewrite).

The confusing and diffused film begins when shipping magnate George Tanner (Brian Keith) asks old friend Harry Kilmer (Mitchum) to rescue his daughter, Louise (Lee Chirillo), kidnapped by Yakuza chieftain Tono Toshiro (Okada Eiji), in an argument over an arms deal. Kilmer reluctantly flies to Tokyo in the company of Tanner's bodyguard, Dusty (Richard Jordan), and moves in with Oliver Wheat (Herb Edelman), an expatriate friend. Kilmer then looks up Tanaka Eiko (Kishi Keiko), his one great love; their postwar romance had been destroyed by the disapproval of her brother, Tanaka Ken (Takakura Ken). The spark, Kilmer finds, is still there, and her young daughter, Hanako (Christina Kokubo), has grown into a beautiful teenager and holds Kilmer in reverent respect.

Eiko agrees to put him in touch with Tanaka Ken, a former Yakuza who has put away his sword and now runs a "kendo" school. Acknowledging his long-time debt to Kilmer for helping Eiko during the occupation, Ken agrees to help rescue Louise Tanner. Their plan backfires, though and several of Tono's men are killed. Ken's older brother, Goro (James Shigeta), arbiter of the Yakuza code of honor, tells Kilmer that Tono will seek revenge on Ken for his part in the affair, and suggests that Kilmer may wish to help his friend. Meanwhile, with his daughter back, Tanner agrees to doublecross Kilmer by allowing

In *The Yakuza*.

the society to kill him. Tono's men attack Wheat's house, and in the ensuing fight with swords and guns, Dusty and Eiko's daughter Hanako are killed. Kilmer responds by shooting Tanner and, spurred by Goro's revelation that Eiko is in fact Ken's wife, pursuades Ken to allow him to join in an attack on Tono.

The two burst into Tono's heavily guarded mansion, and though outnumbered twenty to one, they embark on a murderous orgy, killing all the guards, Tono himself, and Goro's wayward son, Spider (Go Eiji). For killing Spider and violating an oath made to Goro, Ken sacrifices his little finger as penance. Kilmer too realizes that he must atone for the wrong he had done to Ken by living with his wife, so he slices his finger into a white handkerchief and then departs for Los Angeles with Ken's life-long respect.

Rex Reed raved over *The Yakuza*, calling it "an exciting, riveting, totally original motion picture that left me numb. . . . Robert Mitchum looks as ravaged as a bomb site in Hiroshima, as sleepy as a wombat, and as gloriously bigger than life as the Imperial Hotel . . . [his] final act of allegiance is as moving a scene as anything I've seen played between two men in conflict in the history of movies. . . . It is an enormously complex film but I urge you to see it and experience a truly unique cinematic revelation."

Similarly as enthusiastic was Judith Crist, writing in *New York Magazine* that the film was "as absorbing and satisfying as the best of Kurosawa's samurai dramas [and] a uniquely satisfying thriller. . . . Mitchum, looking his age, and angry as ever, goes beyond the macho moments to exhaustion and to a subtle depth of feeling. His scenes with Kishi Keiko . . . have a tender maturity to their silences and appreciations." And in *The New Yorker*, Pauline Kael gave her blessings: "Mitchum's massive head has grown, his face sunk—and he looks great. He doesn't look as if he regretted a wrinkle. He seems to be the only movie star who's becoming a more commanding figure as he ages."

"A cinematic hybrid" is how Lawrence Van Gelder described the film in *The New York Times*. "To come upon it unsuspecting is a little like opening an Almond Joy wrapper and finding inside the arrangement of fish, rice and seaweed known as norimaki. Neither fans of Almond Joy nor of norimaki are likely to be wholly satisfied by *The Yakuza*, but those who don't mind sampling both won't go away famished." In *Newsweek*, Paul D. Zimmerman inscribed: "Imagine *The Big Sleep* shot in the back alleys of modern Tokyo, and you have something of the muddled mood of *The Yakuza*, a cultural cross-breed that is neither suski or Southern-fried chicken. . . . Looking as menacing as a middle linebacker and doing his weary-warrier turn with a nice tension beneath his turtle-necked exterior, Mitchum is backed up by a lot of expensive talent but all this money didn't buy a single witty line or belly-laugh. . . . *The Yakuza* was lavishly financed because of its potential appeal to two audiences—mystery mavens and kung-fu freaks. Instead, it delivers half a film to each."

Jerry Oster, of the New York *Daily News*, begrudgingly gave *The Yakuza* a lonely two stars, and wrote: "For a gangster picture, it is splendidly inert. It takes forever to start and forever to end . . . and winds up as a long, muddled middle. . . . The characters are reduced to anthropologists and the dialogue sounds like the spiel of a tour bus guide."

91
Farewell, My Lovely

Avco-Embassy, 1975

THE CAST:

Philip Marlowe, ROBERT MITCHUM; *Helen Grayle*, CHARLOTTE RAMPLING; *Lt. Nulty*, JOHN IRELAND; *Jessie Florian*, SYLVIA MILES; *Laird Brunette*, Anthony Zerbe; *Billy Rolfe*, Harry Dean Stanton; *Moose Malloy*, Jack O'Halloran; *Nick*, Joe Spinell; *Jonnie*, Sylvester Stallone; *Frances Amthor*, Kate Murtagh; *Lindsay Marriott*, John O'Leary; *Tommy Ray*, Walter McGinn; *Judge Baxter Wilson Grayle*, Jim Thompson; *Cowboy*, Burton Gilliam; *Georgie*, Jimmy Archer; *Roy*, Ted Gehring; *Commissioner*, Logan Ramsey; *Woman*, Margie Hall; *Louis Levine*, Jack Bernardi; *Patron in Pool Hall*, Ben Ohta; *Fence*, Jerry Fujikawa; *Detectives*, Richard Kennedy, John O'Neill, and Mark Allen; *Mulatto Child*, Andrew Harris; *Hotel Clerk*, Napoleon Whiting; *Butler*, John Eames; *Doris*, Rainbeaux Smith; *First Man*, Stu Gilliam; *Second Man*, Roosevelt Pratt: *Bouncer*, Dino Washington; *Bartender*, Harry Caesar; *Hood*, Bill Gentry; *Waiter*, Cory B. Shiozaki; *Girl*, Noelle Worth; *Father*, Wally Berns; *Mother*, Lola Mason; *Woman in Ballroom*, Joan Shawlee; *Singer*, Edra Gale; *Prostitute*, Karen Gaston.

An E. K./ITC Production. *Executive Producers*, Elliott Kastner and Jerry Bick; *Producers*, George Pappas and Jerry Bruckheimer; *Director*, Dick Richards; *Screenplay*, David Zelag; *Based on the Novel by* Raymond Chandler; *Photography*, John A. Alonzo; *Music*, David Shire; *Art Director*, Angelo Graham; *Production Design*, Dean Tavoularis; *Assistant Directors*, Henry Lange, Jr., and David O. Sosna; *Editors*, Walter Thompson and Joel Cox. Panavision and Technicolor. Running time: 96 minutes.

Farewell, My Lovely remains, in the mid-1970s, vintage Raymond Chandler, high quality Philip Marlowe, and definitive Robert Mitchum. Marlowe, in fact, is a role Mitchum should have played two decades earlier as many astute critics pointed out. In 1975, Mitchum put his Marlowe interpretation on the screen. Few were disappointed.

Under the direction of television commercials-turned-theatrical-movie-maker Dick Richards, Mitchum became the personification of Chandler's Marlowe in his longest role in years. He followed a long line of screen and television Marlowes,* but can be compared to none because of his unique artistry and seemingly effortless way in creating a sense of déjà vu. As Marlowe, Mitchum keeps a cherished screen genre—the private-eye film—gloriously alive.

In the incarnation devised by screenwriter David Zelag Goodman, Mitchum's Marlowe is the most violent, though the script basically follows Chandler's 1940 novel (his second Marlowe book). From his hotel room, Marlowe telephones his old friend, Lt. Nulty (John Ireland), of the Los Angeles police. There have been seven unsolved murders and the cops, needing a fall guy, have elected Marlowe. The detective, though, wants to explain his recent activities. He had been hired by a giant lug named Moose Malloy (Jack O'Halloran), an ex-con, to find Moose's girlfriend, Velma "a babe as cute as lace pants." Moose has not seen her since entering prison seven years earlier. The two go first to Florian's saloon where Velma had worked as a singer. When the manager pulls a gun, Moose twists his arm and the poor guy shoots himself. Marlowe suggests that Moose lose himself before he can be collared for a parole violation, and when Nulty arrives, Marlowe tells him that the guy responsible for the manager's demise is his client and that the killing was in self-defense.

Determined to find Velma, Marlowe locates Tommy Ray (Walter McGinn), who had led the band when Velma sang at Florian's. Tommy directs Marlowe to Florian's alcoholic widow (Sylvia Miles, in an Oscar-nominated performance). Several days later, Marlowe is hired to accompany Lindsay Marriott (John O'Leary), to a canyon rendezvous where he is to buy back a stolen jade necklace. At the designated location, Marlowe is knocked unconscious, and later awakens to find Marriott dead. An investigation into wealthy jade collectors brings Marlowe to the home of Judge Lew Lockridge Grayle (Jim Thompson), a powerful political figure in his sixties. Grayle denies owning the necklace, but his much younger wife (Charlotte Rampling) admits to being a friend of Marriott's and hires Marlowe to find his killer.

*Dick Powell in *Murder My Sweet*, Humphrey Bogart in *The Big Sleep*, Robert Montgomery in *Lady in the Lake*, George Montgomery in *The Brasher Doubloon*, James Garner in *Marlowe* (from *The Little Sister*), Elliott Gould in *The Long Goodbye*. On radio, Van Heflin had created the role in 1947 and later was replaced by Gerald Mohr. And on television, Philip Carey had the lead in the Marlowe series (1959–60) while William Eythe starred in a "Philco Playhouse" adaptation of *The Little Sister* in 1950, and Dick Powell played Marlowe once again in *The Long Goodbye* on the "Climax!" series in 1954.

With Sylvia Miles in *Farewell, My Lovely*.

With Charlotte Rampling in *Farewell, My Lovely*.

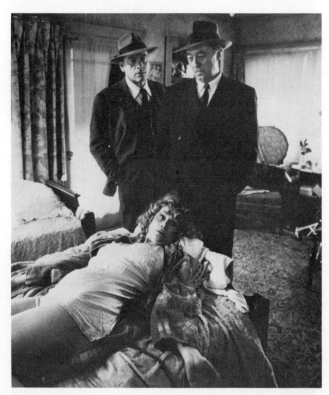

With John Ireland and Sylvia Miles in *Farewell, My Lovely*.

In *Farewell, My Lovely.*

Back at his seedy office, Marlowe is clobbered and taken to a plush brothel run by Frances Amthor (Kate Murtagh), who has him shot full of drugs in an attempt to learn of Moose's whereabouts. In a stupor, Marlowe manages to escape after finding the corpse of Tommy Ray and witnessing the accidental killing of Frances Amthor in a brawl. Two days later, he meets Mrs. Grayle at a political party where he is paid by Laird Brunette (Anthony Zerbe) to bring Moose to his gambling yacht. Marlowe arranges a meeting with Moose through Mrs. Florian, but an unexpected shootout causes Moose again to disappear, and Marlowe finds Mrs. Florian murdered in her flat.

It is at that point that Marlowe summoned Nulty—to pursuade Nulty to tail him when he takes Moose to Brunette's boat. Compromised by payoffs, Nulty at first refuses, but later follows Marlowe and Moose. On the floating casino, Marlowe finds Brunette with Mrs. Grayle, and Moose recognizes her as Velma. She had once been a call-girl for Frances Amthor and had let Moose take the rap for a robbery she had committed. In order to keep Moose from making the connection, she and Brunette had killed Marriott, Ray, and Mrs. Florian, and tried to frame Marlowe for Marriott's murder. Velma then takes a revolver from her purse and shoots

Moose. Marlowe drops to the floor with his gun and kills Velma, just as Nulty and his men break in.

(In the Dick Powell/Marlowe version, called *Murder, My Sweet,* Claire Trevor plays Mrs. Grayle, Mike Mazurki is Moose, Otto Kruger has the part of Amthor, Paul Phillips is Nulty, Miles Mander enacts Grayle, Douglas Walton portrays Marriott, and Esther Howard has the role of Mrs. Florian. Anne Shirley also stars in the extra role of Marlowe's confidant/girlfriend, which is neither in the book nor in the Mitchum version.)*

Following the film's release, Mitchum's fans and his industry boosters began talking about an Academy Award nomination for his performance, particularly after his fine critical notices. Among the more representative:

"Robert Mitchum always takes getting to know in a role. He comes on too strongly at first; too stagey, too droopy of eye, an excessively dangling cigarette. But he settles into his part, his performance drops away, and he moves through the picture with force, humor and unexpected humility" (Richard Eder, *The New York Times*).

". . .neither George Sanders nor Dick Powell, nor Robert Montgomery, George Montgomery, James Garner, nor—dare I say it?—Humphrey Bogart, had quite the weary cynicism, the whisky-soaked wistfulness, the wry humor, and the tender heart that Robert Mitchum brings to the ritual" (Judith Crist, *Saturday Review*).

". . .if you are starved for entertainment, this is something you shouldn't miss. You certainly shouldn't miss Robert Mitchum, who effortlessly sleepwalks through the role of Marlowe. The heavy-lidded eyes, the now-sagging jowls, the stooped and lumbering walk—all are perfect for Marlowe, who is feeling his age and is sick to death of his stinking job. . . . It is Mitchum's movie" (Kathleen Carroll, New York *Daily News*).

Critic Rex Reed raved: "Mitchum's way of playing Philip Marlowe is so sardonic and lazily convincing I found myself beginning to question the presence of a camera. . . . Mitchum has been steadily growing as an actor, giving beautifully modulated performances in *The Friends of Eddie Coyle* and *The Yakuza,* and *Farewell, My Lovely* is a tailor-made showcase for him. . . . I think it's the kind of movie Bogart would have stood in line to

*The Chandler novel also was the basis for *The Falcon Takes Over* in 1942, the third in RKO's "Falcon" series. George Sanders was the Marlowe character and Helen Gilbert had the part of Mrs. Grayle, both under other names. Others, straight out of Chandler, were Ward Bond as Moose Malloy, Anne Revere as Mrs. Florian, Hans Conried as Lindsay Marriott, Selmer Jackson as Laird Brunett, and Turhan Bey as Amthor.

see." And film historian Don Miller, writing in *Focus on Film,* felt: "Mitchum is a good Marlowe, allowing for the age discrepency. . . . He still does the little things superbly, better than almost anyone in the business: a twitch of the eye, a slope of the shoulder, a look of revulsion as he examines a corpse, a patient weary tone of voice during an argument—they are so right, largely because they make the point almost subliminally . . . he can join Powell, Bogart and company without seeming like an intruder."

Invariably, some critical opinion was negative. Representing this faction was Jay Cocks of *Time,* who said: "This time around, Robert Mitchum stars as Marlowe. He is all wrong. For Chandler,

Marlowe was a kind of rogue knight. Mitchum plays him with the same sloppy self-loathing that he has frequently used to demonstrate his superiority to a role. If this contempt suits Mitchum, it ill becomes Marlowe. With the main character deep-sixed, *Farewell, My Lovely* loses its moral center."

Despite the few dissenting voices, *Farewell, My Lovely* did fine business, and was selected among the Best Films of 1975 by the National Board of Review of Motion Pictures, which noted: "Mitchum *is* impressive, in a role that fits him as comfortably as an old pair of shoes. He carries the picture on his own, rare today."

92
Midway

Universal, 1976

THE CAST:

Capt. Matt Garth, CHARLTON HESTON; *Adm. Chester W. Nimitz,* HENRY FONDA; *Capt. Vinton Maddox,* JAMES COBURN; *Rear Adm. Raymond A. Spruance,* GLENN FORD; *Cmdr. Joseph Rochefort,* HAL HOLBROOK; *Adm. Isoroku Yamamoto,* TOSHIRO MIFUNE; *Adm. William F. Halsey,* ROBERT MITCHUM; *Cmdr. Carl Jessup,* CLIFF ROBERTSON; *Lt. Cmdr. Ernest L. Blake,* ROBERT WAGNER; *Rear Adm. Frank J. "Jack" Fletcher,* Robert Webber; *Adm. Harry Pearson,* Ed Nelson; *Vice Adm. Chuichi Nagumo,* James Shigeta; *Haruko Sakura,* Christina Kokubo; *Cmdr. Max Leslie,* Monte Markham; *Capt. Miles Browning,* Biff McGuire; *Ens. George Gay,* Kevin Dobson; *Lt. Cmdr. C. Wade McClusky,* Christopher George; *Lt. Cmdr. John Waldron,* Glenn Corbett; *Capt. Elliott Buckmaster,* George Walcott; *Lt. Tom Garth,* Edward Albert; *Capt. Murray Arnold,* Dabney Coleman; *Adm. Nobutake Kondo,* Conrad Yama; *Vice Adm. Moshiro Hosogaya,* Dale Ishimoto; *Cmdr. Delaney,* Larry Csonka; *Ens. Mansen,* Dennis Rucker; and Pat Morita, Lloyd Kino, Michael Richardson, John Fujioka, Bennett Ohta, Clyde Kusatsu, Erik Estrada, Ken Pennell, Kip Niven, Kurt Grayson, James Ingersoll, David Macklin, Richard Sarradet, Robert Ito, Phillip R. Allen, Sab Shimono, Steve Kanaly.

A Walter Mirisch Production. *Producer,* Walter Mirisch; *Director,* Jack Smight; *Screenplay,* Donald S. Sanford; *Photography,* Harry Stradling, Jr.; *Music,* John Williams; *Art Director,* Walter Tyler; *Technical Advisor,* Vice Adm. Bernard M. Strean, U.S.N. (Ret.); *Special Effects,* Jack McMaster; *Assistant Directors,* Jerome Siegel and Richard Hashimoto; *Editors,* Robert Swink and Frank J. Urioste. Filmed in Sensurround. Panavision and Technicolor. Running time: 132 minutes.

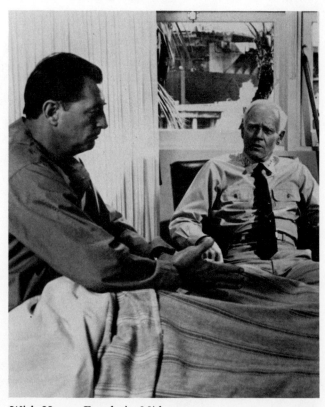

With Henry Fonda in *Midway.*

Mitchum contributed his presence—in two brief scenes—to the action spectacular, *Midway*, a rare seventies all-star throwback to the traditional war movie of an earlier day. The film epic is a multimillion-dollar restaging of the historical naval battle of the spring of 1942 with the formula ingredients of this movie genre—lots of shipboard firepower, aerial dogfights, high command war-planning, and personal heroics. It also is top-heavy with the embellishments of Panavision and the sonics of Sensurround, plus a large cast of expensive "guest stars" alphabetically arranged, putting Mitchum fifth.

Against the wider tapestry of the well-documented historical events is an extraneous subplot involving Charlton Heston as a fictional naval officer (and aide to Admiral Nimitz), Edward Albert as his son, and Christina Kokubo as the Japanese-American girl the son has chosen the wrong time to fall for. As one of the "real" people, Mitchum is Admiral "Bull" Halsey, who missed the battle of Midway when he was hospitalized with a skin ailment. In a part that took no more than one day of filming, Mitchum (as Halsey) plays his entire role sitting up in a hospital

Publicity photo for *Midway*.

With Henry Fonda and Glenn Ford in *Midway*. This scene does not appear in the film, and Mitchum is never seen in uniform.

bed, covered with salve, grousing and scratching as he recommends to Nimitz (Henry Fonda) that Vice Admiral Raymond Spruance (Glenn Ford) be his replacement. A short time later, when Spruance drops by to thank him, Halsey is peering through binoculars and grumbling about a tree outside his window blocking his view of the harbor as the war passes him by. He snarls: "You just find Yamamoto and chew his ass—and find someone to get rid of that damn tree!"

One of the film's unintentional comedy highlights, as hundreds of movie buffs and more than one critic chuckled over somewhat perversely, was the scene in which the Japanese high command, acquainting itself with the enemy through pictures of its leaders, passed around an 8x10 glossy of Mitchum that looked suspiciously like a publicity shot dating back to his RKO days!

"I met Halsey one time after the war," ex-PFC Mitchum has recalled. "He was a great old bird." He drew the line, though, at submitting to a Halsey-style crew cut for one day's work. And for the job: "I told them they could send my salary to charity."

93
The Last Tycoon

Paramount, 1976

In *The Last Tycoon*.

THE CAST:

Monroe Stahr, ROBERT De NIRO; *Rodriguez*, TONY CURTIS; *Pat Brady*, ROBERT MITCHUM; *Didi*, JEANNE MOREAU; *Brimmer*, JACK NICHOLSON; *Boxley*, DONALD PLEASENCE; *Kathleen Moore*, INGRID BOULTING; *Fleishacker*, RAY MILLAND; *Red Ridingwood*, DANA ANDREWS; *Cecilia Brady*, Theresa Russell; *Wylie*, Peter Strauss; *Popolos*, Tige Andrews; *Marcus*, Morgan Farley; *Doctor*, Jeff Corey; *Guide*, John Carradine; *Stahr's Secretary*, Diane Shalet; *Seal Trainer*, Seymour Cassell; *Edna*, Angelica Huston; *Brady's Secretaries*, Bonnie Bartlett and Sharon Masters; *Norman*, Eric Christmas; *Mrs. Rodriguez*, Leslie Curtis; *Butler*, Lloyd Kino; *Assistant Editor*, Brendan Burns; *Lady in Restaurant*, Carrie Miller; *Hairdresser*, Peggy Feury; *Lady Writer*, Betsey Jones-Moreland; *Girl on Beach*, Patricia Singer.

A Sam Spiegel/Elia Kazan Film. *Producer*, Sam Spiegel; *Director*, Elia Kazan; *Screenplay*, Harold Pinter; *Based on the Novel by* F. Scott Fitzgerald; *Photography*, Victor Kemper; *Music*, Maurice Jarre; *Production Design*, Gene Callahan; *Art Director*, Jack Collis; *Costumes*, Anna Hill Johnstone and Anthea Sylbert; *Assistant Director*, Danny McCauley; *Editor*, Richard Marks. Panavision and Technicolor. Running time: 123 minutes.

With Ray Milland in *The Last Tycoon*.

In *The Last Tycoon*.

With Theresa Russell in *The Last Tycoon*.

In *The Last Tycoon.*

Like previous attempts at translating F. Scott Fitzgerald to the screen—the various incarnations of *The Great Gatsby*, *Babylon Revisited* (as *The Last Time I Saw Paris*), and *Tender Is the Night*—the film version by English playwright Harold Pinter of *The Last Tycoon*, Fitzgerald's final, uncompleted novel, frustrated literary purists as well as both audiences and movie critics. Most of the reviewers agreed that Elia Kazan's approach was admirable and the closest yet to capturing Fitzgerald on film,* and that Robert De Niro, in the key role of Monroe Stahr, dreamer and dreammaker whom Fitzgerald patterned after Irving Thalberg, the boy genius production chief of MGM during the thirties, delivered a remarkably sensitive portrayal.

In his first film for Kazan (originally Mike Nichols was to have directed), Robert Mitchum has a fairly brief role—the closest to the story's second male lead—as Pat Brady, the studio head who is Stahr's mentor, friend, boss, almost-

The Last Tycoon had a television incarnation under John Frankenheimer's direction on Playhouse 90 on 3/14/57. Jack Palance starred with Viveca Lindfors, Lee Remick, Keenan Wynn, Peter Lorre, and Robert F. Simon as Pat Brady.

father-in-law, and subsequent rival, reluctantly forced by the board of directors to dismiss his protégé. Early on, an admiring Brady introduces himself as "the strong base on which Stahr rests"; later, increasingly disenchanted with Stahr's obsession with the elusive beauty he is persuing at the expense of his studio loyalties, he sides with the money people from New York and begins tearing down Stahr as "the Jesus of Vine Street."

Most critical attention went, naturally, to De Niro and to Ingrid Boulting, the new actress (found, by and large, to be not only miscast but totally inept) who plays Kathleen Moore, the girl who reminds Stahr of his dead wife. Mitchum and the alphabetically listed veteran actors, most playing merely cameos (Tony Curtis as a matinee idol going though a masculinity crisis; Ray Milland, a suave studio executive; Jeanne Moreau, a fading Continental star; Jack Nicholson, a tough union organizer; Donald Pleasence, a highbrow screenwriter; Dana Andrews, a washed-up director), generally received only passing mention in the reviews. Vincent Canby, in *The New York Times,* however, singled out Mitchum's performance as "extremely effective," and William Wolf, critic for *Cue,* judged that "Mitchum, growing more persuasive with age, makes producer Pat Brady richly credible."

Charles Champlin's unkind comments about *The Last Tycoon* in the *Los Angeles Times* included the negative view that Mitchum gives "a dull, wooden and unconvincing performance that never, thanks to Pinter or Kazan or both, captures the feral vulgarity you would have thought was called for."

The tenor of the reviews, though, paralleled the comments by Kathleen Carroll of the New York *Daily News*, who had nothing but praise for De Niro and then noted: "The other actors, particularly Robert Mitchum . . . look as if they had wandered in from another set and were wondering where the closest exit is. At one point in the film, the studio executives are in a screening room examining footage. 'It just lays there and goes to sleep,' complains Mitchum. He could just as well be critiquing *The Last Tycoon.*"

94
The
Amsterdam Kill

(also called
Quinlan Must Die!)

Golden Harvest, 1977

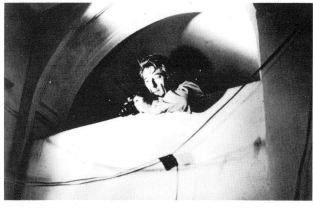

In *The Amsterdam Kill.*

THE CAST:

Quinlan, ROBERT MITCHUM; *Odums,* Bradford Dillman; *Ridgeway,* Richard Egan; *Knight,* Leslie Nielsen; *Chung Wei,* Keye Luke; *Jimmy Wong, George Cheung; Assassin,* Chan Sing; *Police Chief,* Stephen Leung.

Executive Producer, Raymond Chow; *Producer,* Andre Morgan; *Director,* Robert Clouse; *Screenplay,* Robert Clouse and Gregory Tiefer; *Photography,* Alan Hume; *Special Effects,* Gene Grigg; *Editor,* Alan Holtzman. In color. Running time: 93 minutes.

With Bradford Dillman in *The Amsterdam Kill.*

An ambitious action story about worldwide drug trafficking, filmed on several continents and teeming with the traditional spies, narcotics peddlers, cryptic notepads, and all manner of violence, *The Amsterdam Kill* represented the latest effort to buy a larger slice of the international cinema market by Raymond Chow's Golden Harvest Group—responsible in the early seventies for the King Fu movie craze and the stardom its *Enter the Dragon* had brought to Bruce Lee. In appreciation of Robert Mitchum's importance as a marquee name virtually everywhere, Chow had the film's lead role tailored to Mitchum's familiar tough guy/loner image and signed him to head a multinational cast as the discredited drug agent given the assignment of unmasking a powerful narcotics czar.

Set against the colorful backgrounds of London's Soho district, Hong Kong's drug centers, Amsterdam's Chinatown, and the Utrecht flower auction, *The Amsterdam Kill* is involved with East-West treachery and intrigue when the European drug market shifts from Marseilles to Amsterdam with Hong Kong at the other end of

the axis. Quinlan (Mitchum), a former agent for the U.S. Drug Enforcement Agency (DEA), who has been rotting in London after having been fired because of his own involvement with drugs, is contacted by aging Amsterdam syndicate head, Chung Wei (Keye Luke), who wants to retire and is willing to sell vital information about the drug network in exchange for protection. Aware that alone he has no credibility, Quinlan flies to Hong Kong to meet with an old colleague, Odums (Bradford Dillman), the one DEA operative he trusts. Odums convinces his boss, Ridgeway (Richard Egan), and Knight (Leslie Nielsen), one of Quinlan's rivals from the old days who now heads the DEA office in Amsterdam, to accept Wei's offer, but tells them that Quinlan insists on working alone.

Quinlan brings long-time friend Jimmy Wong (George Cheung), an ex-cop from New York, to protect Wei and then goes about checking the names Wei had listed in his detailed notebook.

In *The Amsterdam Kill.*

When some of the information is mysteriously leaked, Quinlan finds himself the target not only of the syndicate but of the DEA and the Hong Kong police. He is mugged several times, kidnapped, and then faced with Wei's murder. Realizing he has been betrayed, Quinlan doggedly stays on the trail to clear himself and, with Jimmy, goes to Amsterdam armed with a single clue, the name "Juliana," that ultimately leads them to a Dutch flower farm where the syndicate processes heroin for distribution to North America under the guise of the flower auctions.

Spotted by the dealers, Quinlan and Jimmy become embroiled in a gun battle, and in the melee that follows, the farm and the men running the operation are destroyed. The Hong Kong leak is exposed and Quinlan uncovers the identity of the drug network's head man, his friend Odums. Odums commits suicide and Quinlan comes in from the cold, his image restored.

Variety reported that "The film's acting asset belongs to Mitchum. He is sympathetic and has sensitive moments of middle-aged knowingness and is masterly, believable and downbeat." Its critic was less complimentary toward the movie itself.

95
The Big Sleep
United Artists, 1978

THE CAST:

Philip Marlowe, ROBERT MITCHUM; *Charlotte Sternwood,* SARAH MILES; *Lash Canino,* Richard Boone; *Camilla Sternwood,* Candy Clark; *Agnes Lozelle,* Joan Collins; *Joe Brody,* Edward Fox; *Inspector Carson,* Sir John Mills; *Eddie Mars,* Oliver Reed; *General Sternwood,* James Stewart; *Norris,* Harry Andrews; *Harry Jones,* Colin Blakely; *Mona Grant,* Diana Quick; *Inspector Gregory,* James Donald; *Commander Barker,* Richard Todd; *Arthur Geiger,* John Justin; *Karl Lundgren,* Simon Turner; *Owen Taylor,* Martin Potter; *Rusty Regan,* David Savile.

An E.K./ITC Production. *Executive Producers,* Elliott Kastner and Jerry Bick; *Producer/director,* Michael Winner; *Screenplay,* Michael Winner; *Based on the Novel by* Raymond Chandler; *Photography,* Robert Paynter; *Music,* Jerry Fielding; *Production Design,* Harry Pottle; *Art Director,* John Graysmark; *Editor,* Freddie Wilson. Color by DeLuxe. Running time: 99 minutes.

The enthusiastic reception given to Mitchum for his portrayal of Philip Marlowe in *Farewell, My Lovely* prompted producers Elliott Kastner and Jerry Bick to sign him to reprise his interpretation of Raymond Chandler's quintessential gumshoe in a new version of *The Big Sleep,* updated to London of the seventies. Filmed in the latter part of 1977 and not yet completed as this book was being published, this contemporary adaptation of Chandler's novel promised to generate more than ordinary interest by its inevitable comparison to the fondly remembered 1946 Howard Hawks classic that starred Humphrey Bogart.

Bogart was just forty-six when he played Marlowe; Mitchum had already turned sixty at the time the latest *The Big Sleep* was going into production. But as was generally conceded at the time *Farewell, My Lovely* was released, once the viewer as well as the Philip Marlowe-phile accepts the age discrepancy between the real-life, actor and the fictional detective, Mitchum is seen as the ideal Marlowe, fitting comfortably alongside the legendary screen incarnations of the past.

Reunited in London with his *Ryan's Daughter* costars, Sarah Miles (in the old Lauren Bacall role) and John Mills, and working for the first time with fellow veteran Jimmy Stewart, Mitchum discovered that moving the Chandler thriller from the Los Angeles of the forties permitted him to wear a Savile Row wardrobe. "I plan to steal most of it," he allowed during the filming. "The last time I played Marlowe I was given a suit once worn by Michael Caine and originally by Victor Mature. It hadn't been cleaned since." About switching the action from America, Mitchum admitted: "I like working in England. I speak the language. Actually I like location pictures. You get a free lunch. An if it's a British picture working a twelve-hour day, sometimes you get a radish thrown at you around seven." He was asked how he felt Chandler would have reacted to *The Big Sleep* being made in England. "I'm sure he

would have gone along for the ride. I met him back in the forties. He was a fellow who drank and who found himself confused by questions like 'What is the script about?' That never failed to stop him."

Producer/director/writer Michael Winner offered these words on remaking so famous a film and doing it in England. "We're not giving you the tourist London, with the Tower and Piccadilly Circus in the background whenever two people talk. Rather a strange, amorphous London made up of odd and little-known locations, a sort of magical city that could be anywhere, a timeless setting for Marlowe to crusade against evil and corruption. And it's less a remake than simply another film from the book. Great films have been the second or even third versions of classic stories. Sir Henry Irving did a legendary *Hamlet* in 1874 but people still went on to try it again!"

It will remain the judgment of future moviegoers about where this version of *The Big Sleep* stands in screen history. And how Robert Mitchum holds up as Marlowe, or Sarah Miles as the beautiful, elusive Charlotte Sternwood, or Richard Boone as the sinister "man in brown," Lash Canino, or Oliver Reed (a frequent Michael Winner player) as Eddie Mars, the underworld gambling boss. And how timeless *The Big Sleep* really is.

With Sarah Miles.

With James Stewart.

With Joan Collins.

A Mitchum Portrait Gallery

1943

1944

1949—the definitive Mitchum.

1955

1952

1957

1959

1967

1968

1969

1972

1973

1975

1975

Appendix

MITCHUM ON RADIO

"Lux Radio Theatre" (CBS 1/6/47): As Bill Tabeshaw in *Till the End of Time* with Laraine Day, Guy Madison and Bill Williams

"Reader's Digest" (CBS 2/27/47): As Caster in *We Were Expecting You At Dakar*

"Suspense" (CBS 5/14/47): As David In *Death at Live Oak*

"Studio One" (CBS 11/18/47): As Toby McLean in *Young Man in Manhattan*

"Theatre Guild on the Air" (Mutual 11/23/47): In Eugene O'Neill's *The Straw* with Mary Anderson

"Studio One" (CBS 5/11/48): As Charles in *Wine in the Country*

"We the People" (CBS 1/13/48): Interviewed by Francis X. Bushman

AND ON TELEVISION

"Stage Show with Tommy and Jimmy Dorsey" (CBS 10/23/55)

"The Jimmy Durante Texaco Star Theatre" (NBC 2/11/56)

"Climax" (CBS 3/8/56): As himself in *The Louella Parsons Story* with Teresa Wright

"The Ed Sullivan Show" (CBS 1/17/57)

"It Could Be You" (Game Show) (NBC 5/3/57)

"The Frank Sinatra Show" (ABC 1/10/58)

"Here's Hollywood" (NBC 6/21/61)

"The Dick Powell Theatre" (NBC 1/15/63): Guest host following Powell's death

"The Ed Sullivan Show" (CBS 6/23/63)

"What's My Line" (CBS 3/28/65)

"Truth or Consequences" (NBC 4/13/65)

"Celebrity Game" (CBS 6/3/65)

"NBC Sports in Action" (NBC 11/6/65): As analyst for all-America Quarter Horse Futurity

"The Dean Martin Show" (NBC 4/8/68)

"The Tonight Show" (NBC 10/16/70): Discussing experiences with the law since 1948

"The Tonight Show" (NBC 7/7/72)

"The Jim Stafford Show" (NBC 9/3/75)

"Dean's Place" ("The Dean Martin Show") (NBC 9/6/75)

"33rd Annual Golden Globe Awards" (Metromedia 1/26/76): As presenter

"People's Choice Awards" (CBS 2/19/76): As presenter

MITCHUM-narrated television documentaries for Airlie Productions of the George Washington University Medical Center

"A MOVABLE SCENE"
A television special on youth and narcotics in "The Distant Drummer" series, 1968.

Lawrence Laurent, *The Washington Post:* "Mitchum's role as the narrator is a new facet to an acting career that has commanded growing respect.... He makes a restrained narrator. He talks in a matter-of-fact tone about the rising rate of drug addiction among the young."

"AMERICA ON THE ROCKS"
A television film about the use and abuse of alcohol in America, 1973.

242

John Carmody, *The Washington Post:* "Narrated by Robert Mitchum (a marvelous choice, incidentally), the film neither scolds nor tries to scare. But when it's over, the dimensions of this national problem have been spelled out as succinctly as a 'fair' film on this subject is ever likely to."

Variety: "The middle-class is the target of this fine documentary on alcoholism, and the point is effectively made. . . . Narrated by Robert Mitchum— whose voice suggests that only Dean Martin would have been a more inspired choice to host the show—explains that alcohol is such a problem in this country partly because as a society we have no general ground-rules on drinking . . . producer/director Frank Kavanaugh has brought the material to life with imaginative filming, a central visual theme that holds the material together, and the production values that a generous $125,000 budget helps buy."

Index

Pages on which photos appear are set in bold face.

Acosta, Rodolfo, 147
Aerial Gunner, 53–54, 65
Aherne, Brian, **92**
Aldrich, Robert, 36, 160, 161
Ames, Leon, 127
Amsterdam Kill, The, 43, 233–34
Anderson, Judith, **96**, 97
Anderson, Michael Jr., 37, 166, **167**
Angel Face, 31, 126–27
Angry Hills, The, 36, 160–61
Anzio, 41, 198–200
Arlen, Richard, 53, 54, 65, 175
Armendariz, Pedro, **162**
Armstrong, Robert, 74
Asner, Edward, 196
Aubrey, James, 42, 217

Bacall, Lauren, 34, 235
Bacon, Lloyd, 132
Bainter, Fay, 63
Baker, Carroll, 191, **192**, 193
Baker, Kenny, **70**
Baker, Stanley, 160, 161
Balsam, Martin, 176, 210, **211**
Bancroft, Ann, 180
Bandido!, 35, 147–49
Barry, Gene, 156
Bar 20, 25, 57–58
Battle Hymn, 36
Beery, Noah Jr., **59, 60,** 61
Belafonte, Harry, 36
Bel Geddes, Barbara, 104, **105**
Bendix, William, **109, 120,** 121
Bergen, Polly, 38, 176
Best Years of Our Lives, The, 27, 89
Beyond the Last Frontier, 25, 66–67
Bickford, Charles, 138
Big Sleep, The, 224, 234–35
Big Steal, The, 29, 30, 31, 108–9
Bikel, Theodore, 160
Blondell, Joan, 63

Blood Alley, 34, 137
Blood on the Moon, 28, 104–6
Blyth, Ann, 36, **122**, 123
Bogart, Humphrey, 234
Bolt, Robert, 212
Bondi, Beulah, **137**
Border Patrol, 25, 47–48
Boyd, William, 47, **48, 49,** 50, 55, **56,** 57, **64, 71,** 72
Boyle, Peter, 220, **221**
Boy on a Dolphin, 36
Brennan, Walter, 104, 196
Britt, May, **158**
Brodie, Steve, **26, 94,** 101
Bronson, Charles, **203,** 204
Brooks, Richard, 93
Brown, Clarence, 57
Brown, Johnny Mack, **62**
Brown, Wally, 26, 75, **76**
Brynner, Yul, 42, **203, 204**
Buchanan, Edgar, 132
Buono, Victor, **217,** 218
Burnette, Smiley, 66
Burr, Raymond, 116
Burton, Richard, 43
Busch, Niven, 89, 95
Buttons, Red, 180

Caan, James, 195
Cabot, Sebastian, **160**
Cagney, James, **37**
Cain, James M., 101
Calhern, Louis, 107
Calhoun, Rory, 135
Cameron, Rod, 74
Cape Fear, 38, 175–77
Carney, Alan, 26, 75, **76**
Carradine, David, 207, 210
Carradine, John, 207, 210
Carter, Janis, **114,** 115
Castle, William, 25

Cattle Queen of Montana, 31
Chandler, Raymond, 225, 234, 235
Chase, Barrie, **176**
Clyde, Andy, 47, **48, 49, 56, 64**
Colbert, Claudette, 122
Collins, Ray, 118
Colt Comrades, 25, 55–57
Conrad, William, 118
Cooper, George, **94**
Copland, Aaron, 107
Corey, Wendell, 110
Corvette K-225, 25, 60–61
Cowan, Douglas, **83**
Cowan, Lester, 26
Crane, Richard, 71
Crawford, Broderick, 34, 138
Cromwell, John, **32,** 118
Crossfire, 27, 41, 93–95, 199
Cry Havoc, 63
Cukor, George, 27, **28,** 97, 98
Cunningham-Morris, Hugh, 21, 26, **41**
Curtis, Tony, 183, 232

Dancing Masters, The, 68–69
Darnell, Linda, **129, 130**
Day, Laraine, 27, **92,** 93
DeFore, Don, **52,** 53, **83,** 84
de Havilland, Olivia, **138, 139**
Dekker, Albert, 163
DeNiro, Robert, 232
Desire Me, 27, 91, 97–99
Devine, Andy, 61
Dew, Eddie, **66**
Dickinson, Angie, 196, **207,** 208, 209
Dillman, Bradford, **233**
Dinehard, Alan, 78
Dmytryk, Edward, 27, 41, 88, 93, 95, 199
Domergue, Faith, 31, **112, 113**
Donen, Stanley, **38,** 171, 173
Donnell, Jeff, **70**
Dorsey, Jimmy, 36

Dorsey, Tommy, 36
Doughboys in Ireland, 25, 70
Douglas, Gordon, 75
Douglas, Kirk, 39, **100,** 101, 183, 185, **194**
Douglas, Melvyn, **115**
DRM Productions, 35, 36, 37, 162
Dunn, James, 88

Egan, Richard, **158,** 233
El Dorado, 39, 195–98, 217
Ellison, James, 47, **77**
Enemy Below, The, 36, 154–55
Errol, Leon, 55

Falk, Peter, **198**
False Colors, 64–65
Farewell, My Lovely, 21, 43, 101, 225–28
Farnum, Dustine, **57,** 58
Farrow, John, 112, 116
Farrow, Mia, 205, **206,** 207
Faylen, Frank, 104, **105**
Feldman, Charles K., 106
Fire Down Below, 36, 149, 151–53
Fitzgerald, Barry, **61**
Fitzgerald, F. Scott, 43, 232
Five Card Stud, 39, 41, 42, 200–202, 218
Fix, Paul, **196**
Follow the Band, 25, 54–55
Fonda, Henry, 107, 108, **228, 229,** 230
Ford, Glenn, **229,** 230
Ford, John, 193, 197
Foreign Intrigue, 35, 145–47
Foster, Norman, 102
Fowley, Douglas, **56**
Frederick, Reva, 42
French Line, 31
Friends of Eddie Coyle, The, 42, 220–22, 227

Gable, Clark, 37, 164
Gardner, Ava, 31, **114, 115**
Garson, Greer, 27, **28,** 97, 98, **99**
Gates, Nancy, **79,** 80
Geisler, Jerry, **29, 30,** 35
Girl Rush, 26, 75–77
Gish, Lillian, 36, 141, 142
Going Home, 42, 214–27
Goldwyn, Samuel Jr., **35,** 142
Good Guys and the Bad Guys, The, 42, 209–11
Gomez, Thomas, **60, 61,** 121
Grahame, Gloria, 93, **120,** 121, 138, 139
Grant, Cary, **171, 172,** 173
Grass Is Greener, The, 9, 37, 171–73
Gray, Gary, **103**
Greer, Jane, **26, 100,** 101, **108, 109**
Gregory, Paul, 34, 35, 140
Grey, Zane, 26, 77, 79, 80, 84, 85
Gung Ho!, 25, 72–74
Gwynne, Anne, 59

Hack, Herman, **48, 71**
Hale, Barbara, **26, 84, 85**
Hall, Thurston, **84, 85**
Hamilton, George, **164,** 165
Hamilton, Neil, **81**
Hardy, Oliver, 68, **69**
Harris, Richard, **169**
Hart, Richard, 27, **98**
Hathaway, Henry, 30, 128, 200, 202
Hawkins, Jack, 185
Hawks, Howard, 39, 60, 195, 196, 197, 198, 217, 234
Hayden, Russell, 47, 65
Hayes, George "Gabby," 47
Hayward, Susan, 31, **124, 128**
Hayworth, Rita, 36, **152, 153, 218,** 219

Heaven Knows, Mr. Allison, 9, 10, 36, 37, 149–51, 155
Hedison, Al (David), 155
Hepburn, Katharine, 27, **90, 91**
Heston, Charlton, 229
Heywood, Anne, **169**
Hinda, Samuel S., **54, 55**
His Kind of Woman, 31, 116–17
Holden, William, 28, **102, 103**
Holiday Affair, 31, 110–111
Holliman, Earl, **199**
Holt, Jennifer, **62**
Holt, Tim, 116
Home from the Hill, 164–65
Hopper, Hedda, 31, 131
Hopper, William, **137**
Hoppy Serves a Writ, 25, 49
Howard, Trevor, 42, 188, **212,** 213
Howe, James Wong, 95
Hudson, Rock, 36
Hughes, Howard, 29, 31, 32, 106, 108, 112, 114, 116, 118, 120, 124, 125, 126, 132
Hull, Henry, 144
Human Comedy, The, 25, 51–53
Hunnicutt, Arthur, 132, 196, **197**
Hunter, Kim, **80, 81**
Hunters, The, 36, 158–59
Hunter, Tab, **136, 137**
Hurst, Paul, 75, **76**
Huston, John, 36, 37, 38, 149, 150, 151, 183
Hutchison, Ken, **217,** 218, 219
Hyer, Martha, 175

In Which We Serve, 60
Ireland, John, 225, **226**

Jackpot, 42
Jagger, Dean, 81, 96
James, John, **72, 73**
Jeffreys, Anne, **26, 79**
Jet Pilot, 120
Johnny Doesn't Live Here Anymore, 77–78
Johns, Glynis, 166
Johnson, Van, **82, 83,** 84
Jordan, Richard, 220, 223
Jory, Victor, 49, **50,** 55, **56, 57, 58**
Jurgens, Curt, 154, 155

Kazan, Elia, **43,** 232
Keats, Steven, 220, **221**
Keiko, Kishi, **223**
Keith, Brian, **222,** 223
Kelly, Gene, 189
Kennedy, Arthur, **32, 124, 125, 198**
Kennedy, Burt, 42, 207, 208, 209, 211
Kennedy, George, 209, **210,** 211
Ken, Takakura, **222,** 223
Kerr, Deborah, **9,** 36, 37, **38,** 43, **149, 150,** 151, **166, 167, 171,** 172, 173
King Brothers, 77, 81
Kirby, Jay, 47, **48, 49, 56,** 57
Knight, Fuzzy, **60,** 61, **62**
Knight, Sandra, **36**
Knowles, Patric, 109
Knox, Alexander, 188, 191, 204
Kramer, Stanley, **34,** 138
Krasna, Norman, 116
Kulik, Buzz, 203, 204

Ladd, Alan, 36, 160
Lancaster, Burt, 183
Langella, Frank, 218, **219**
Langford, Frances, **75, 76**
Last Time I Saw Archie, The, 38, 39, 173–75
Last Tycoon, The, 43, 230–32

Laughton, Charles, **35,** 140, 142, 217
Laurel, Stan, 68, **69**
Lawrence, Barbara, **144**
Lean, David, 42, 212, 214
Leather Burners, The, 50–51
Lee, Bruce, 233
Leeds, Lila, 29, **30,** 31
Leigh, Janet, **110,** 111
Lembeck, Harvey, 175
Lemmon, Jack, 36, **151, 152, 153**
LeRoy, Mervyn, 27, 82, 98
Levene, Sam, 93
List of Adrian Messenger, The, 38, 182–85
Livingston, Bob, 66
Locket, The, 27, 91–93
London, Julie, **162,** 163
Lonely Passion of Judith Hearne, The, 43
Lone Star Trail, The, 62–63
Longest Day, The, 38, 177–80
Losey, Joseph, 42, 205
Loy, Myrna, **106, 107**
Luke, Keye, 233
Lusty Men, The, 31, 32, 124–25
Lyden, Pierce, **48**
Lynn, Diana, 136, **137**

Macao, 31, 120–21
McDowall, Roddy, **201,** 202
McGraw, Charles, 116, **117, 122, 123**
McGuire, Dorothy, 89
MacKenzie, Joyce, **32**
McLaglen, Andrew, 37, 193
MacLaine, Shirley, 38, **39, 40, 180, 181, 189, 190,** 191
Madison, Guy, **27, 88, 89**
Mainwaring, Daniel, 100, 101
Man in the Middle, 38, 187–88
Man with the Gun, 35, 36, 142–44
Marshall, Herbert, 127
Marshall, Trudy, 68
Martin, Dean, 39, **41,** 195, 200, **201,** 202, 207, 209
Martin, Deana, 207
Martinelli, Elsa, 185, **186**
Martin, Lori, **176**
Martin, Richard, **79,** 80, 84, 85
Marvin, Lee, 34, 43
Mature, Victor, 31
Meredith, Burgess, **86,** 88
Merrill, Gary, 163
Midway, 43, 228–30
Miles, Peter, **106**
Miles, Sarah, **212,** 213, **235**
Miles, Sylvia, **217,** 225, 226
Milestone, Lewis, 107
Milland, Ray, **231,** 232
Mills, John, 213, 214, 235
Minesweeper, 65
Minnelli, Vincente, **27,** 37, **90, 91,** 164, 165
Mister Moses, 38, 191–93
Mitchum, Anne (mother), 21, 23, **41**
Mitchum, Carol (sister), 21, 23
Mitchum, Christopher (son), **25, 29, 33,** 42, 198
Mitchum, Dorothy (wife), 23, **24,** 25, 28, **29, 33, 37,** 39, 42. *See also* Spence, Dorothy
Mitchum, James (father), 21
Mitchum, James (son), 24, **25, 29, 32, 33, 36,** 38, **39, 155, 156,** 157
Mitchum, John (brother), 21, 23, 39
Mitchum, Julie (sister), 21, 23
Mitchum, Petrine (daughter), **33, 42**
Monroe, Marilyn, 24, 33, 37, **134, 135,** 136, 139
Montgomery, Robert, 27, 97

Moreau, Jeanne, **43**
Morgan, Frank, **52,** 53
Morris, Chester, 53, 54
Morris, Dorothy, **52,** 53
Mr. Winkle Goes to War, 74–75
Mueller, Elisabeth, 160
Murray, Forbes, **50**
My Forbidden Past, 31, 114–15

Naish, J. Carrol, 72, **73**
Neame, Ronald, 193
Nelson, Barry, **52,** 53
Nelson, Ralph, 42, 218, 219
Nettleton, Lois, **209, 210**
Nevada, 26, 79–80
Newley, Anthony, **153**
Newman, Paul, 180, 189
Nicholson, Jack, 232
Nielsen, Leslie, 233
Night Fighters, The, 37, 169–71
Night of the Hunter, The, 35, 36, 140–42, 177, 217, 218
North, Alex, 144
Not As a Stranger, 34, 138–39
Nuyen, France, **173,** 175, 187, **188**

O'Hara, Maureen, 107
O'Herlihy, Dan, 169
One Minute to Zero, 31, 36, 122–23
O'Sullivan, Maureen, 112
O'Toole, Peter, 43
Out of the Past, 28, 100–101

Page, Genevieve, **145, 146**
Paige, Leroy "Satchel," **163**
Palance, Jack, **130,** 131
Parker, Eleanor, **164,** 165
Parker, Jean, 65
Patten, Luana, 165
Peck, Gregory, 38, 176, **177**
Peckinpah, Sam, 209
Peppard, George, **164,** 165
Phillips, Leslie, **161**
Pine, William, 53, 54, 65
Pinter, Harold, 43, 232
Pollack, Sydney, 43
Porter, Jean, **89**
Powell, Dick, 36, 154, 155, 158, 159, 227
Preminger, Otto, 31, 33, 42, 43, 126, 127, 134, 136
Preston, Robert, **104,** 106
Price, Vincent, 116
Pursued, 95–97

Quillan, Eddie, **54, 55**
Quine, Richard, **59**
Quinn, Anthony, 162

Rachel and the Stranger, 28, 31, 36, 102–3
Racket, The, 31, 32, 118–19
Raft, George, 109
Raines, Ella, 63
Rains, Claude, **112**
Rampage, 38, 185–87
Rampling, Charlotte, 43, 225, **226**
Raymond, Gene, 92
Ray, Nicholas, 31, 121, 124, 125
Reagan, Ronald, 31
Redgrave, Vanessa, 43
Red Pony, The, 28, 30, 106–8
Reed, Donna, **52,** 53
Reeves, George, 48, 51, 55, 56, 58

Reilly, John R., **83,** 84
Rettig, Tommy, **134, 135**
Reynolds, Marjorie, 116
Reynolds, Sheldon, 35, 145
Richards, Dick, 43
Richter, Carroll, 24
Riders of the Deadline, 71–72
Rio Bravo, 195, 197
Rio Lobo, 197
Ripley, Arthur, 156, 157
Ritter, Tex, **62,** 63
River of No Return, 33, 134–36
Robe, The, 26
Robinson, Edward G., 74, 75, 118
Rogell, Sid, 25, 26, 75
Roland, Gilbert, **147,** 148
Rooney, Anne, **54, 55**
Rooney, Mickey, 51, 53
Rosebud, 42, 136
Ross, Frank, 26
Rosson, Richard, 60
Russell, Jane, 31, 116, **117, 120,** 121
Russell, Theresa, **231**
Ryan, Robert, 93, 94, 118, **119,** 199
Ryan's Daughter, 42, 212–14

Saroyan, William, 53
Savalas, Telly, 176
Scala, Gia, **160,** 161
Schary, Dore, 27, 30, 89, 93, 100, 103
Scott, George C., 183
Scott, Lizabeth, 109, **118,** 119
Scott, Randolph, 60, 61, 72, **73,** 74
Scott, Zachary, **148**
Second Chance, 31, 129–31
Secret Ceremony, 42, 205–7
Selznick, David O., 27, 31, 89, 91
She Couldn't Say No, 31, 131, 132–33
Sheridan, Ann, 114
Sherman, Harry, 25, 47
Shigeta, James, 223
Siegel, Don, 29, **30**
Silva, Simone, 33, **34**
Simmons, Jean, 31, **126, 127,** 132, **133,** 171, 172, 173
Simon, Simone, 77, 78
Simpson, Russell, 47, **48**
Sinatra, Frank, **34,** 115, **138,** 139, 183, 189
Slezak, Walter, **128**
Sloane, Everett, 165
Smith, Keely, 36, **157**
Sothern, Anne, 63
Spence, Dorothy, 23, 24. *See also* Mitchum, Dorothy
Spiegel, Sam, 43
Stack, Robert, 60
Stanwyck, Barbara, 31
Steele, Freddie, **86,** 87
Steinbeck, John, 28, 107
Sterling, Jan, **142, 143,** 144
Stevens, Inger, 200
Stewart, James, **235**
Story of G.I. Joe, The, 26, 34, 35, 41, 86–88, 136, 151, 161
Strauss, Robert, 175
Sullavan, Margaret, 63
Sundowners, The, 9, 37, 165, 166–68

Talbot Productions, 37, 42, 174
Taylor, Elizabeth, 180, **205,** 206, 207
Taylor, Robert, **27,** 90, 91
Terry, William, **77**

Thaxter, Phyllis, 84, 104
Thiess, Ursula, **148,** 149
Thirty Seconds Over Tokyo, 25, 82–84
Thomas, William, 53, 54, 65
Thompson, J. Lee, 176, 191
Thunder Road, 36, 155–57
Till the End of Time, 27, 41, 88–89, 199
Tourneur, Jacques, 28, 101
Track of the Cat, 34, 136–37
Tracy, Spencer, 84
Trevor, Claire, 109
Tulean, Ingrid (Ingrid Thulin), **146,** 147
Tully, Tom, 104, **105**
Two for the Seesaw, 38, 180–82

Undercurrent, 90–91
Uris, Leon, 160
Ustinov, Peter, 166, 168

Vaccaro, Brenda, 215, **216,** 217
Vague, Vera, 75, **76**
Van Dyke, Dick, 189
Villa Rides!, 41, 202–4
Vincent, Jan-Michael, **215,** 217
Von Sternberg, Josef, 120, 121

Wagner, Robert, 158
Wald, Jerry, 116
Walker, Robert, 207, **208,** 209
Walsh, Raoul, 95
Wanamaker, Sam, **188**
Wanger, Walter, 59, 72
Warde, Anthony, **71**
Warren, James, **26,** 79
Warrick, Ruth, 74
Watson, Moray, **172,** 173
Wayne, John, 34, 39, 72, 137, 178, **195, 196, 197**
Way West, The, 39, 193–95
Webb, Jack, 38, **174,** 175
Welles, Orson, 24
Wellman, William A., 26, 34, 86, 136, 137, 161
West of the Pecos, 26, 84–85
We've Never Been Licked, 25, 59–60
What a Way to Go!, 38, 40, 189–91
When Strangers Marry, 25, 80–81
Where Danger Lives, 31, 112–13
White Witch Doctor, 31, 124, 128–29
Widmark, Richard, 39, **194**
Williams, Bill, **26,** 27, 89
Wilson, Richard, 142
Winner, Michael, 235
Winters, Shelley, **140,** 141
Wise, Robert, 28, 38, **39,** 104, 180
Wonderful Country, The, 36, 162–63
Wrath of God, The, 42, 217–19
Wright, Teresa, 89, **95, 96,** 97, **137**
Wyler, William, 150
Wynn, Keenan, **187**

Yakuza, The, 43, 203, 222–24, 227
Yates, Peter, 220
Young Billy Young, 42, 207–9
Young, Loretta, 28, **102, 103**
Young, Terence, 42, 43
Young, Robert, **93,** 94, 95, 114

Zanuck, Darryl F., 38, 93, 124, 129, 134, 178, **179**
Zinnemann, Fred, 10, 37, 166, 168